THE

# "WHITE CROSS"

## TOURING ATLAS

OF THE

## WESTERN BATTLEFIELDS

By ALEXANDER GROSS, F.R.G.S.

The Naval & Military Press Ltd

*Published by*

**The Naval & Military Press Ltd**
Unit 5 Riverside, Brambleside
Bellbrook Industrial Estate
Uckfield, East Sussex
TN22 1QQ England

Tel: +44 (0)1825 749494

www.naval-military-press.com
www.nmarchive.com

*In reprinting in facsimile from the original, any imperfections are inevitably reproduced and the quality may fall short of modern type and cartographic standards.*

*In reprinting this Atlas we have taken the opportunity, for clarity, to increase the map size over the original.*

# Contents.

|  | PAGE |
|---|---|
| KEY MAP OF SECTIONAL MAPS OF WESTERN FRONT .. | 1 |
| SECTIONAL MAP OF WESTERN FRONT .. | 2 - 38 |
| KEY MAP OF SECTIONAL MAPS OF BRITISH FRONT | 39 |
| SECTIONAL MAP OF BRITISH FRONT | 40 - 64 |
| INDEX TO THE TOWNS AND VILLAGES MENTIONED IN THE DESCRIPTION OF THE BATTLEFIELDS .. | 66 - 67 |
| DESCRIPTION OF THE BATTLEFIELDS .. | 69 - 109 |
| WAR GRAVES INDEX .. | 111 - 145 |
| INDEX TO PHOTOGRAPHS OF TOWNS AND VILLAGES IN FRANCE AND BELGIUM .. .. | 147 |
| PHOTOGRAPHS OF TOWNS AND VILLAGES IN FRANCE AND BELGIUM .. .. .. | 148 - 166 |

# INDEX TO WESTERN FRONT

1

COPYRIGHT. "GEOGRAPHIA" LTD, 55 FLEET STR., LONDON, E.C.4.

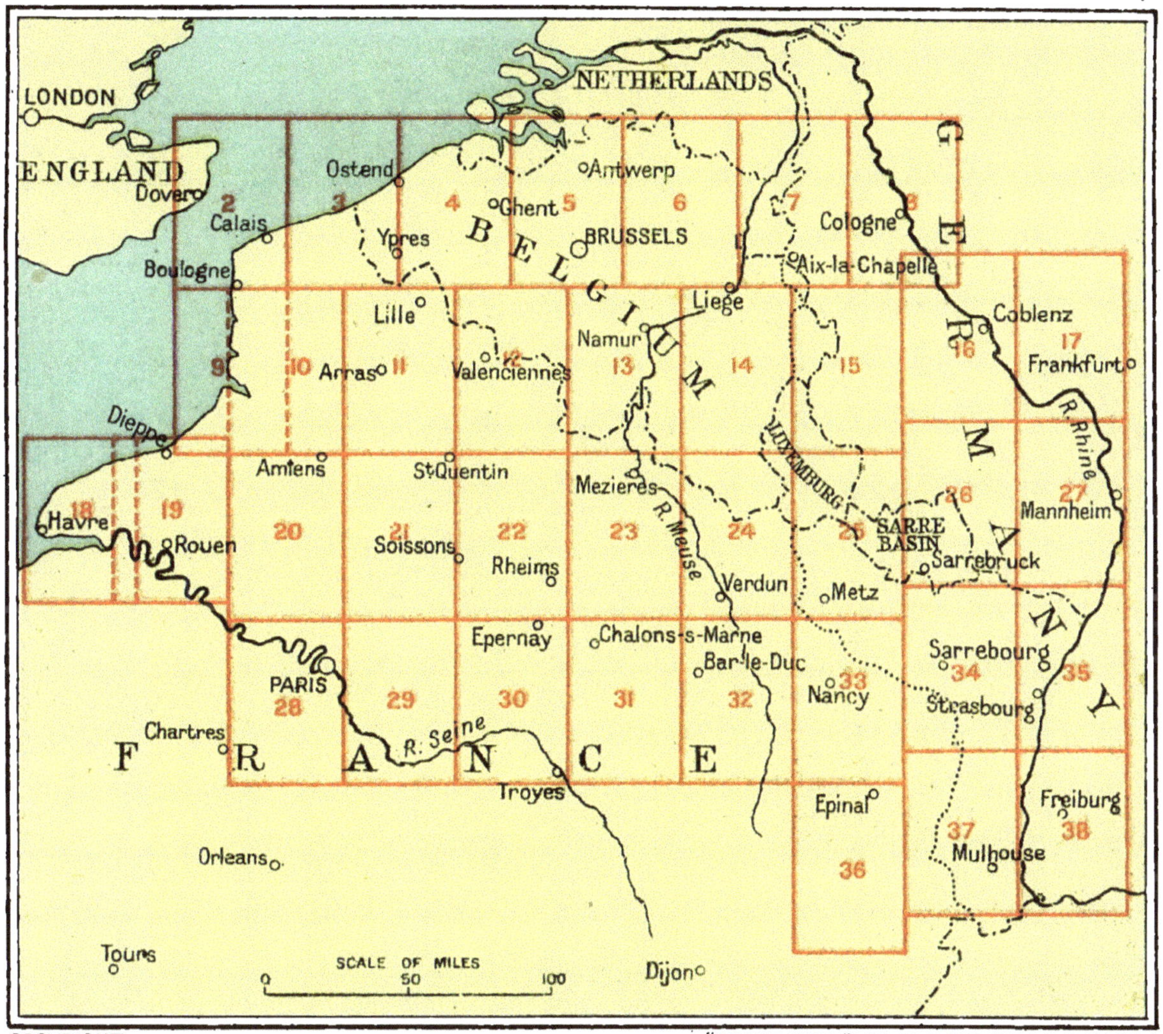

## REFERENCE TO WESTERN FRONT

Railways

Roads

Canals

Forts

International Boundaries

International Boundaries in 1914

Divided into twenty mile squares.

Heights in Feet.

*The red dots indicate the positions of the Cemeteries, the names of which will be found in the Index with the corresponding number to that on the map.*

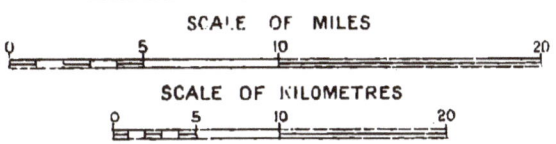

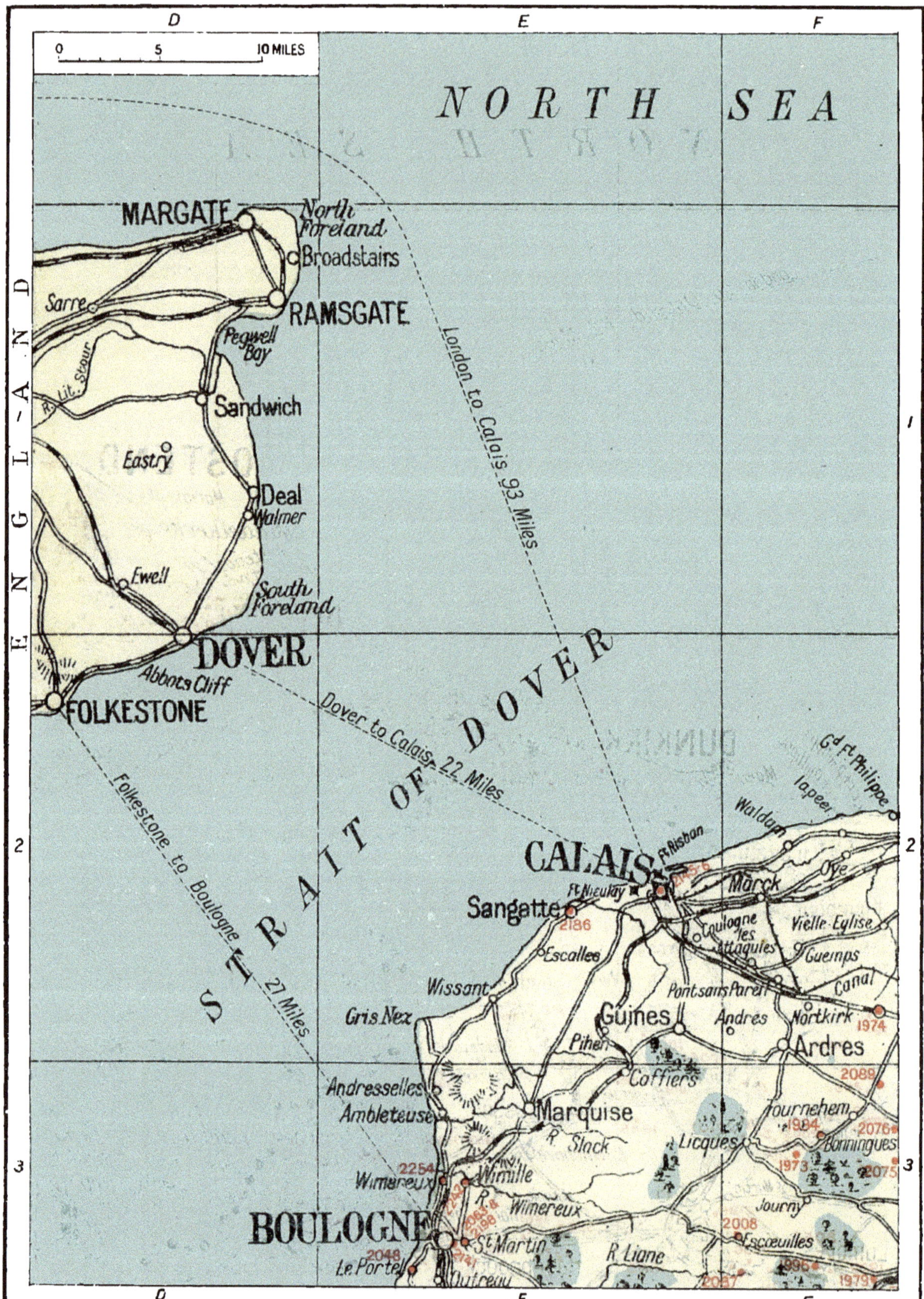


Continued on page 3.



Continued on pages 9. & 10.

"GEOGRAPHIA" LTD. 55 FLEET STREET LONDON E.C. 4.

Continued on page 4.
Continued on page 6.



Continued on pages 12. & 13.

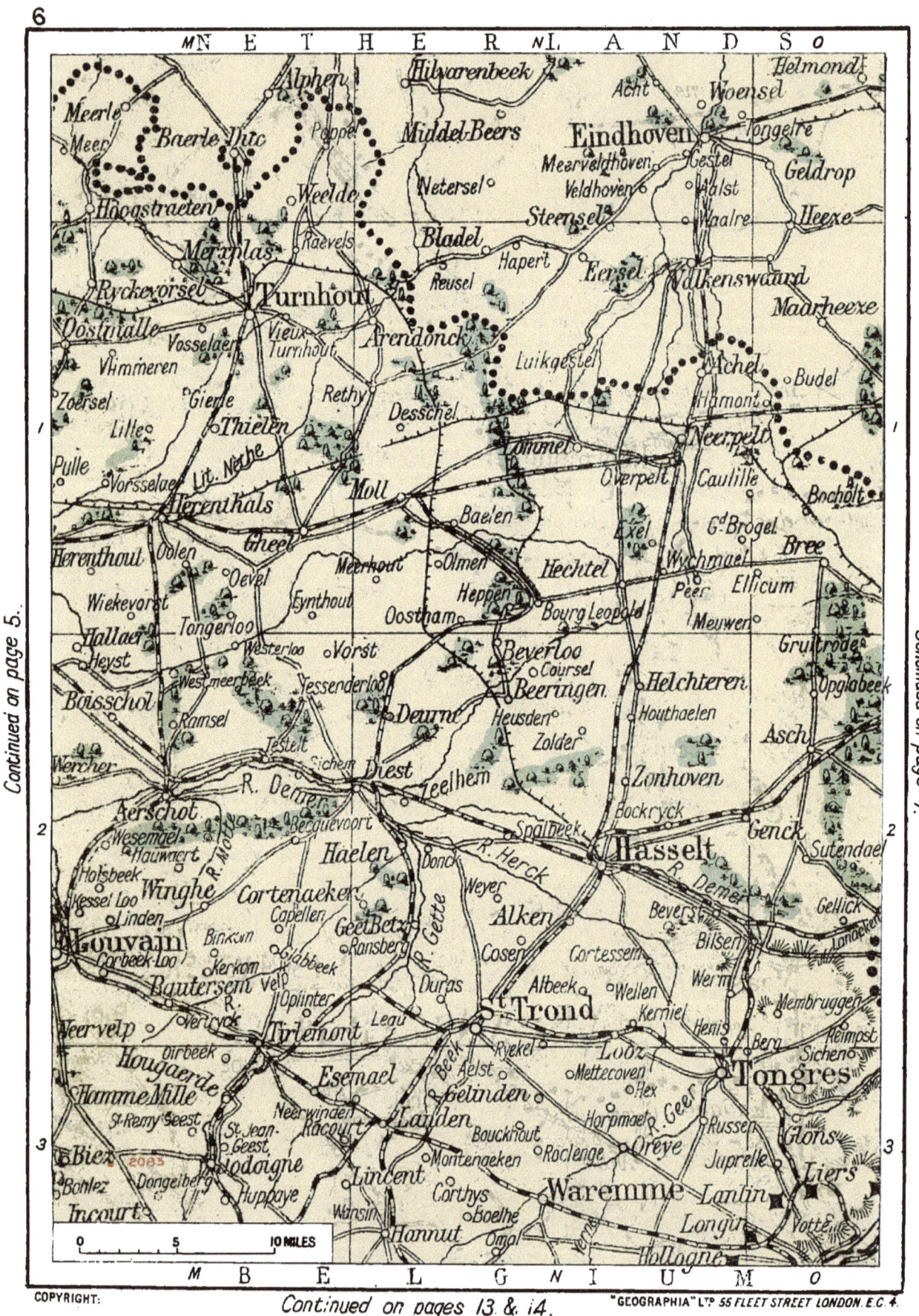

Continued on page 7.

Continued on pages 15. & 16.



"GEOGRAPHIA" L<sup>TD</sup> 55 FLEET STREET LONDON. E.C. 4.

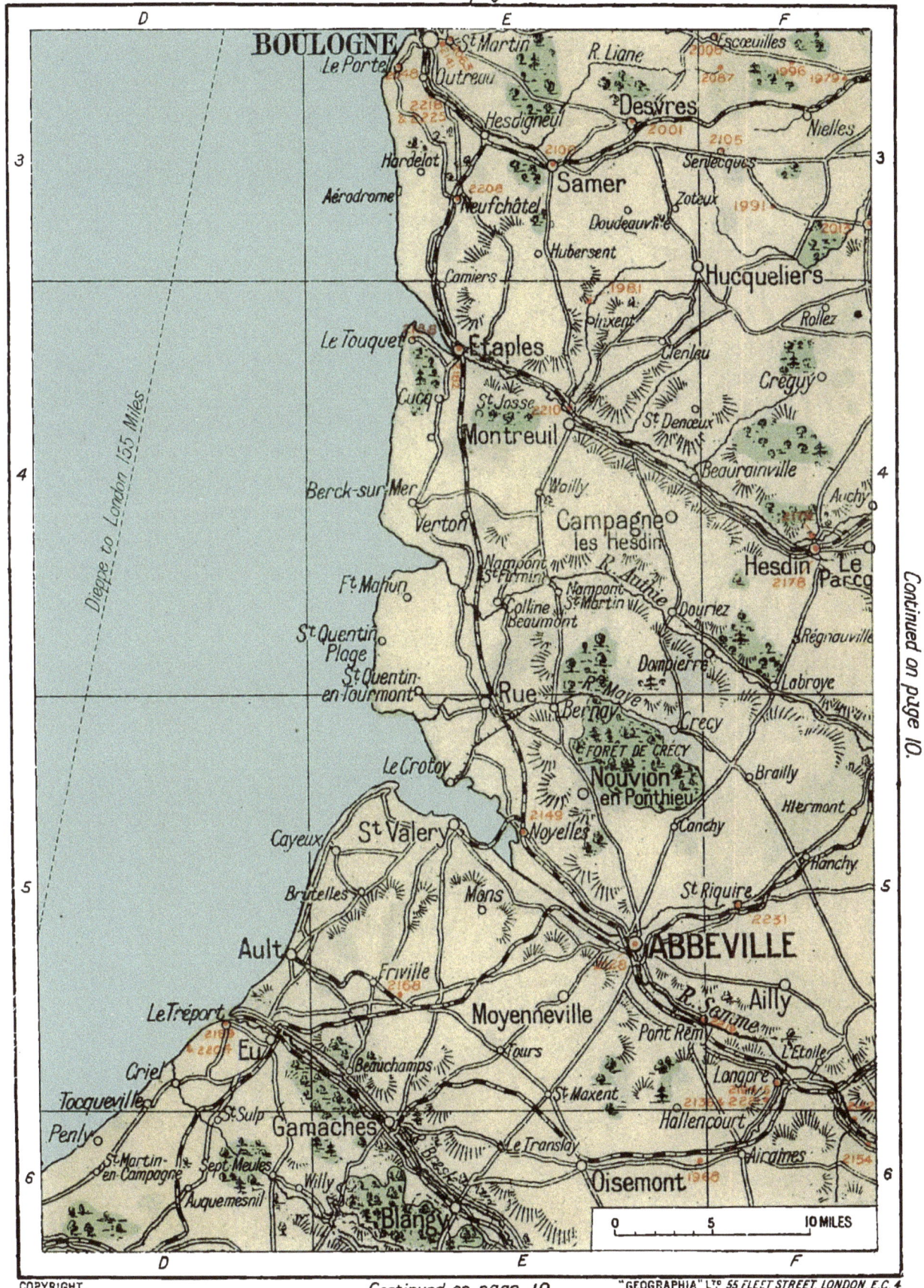

Continued on page 3.

Continued on page 4.



Continued on page 10.

Continued on page 12.



Continued on page 21.

"GEOGRAPHIA" LTD. 55 FLEET STREET LONDON E.C. 4.

Continued on page 5. Continued on page 6. 

Continued on page 12.

Continued on page 14.

 Continued on page 23. "GEOGRAPHIA" LTD 55 FLEET STREET LONDON. E.C 4

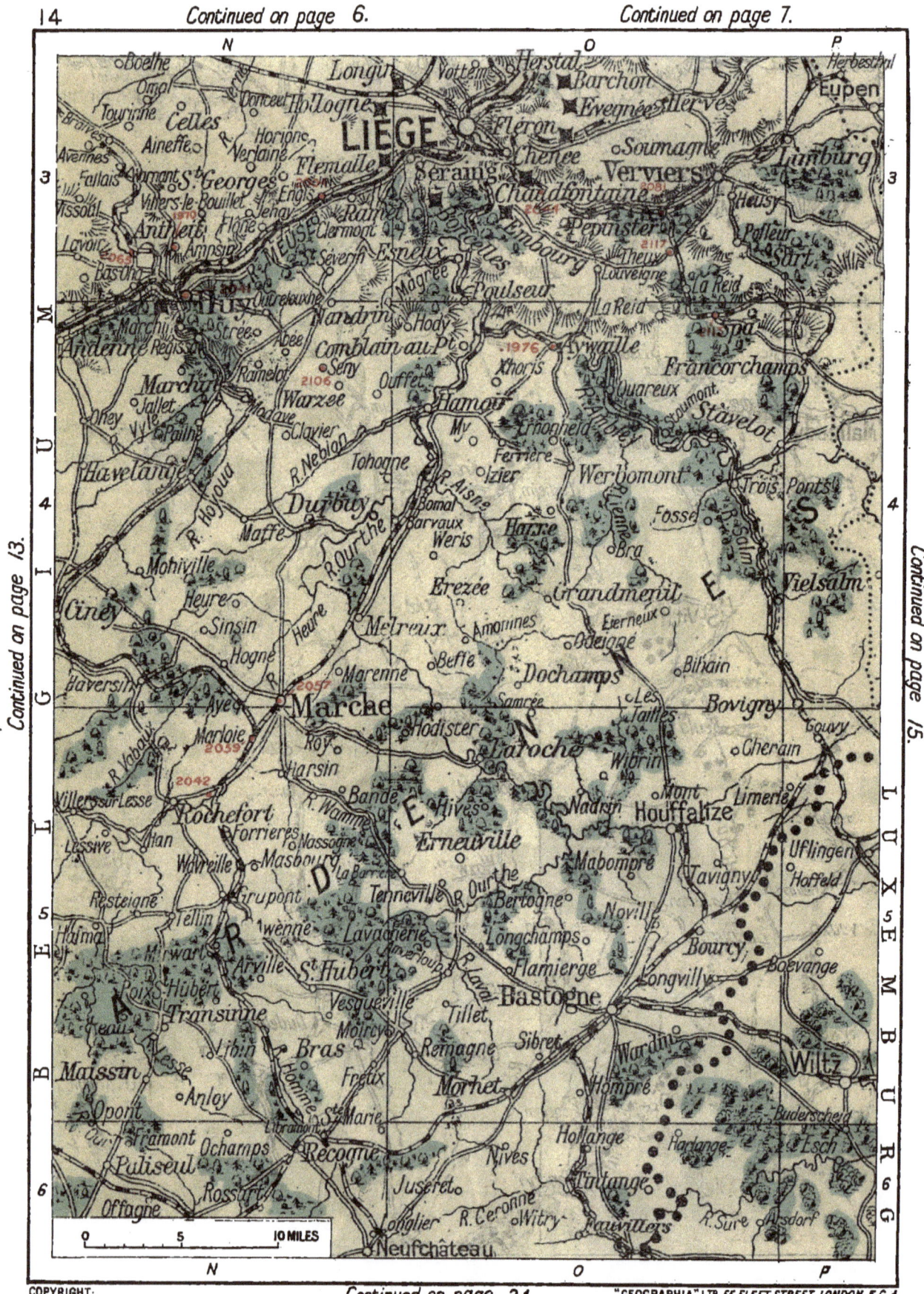

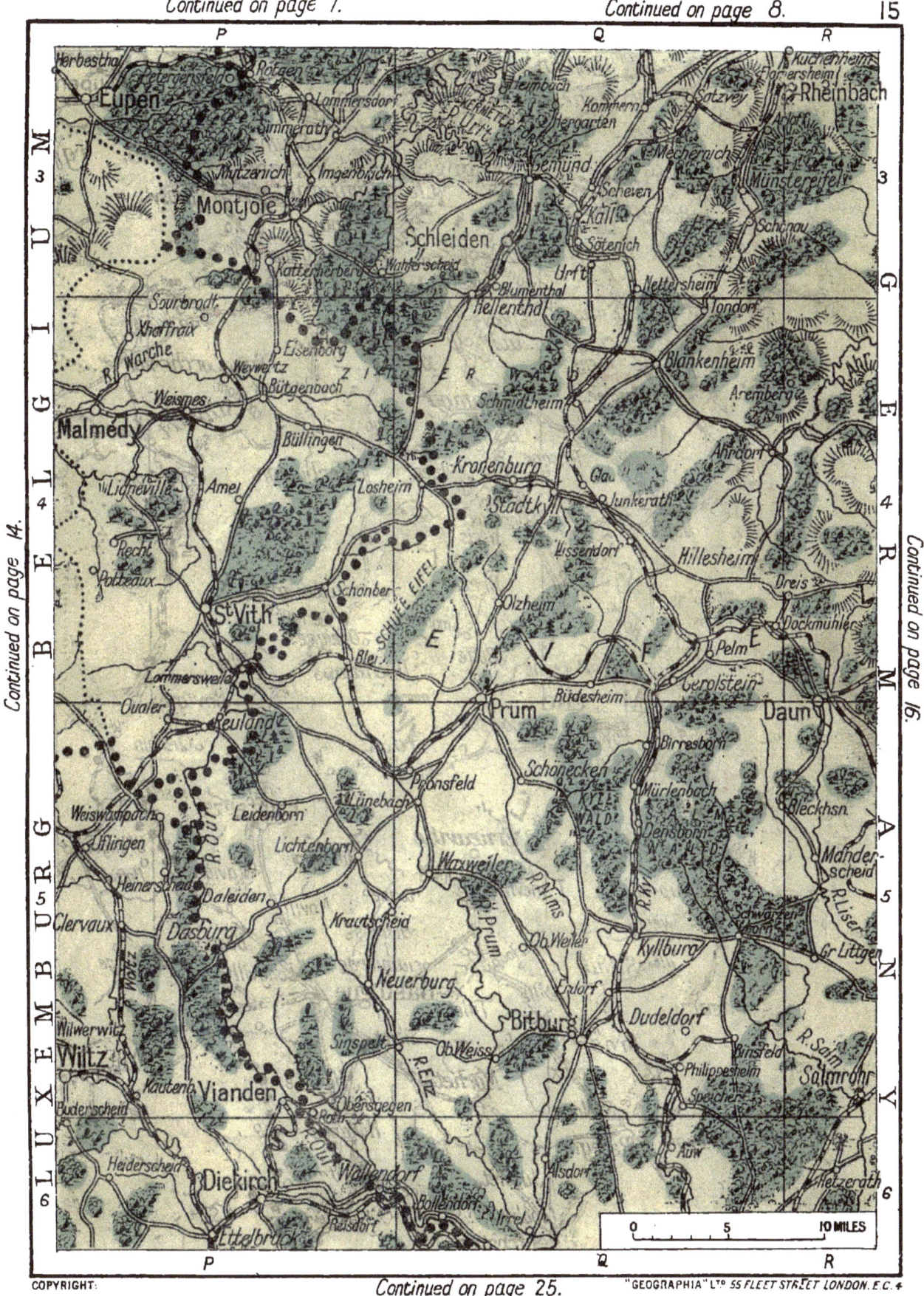

Continued on page 8.

Continued on pages 15. & 8.

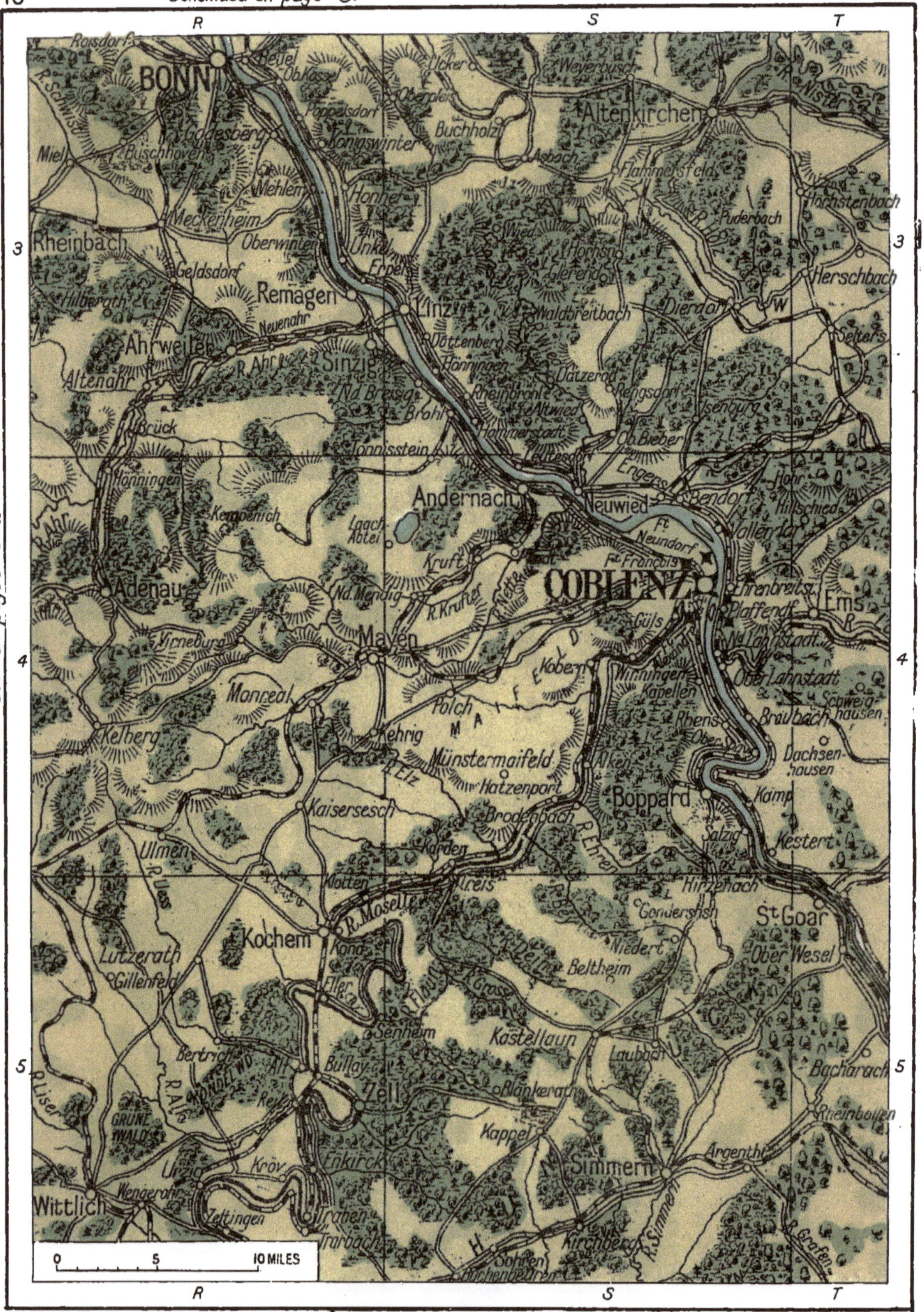

Continued on page 9.



Continued on page 18.

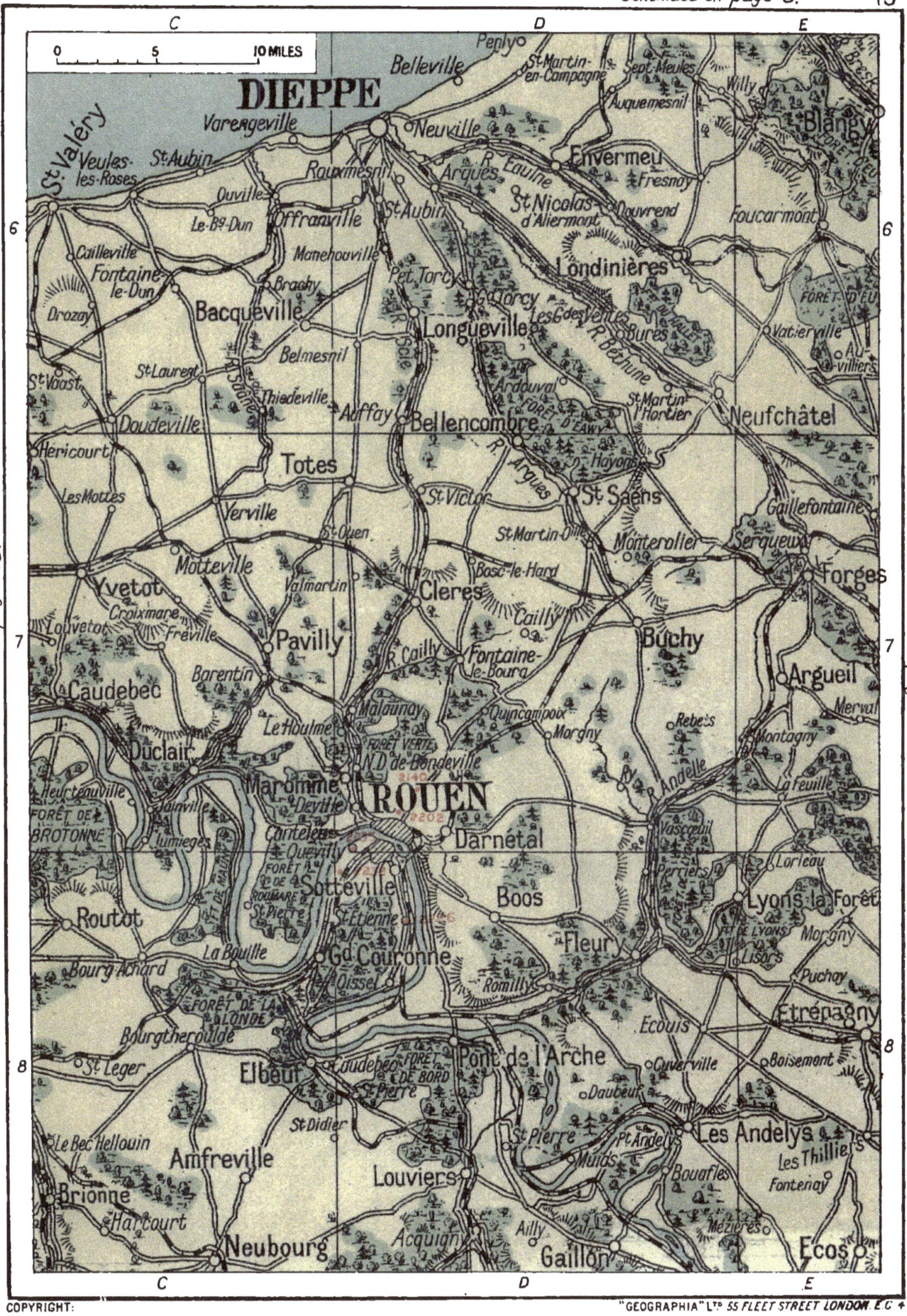


Continued on page 20.



"GEOGRAPHIA" L^TD 55 FLEET STREET LONDON. E.C. 4

Continued on pages 9. & 10.

Continued on page 19.

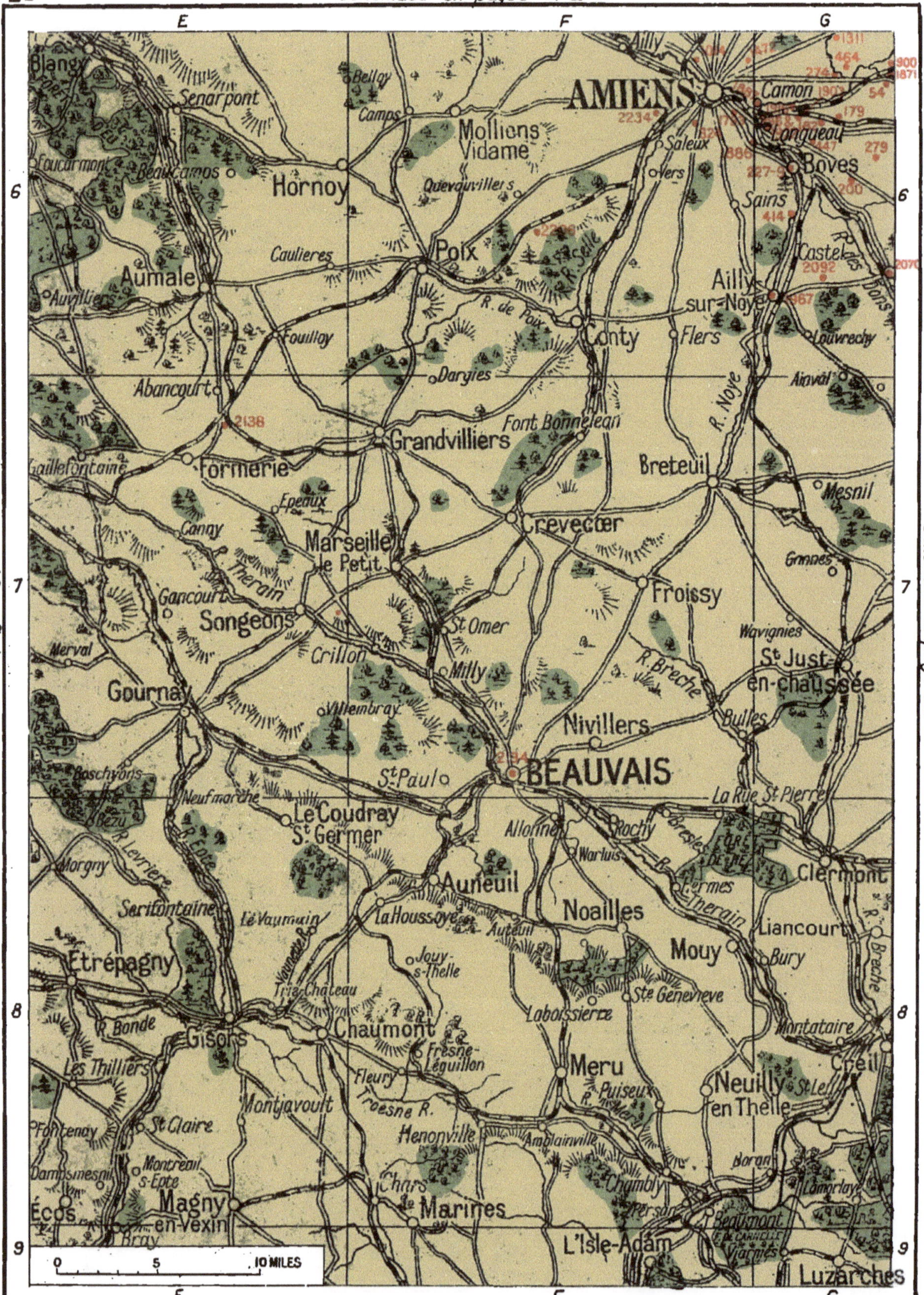


Continued on page 21.



Continued on page 28.

"GEOGRAPHIA" LTD 55 FLEET STREET. LONDON. E.C.4

Continued on page 11.



Continued on page 20.

Continued on page 22.

Continued on page 28.



"GEOGRAPHIA" LTD 55 FLEET STREET LONDON E.C.4.

Continued on page 12.

Continued on page 21.

Continued on page 33.



Continued on page 30.

"GEOGRAPHIA" LTD 55 FLEET STREET LONDON E.C.4

Continued on page 13.

Continued on page 22.
Continued on page 24.


Continued on page 31.
"GEOGRAPHIA" LTD 55 FLEET STREET LONDON. E.C. 4.

Continued on page 17.


Continued on page 26.

Continued on page 35.

Continued on page 21.



Continued on page 28.

Continued on page 30.

 "GEOGRAPHIA" LTD 55 FLEET STREET. LONDON. E.C. 4.

Continued on page 22.

Continued on page 29.

Continued on page 31

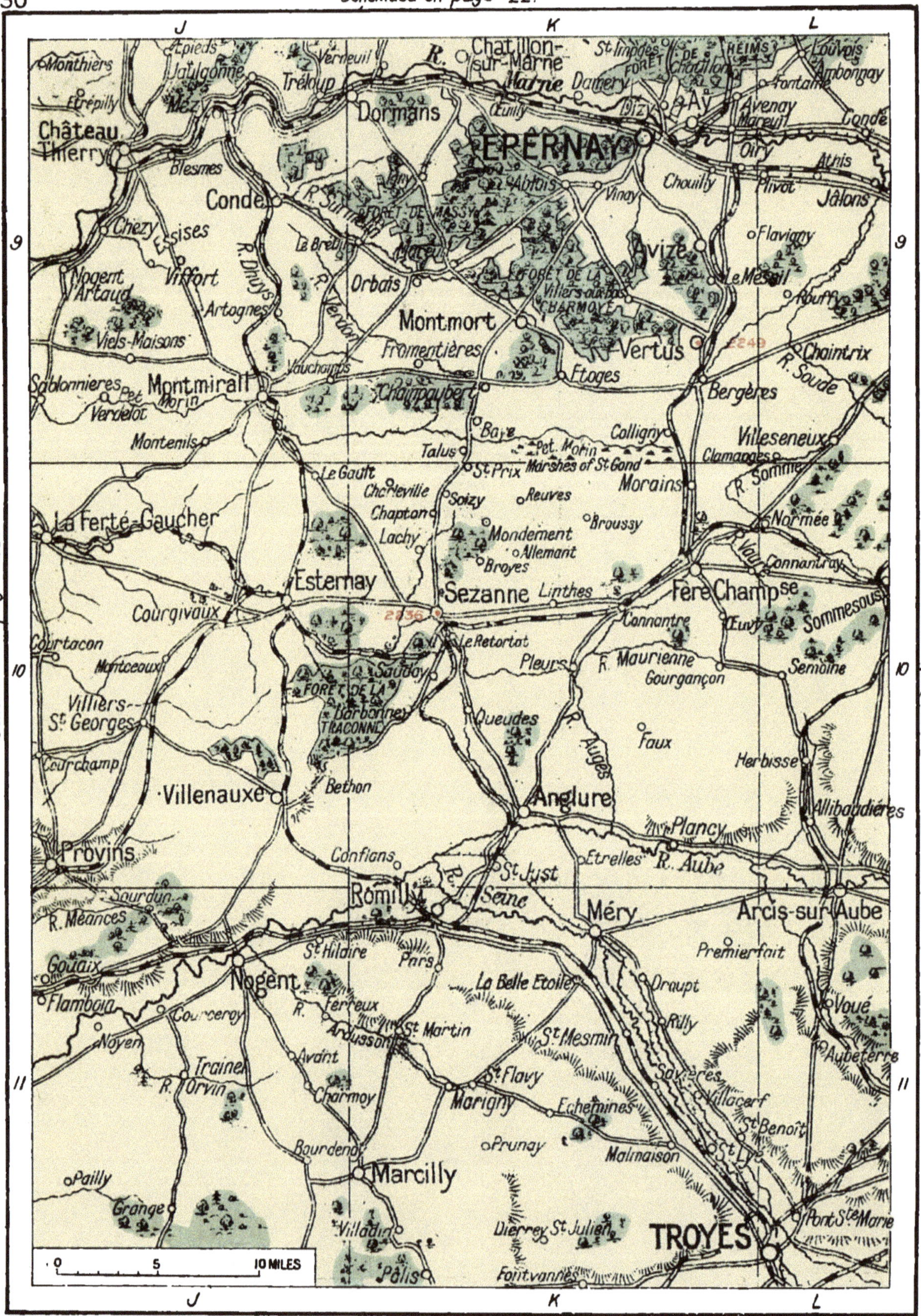




"GEOGRAPHIA" LTD 55 FLEET STREET LONDON E C 4

Continued on page 23.


Continued on page 30.
Continued on page 32.

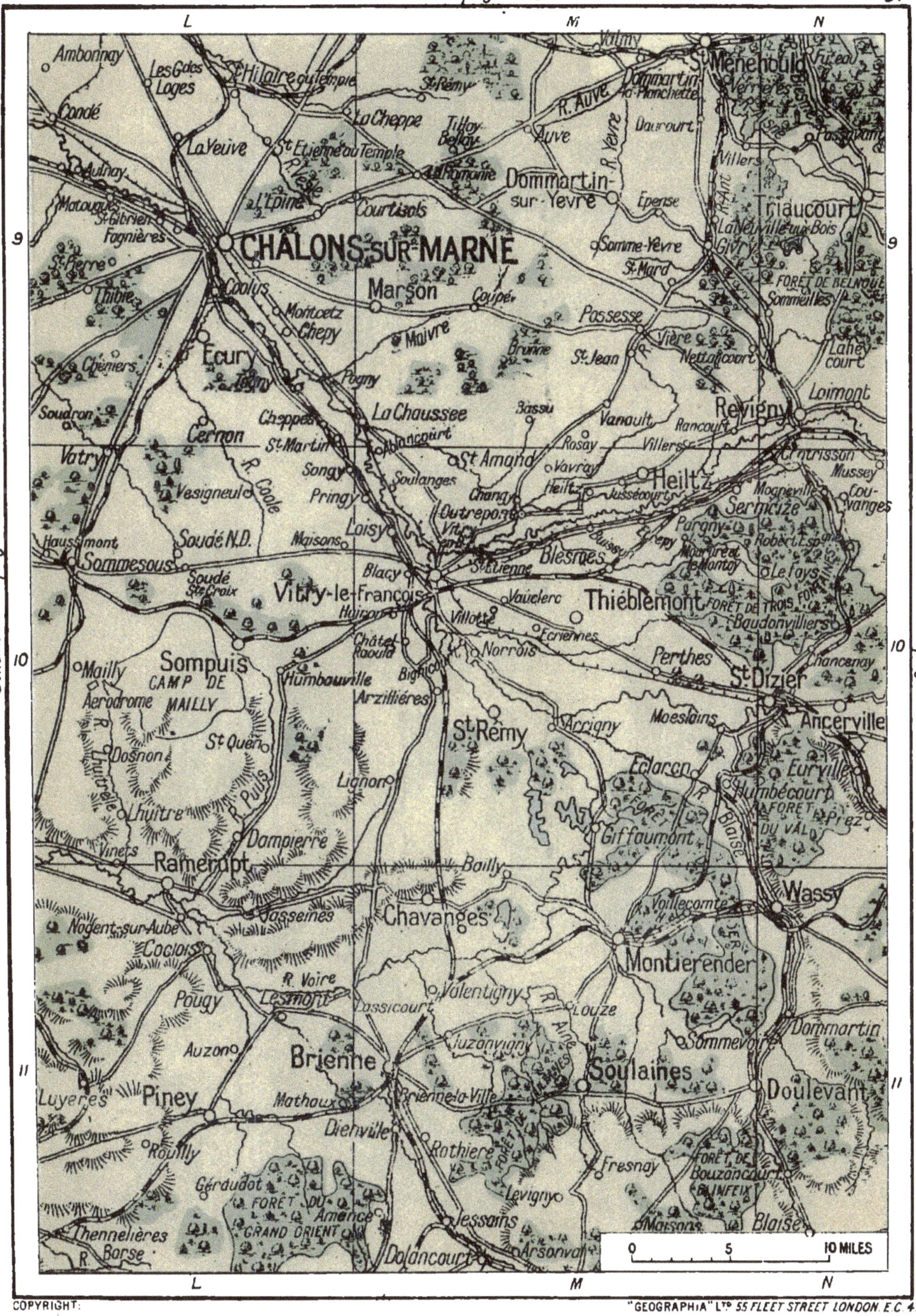



"GEOGRAPHIA" LTD 55 FLEET STREET LONDON. E.C. 4.

Continued on page 24.

Continued on page 31.

Continued on page 33.



"GEOGRAPHIA" LTD. 55 FLEET STREET LONDON. E.C. 4.

Continued on page 25.



Continued on page 32.

Continued on pages 34 & 37.



Continued on page 36.

"GEOGRAPHIA" LTD 55 FLEET STREET. LONDON. E.C. 4.

Continued on page 26.

Continued on pages 33 & 25.

Continued on page 35.



Continued on page 37.

"GEOGRAPHIA" LTD 55 FLEET STREET. LONDON. E.C. 4.

Continued on page 34.

Continued on pages 36. & 33.

Continued on page 38.

 "GEOGRAPHIA" LTD 55 FLEET STREET LONDON E.C.4

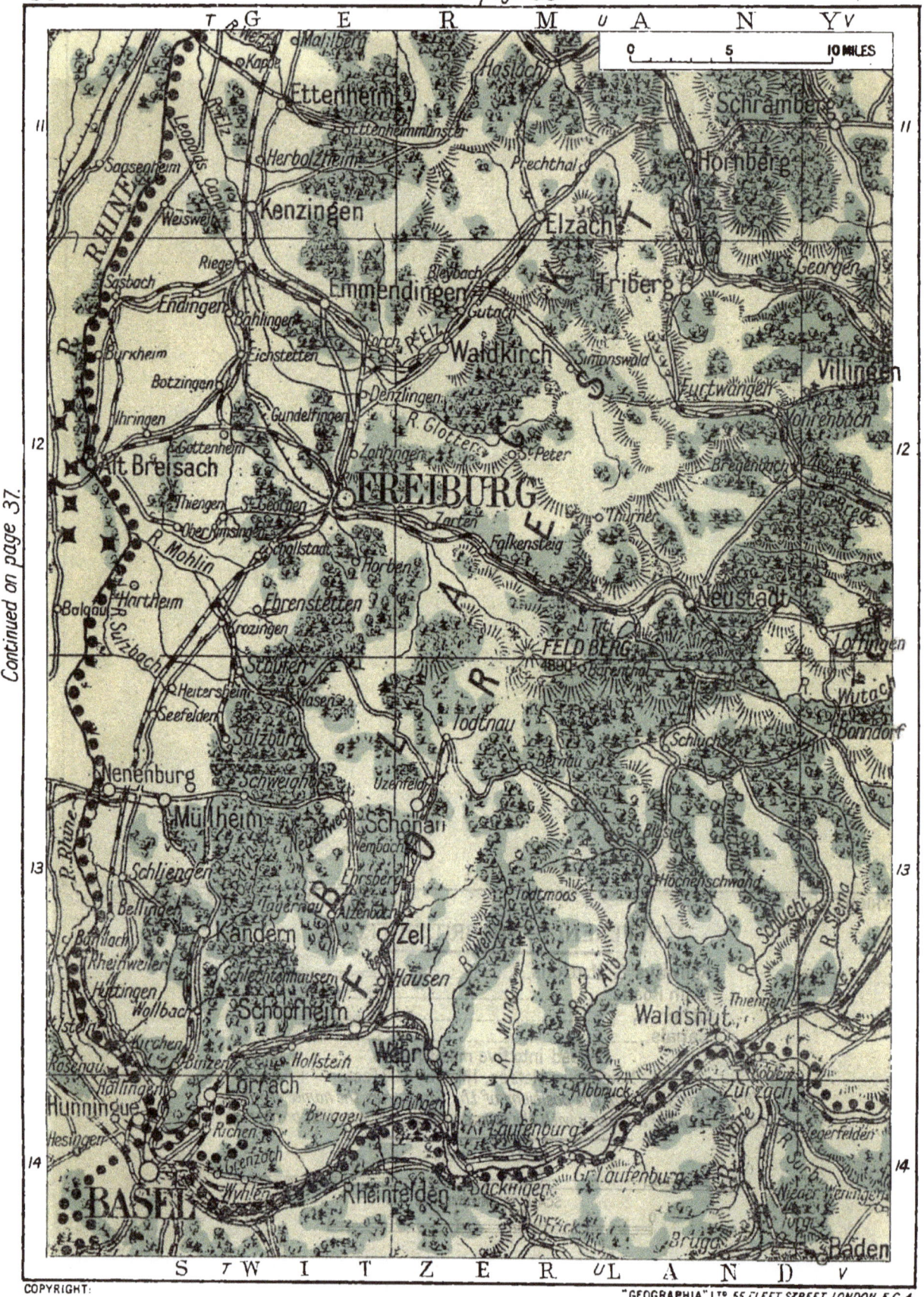

# INDEX TO BRITISH FRONT

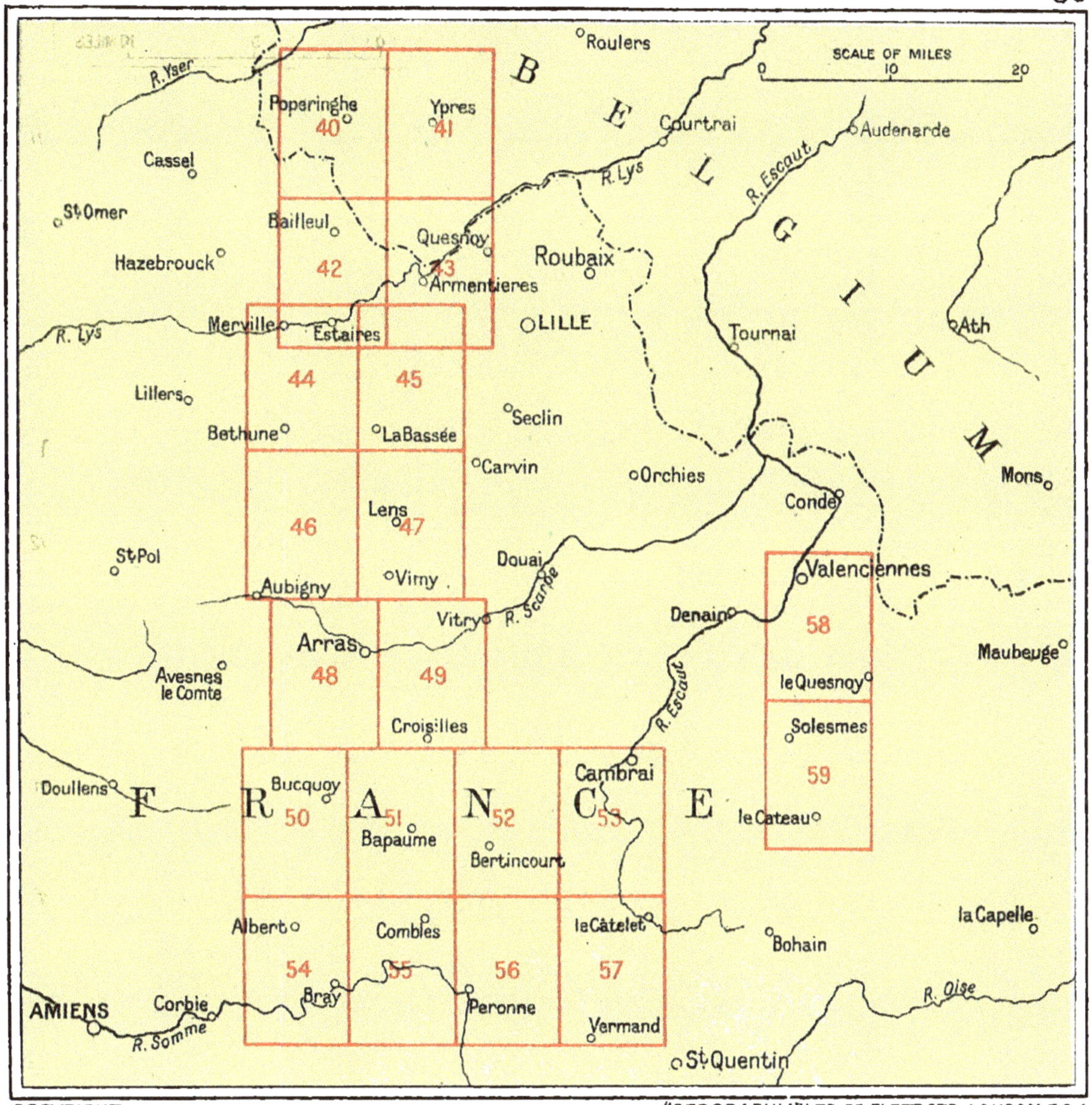

## REFERENCE TO BRITISH FRONT

Railways & Stations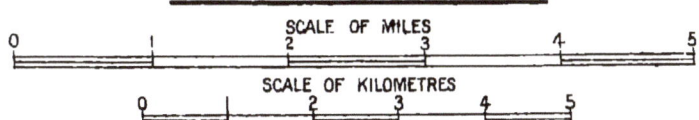
Main Roads
Other "
Canals

Divided into five mile squares.
Heights in Metres, 1 Metre = 3·28 Feet.
*The red dots indicate the positions of the Cemeteries, the names of which will be found in the Index with the corresponding number to that on the map.*

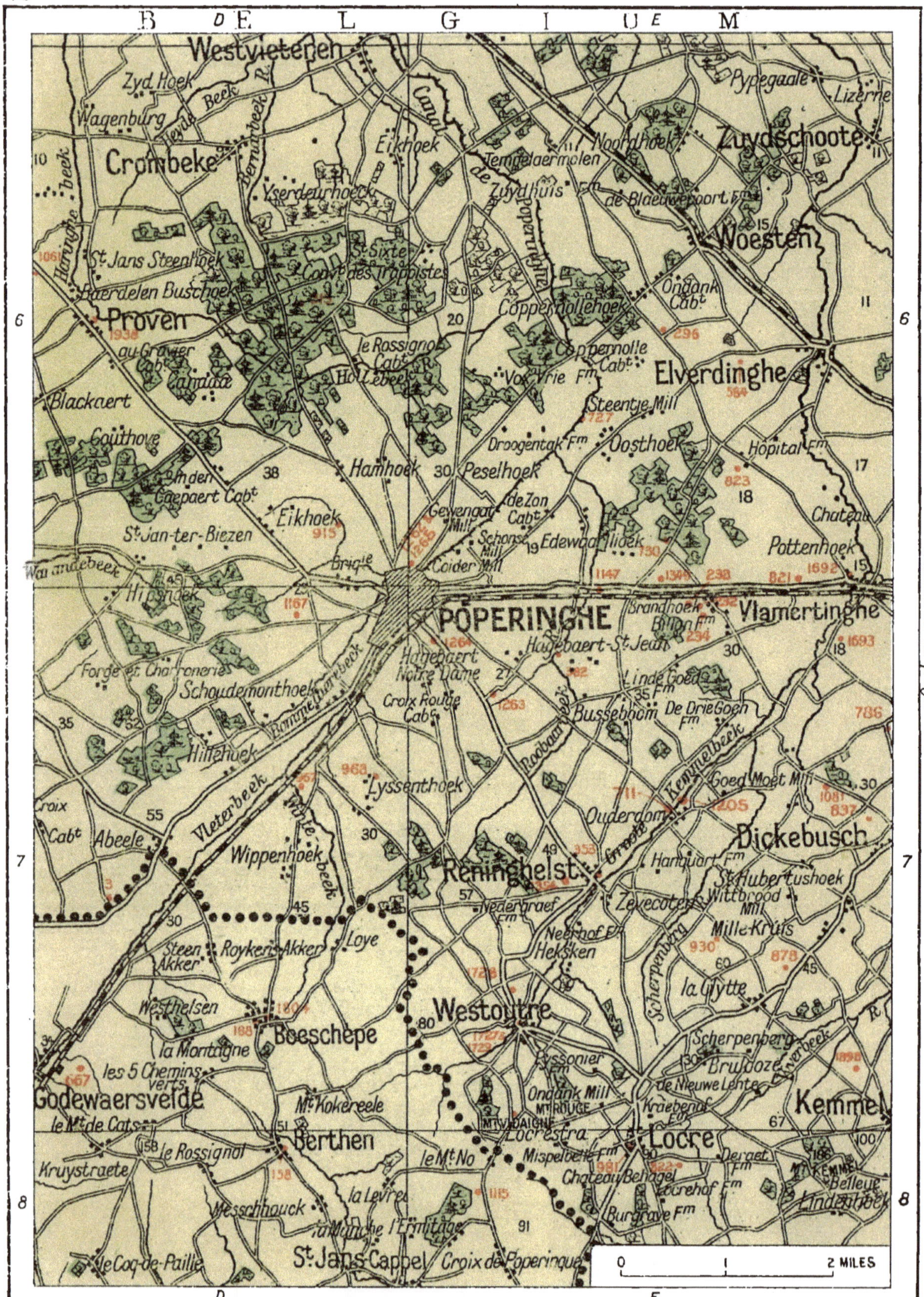


Continued on page 41.



Continued on page 42.

Continued on page 40.

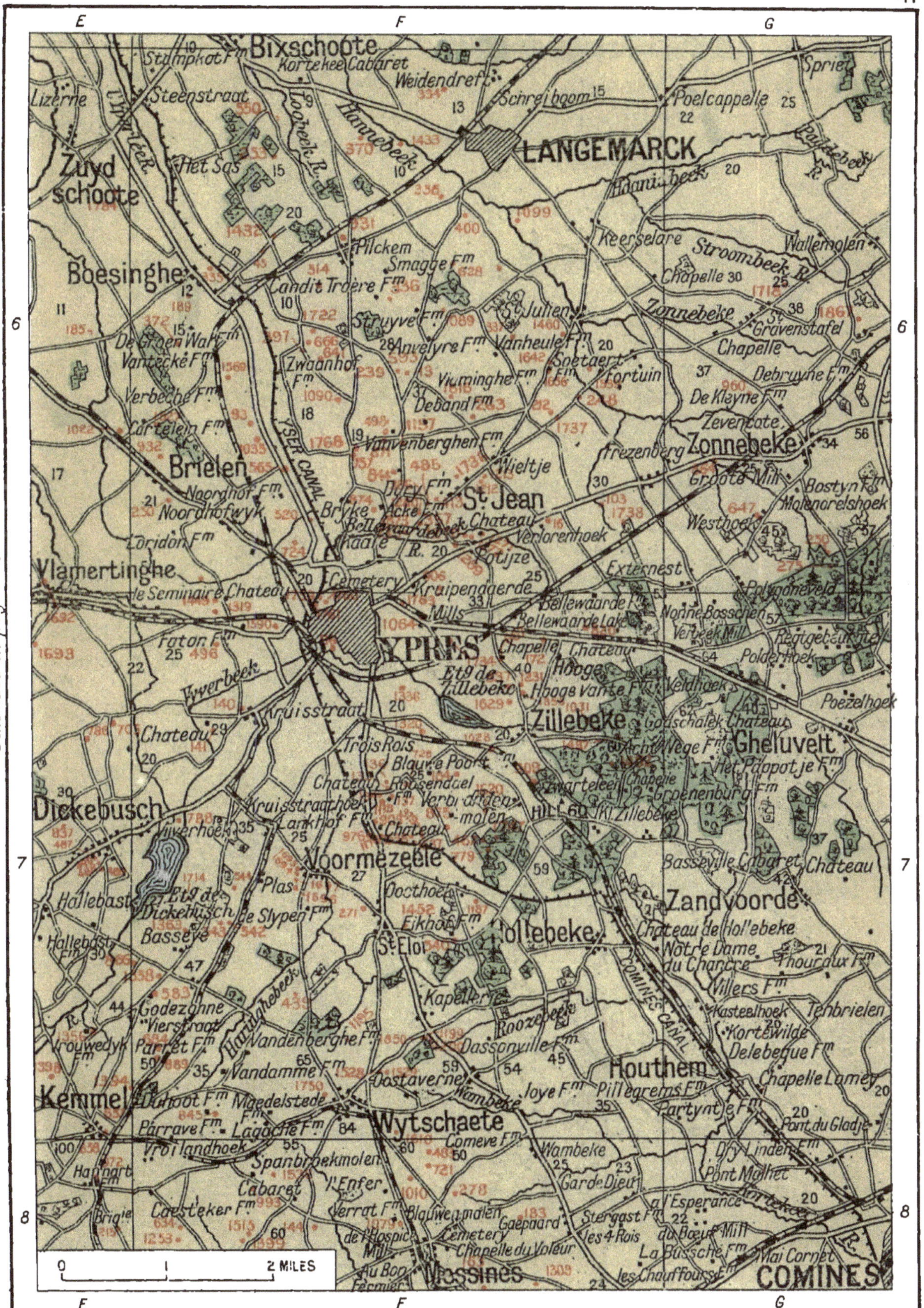


COPYRIGHT:

Continued on page 43.

"GEOGRAPHIA" LTD 55 FLEET STREET LONDON E.C. 4.

Continued on page 40.

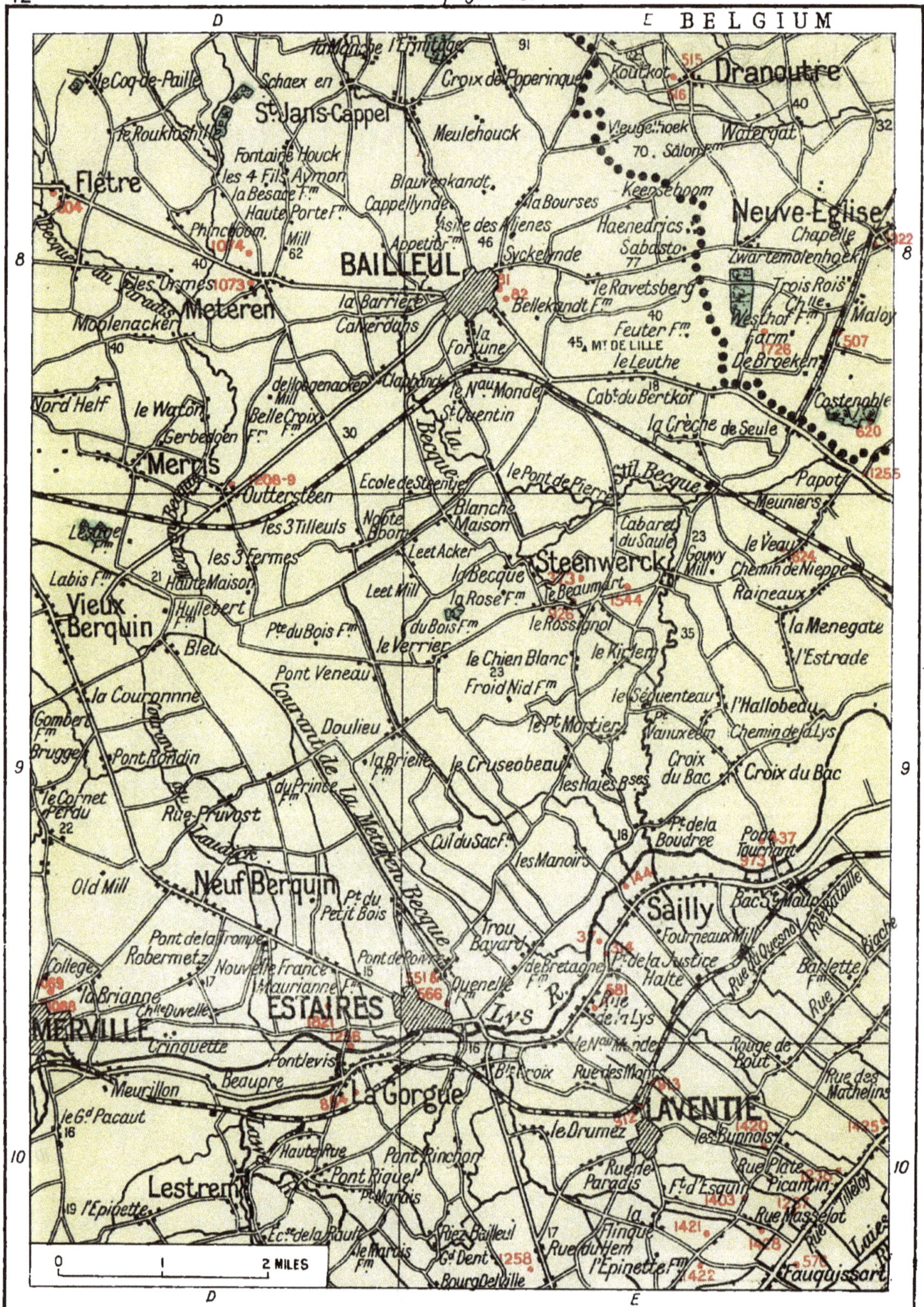


Continued on page 43.


Continued on pages 44. & 45
"GEOGRAPHIA" LTD. 55 FLEET STREET LONDON E.C. 4.

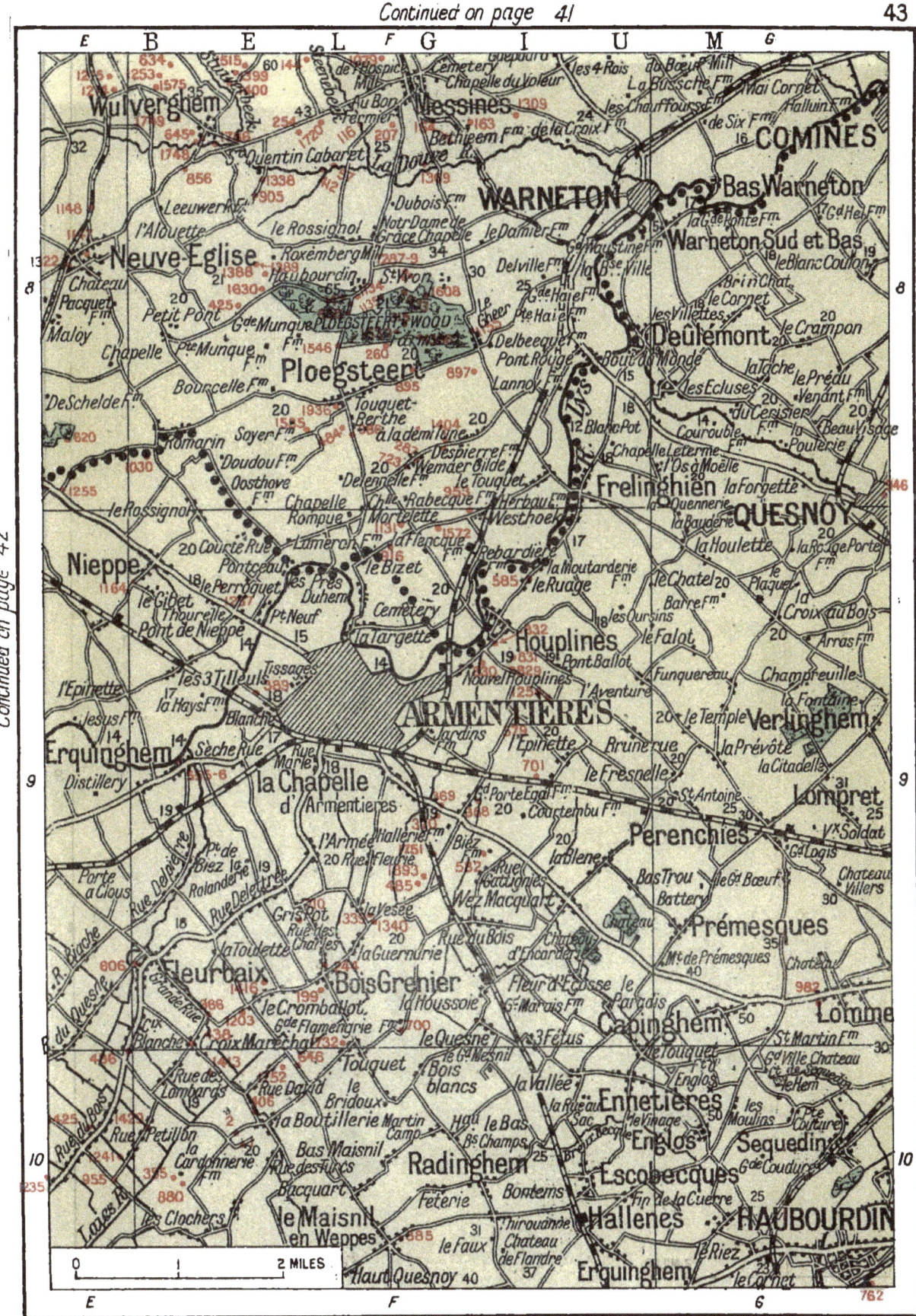

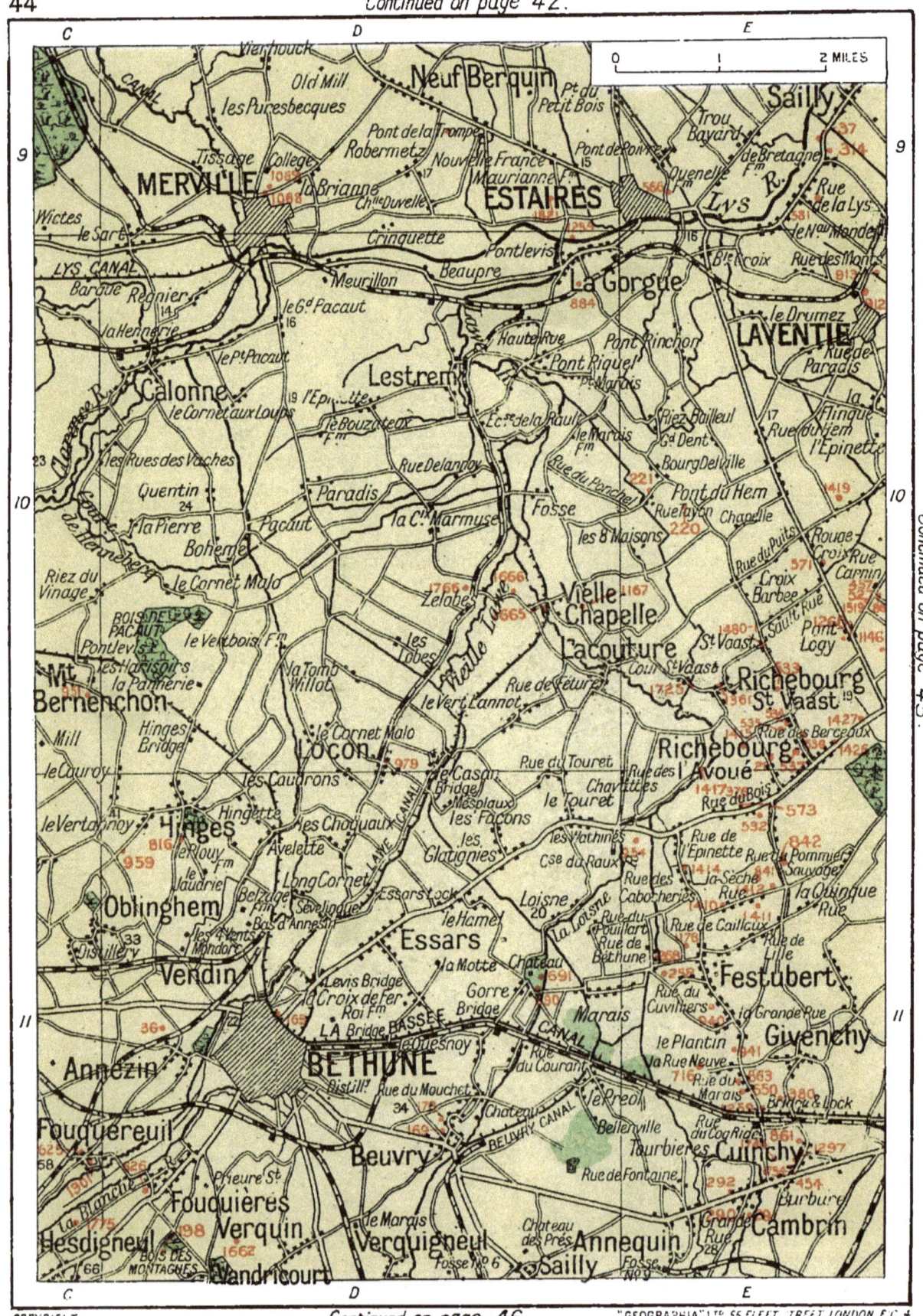

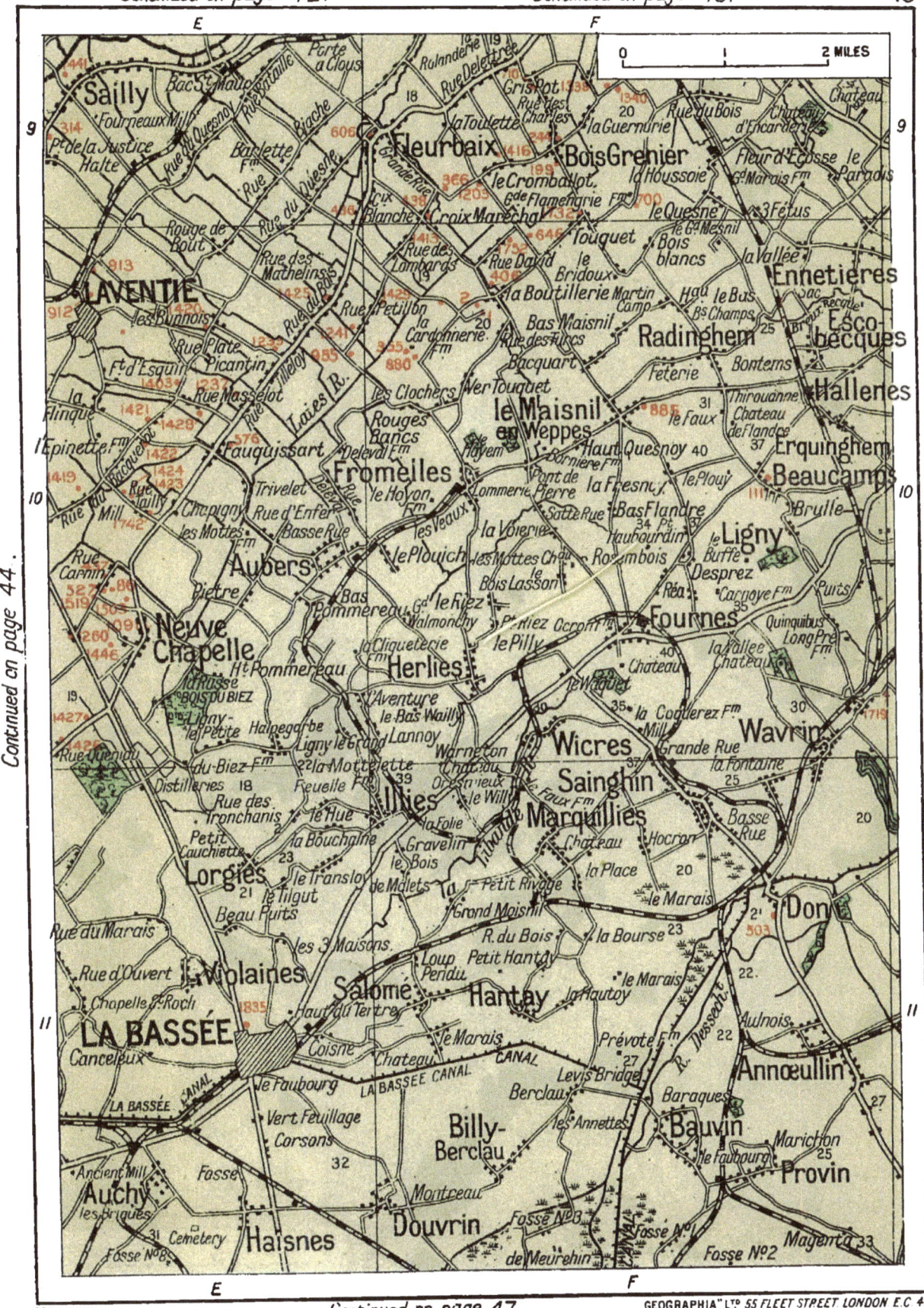

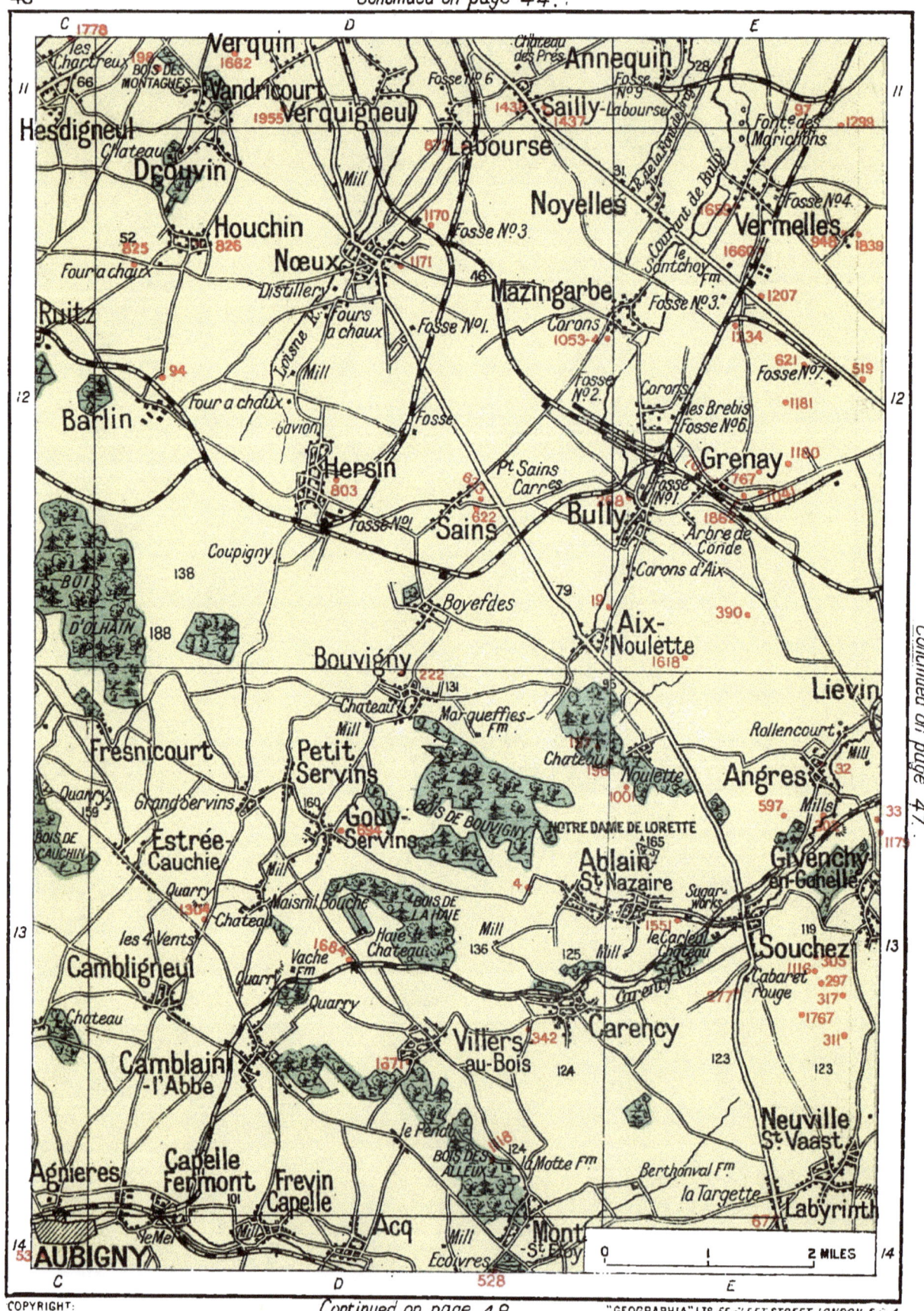

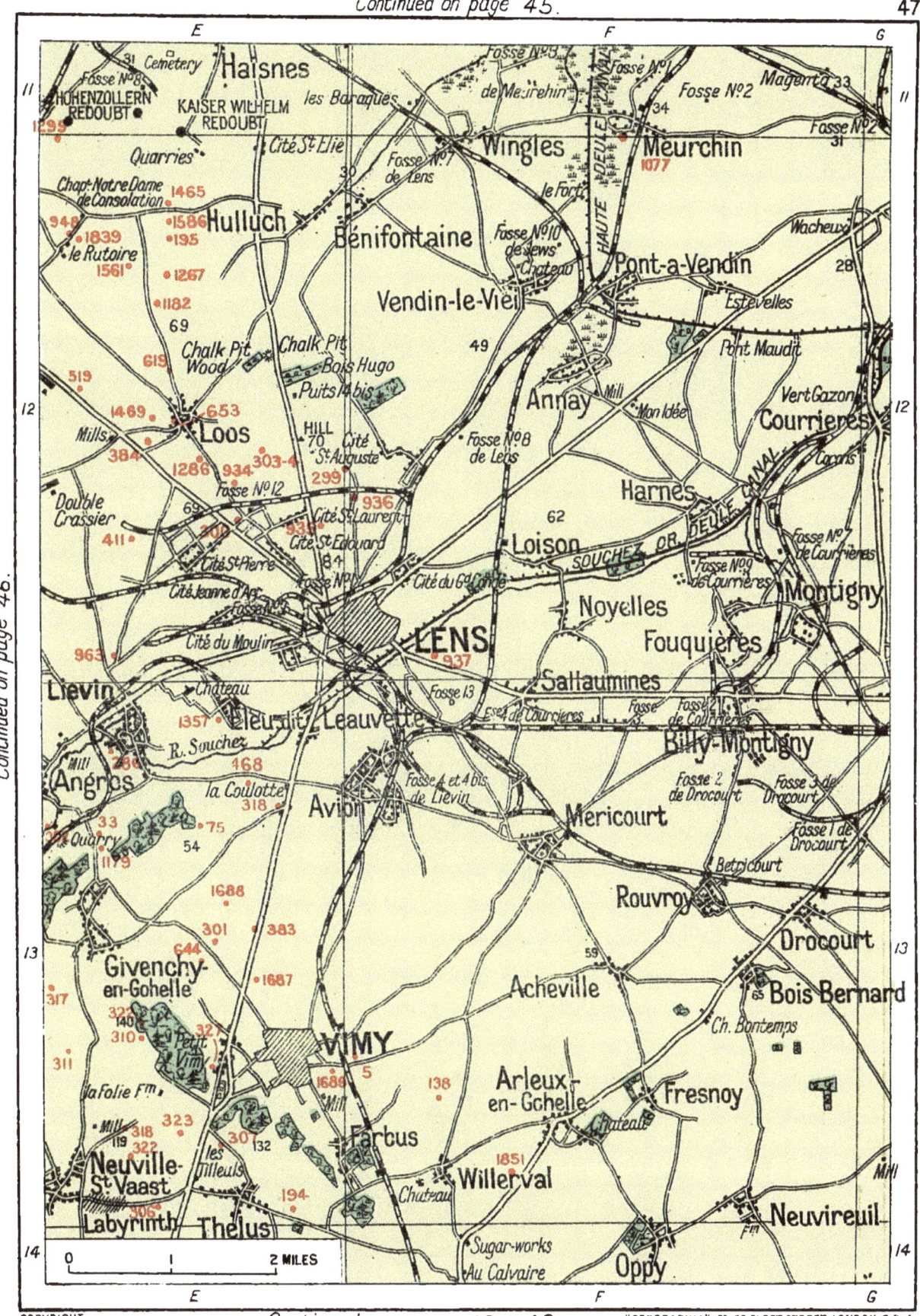

Continued on page 46.
Continued on page 47.

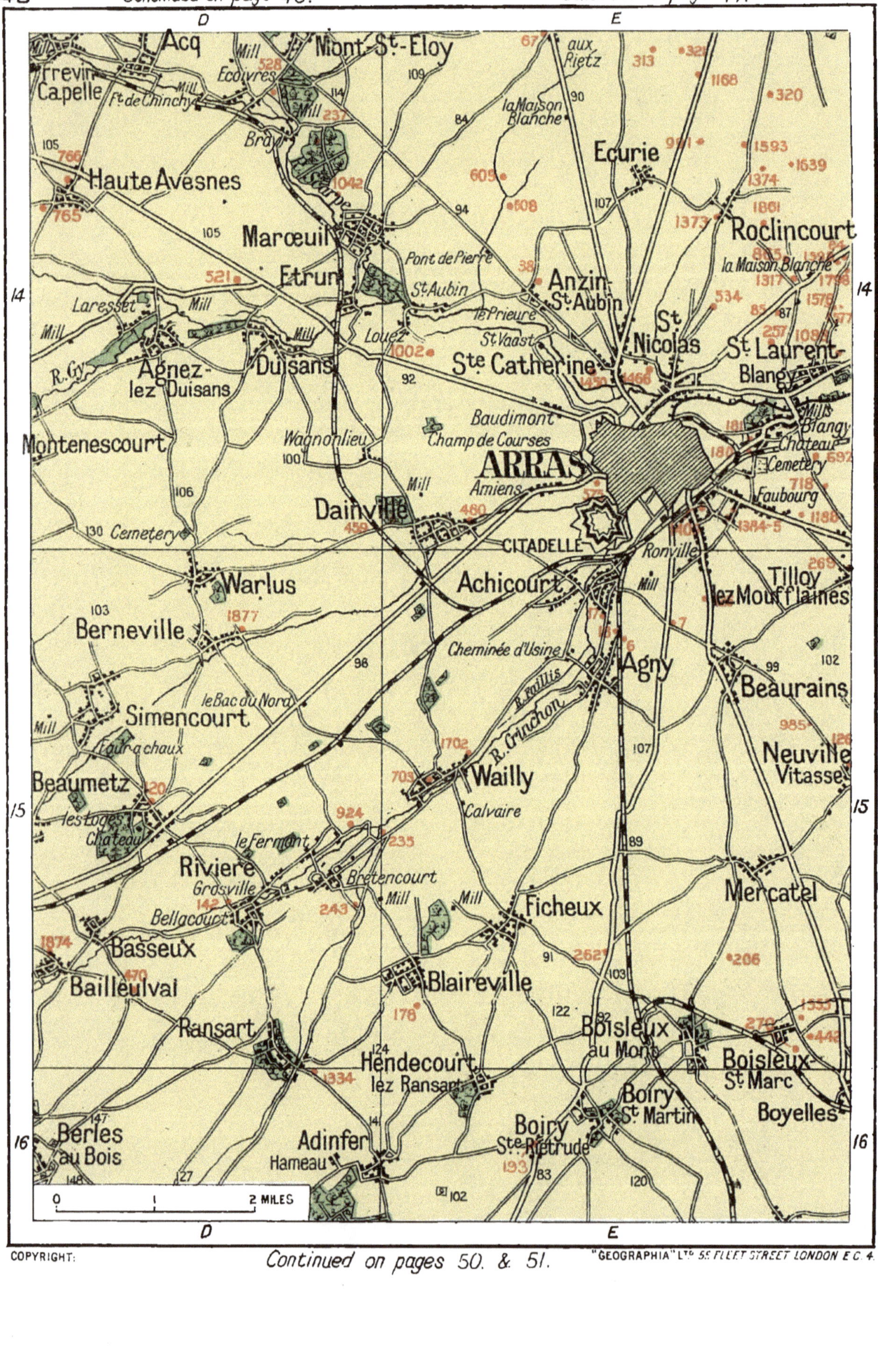


Continued on page, 49.


Continued on pages 50. & 51.

Continued on page 47. 

Continued on page 48.

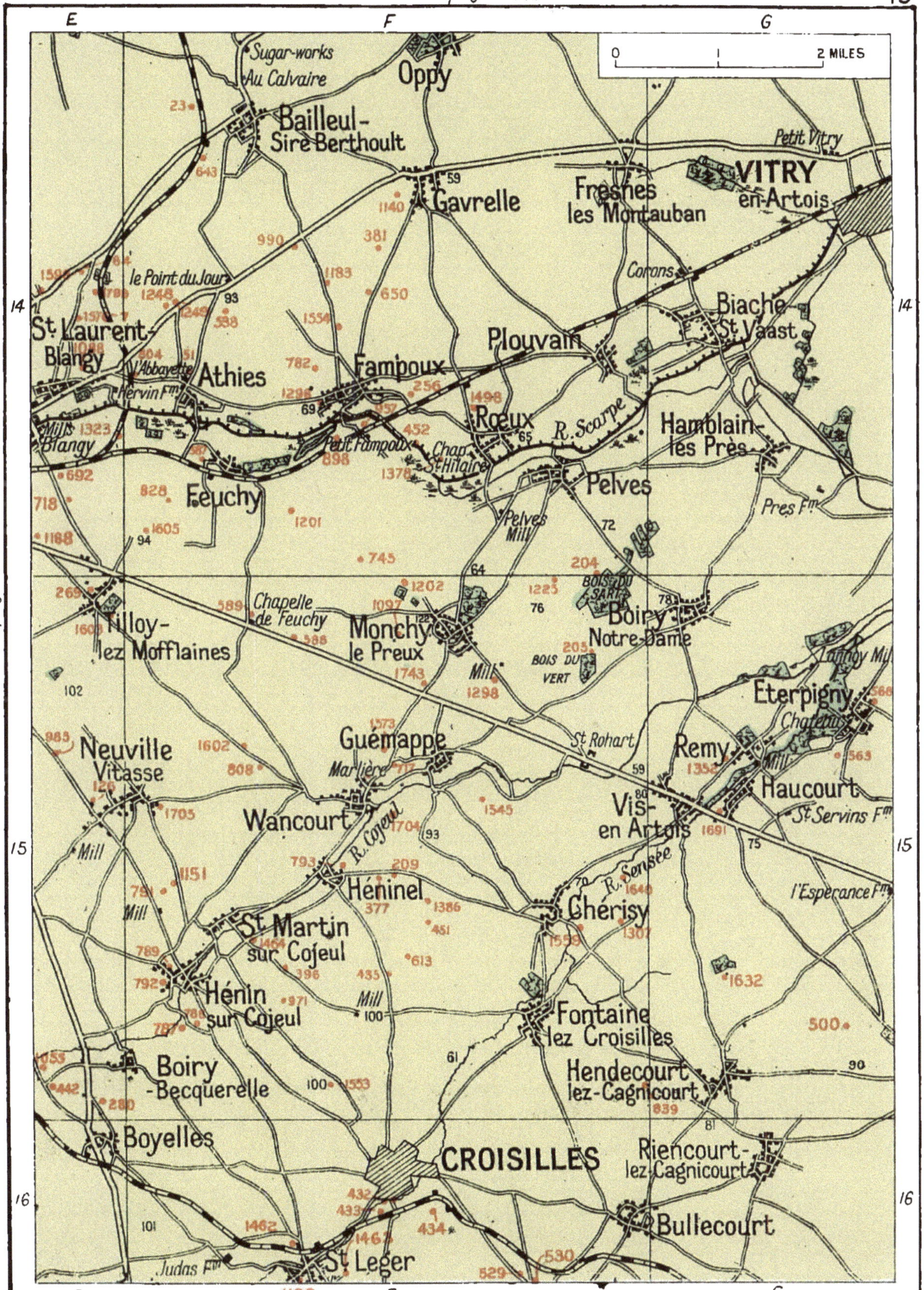


 Continued on pages 51 & 52. 

Continued on page 48.

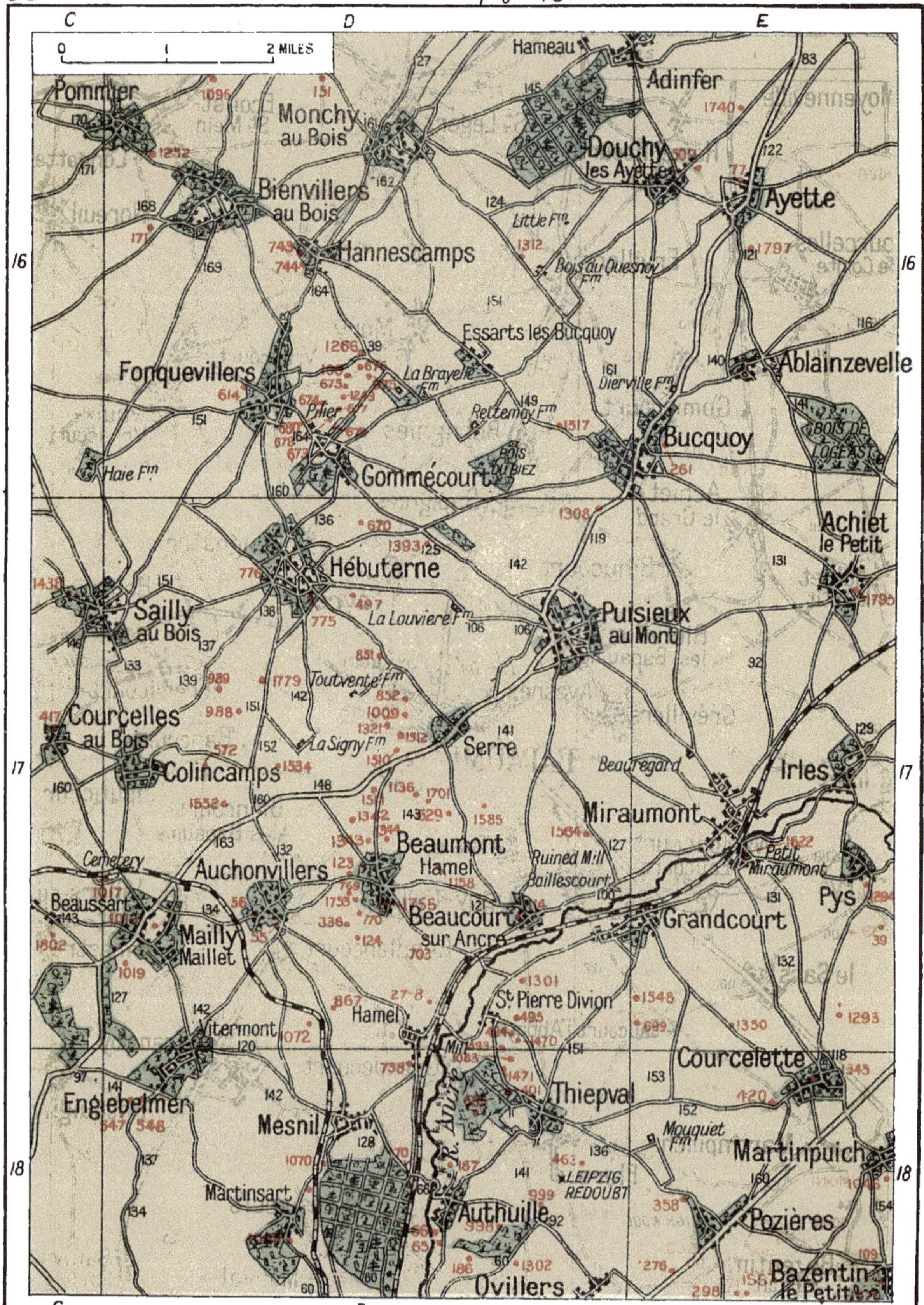

Continued on page 48. Continued on page 49. 

Continued on page 50.

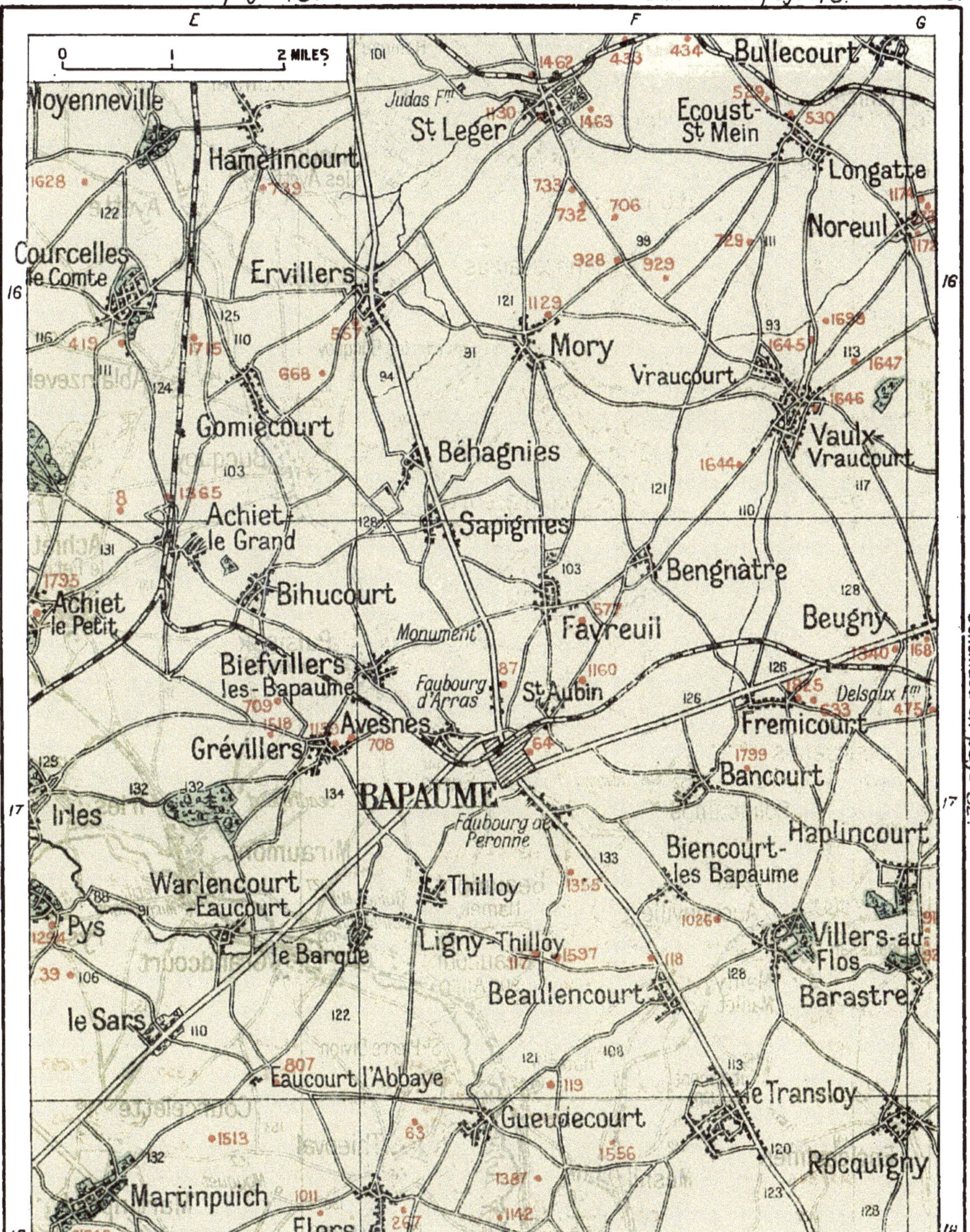


Continued on page 52.

 Continued on page 55. "GEOGRAPHIA" LTD 55 FLEET STREET LONDON E.C. 4

Continued on page 49.

Continued on page 51.

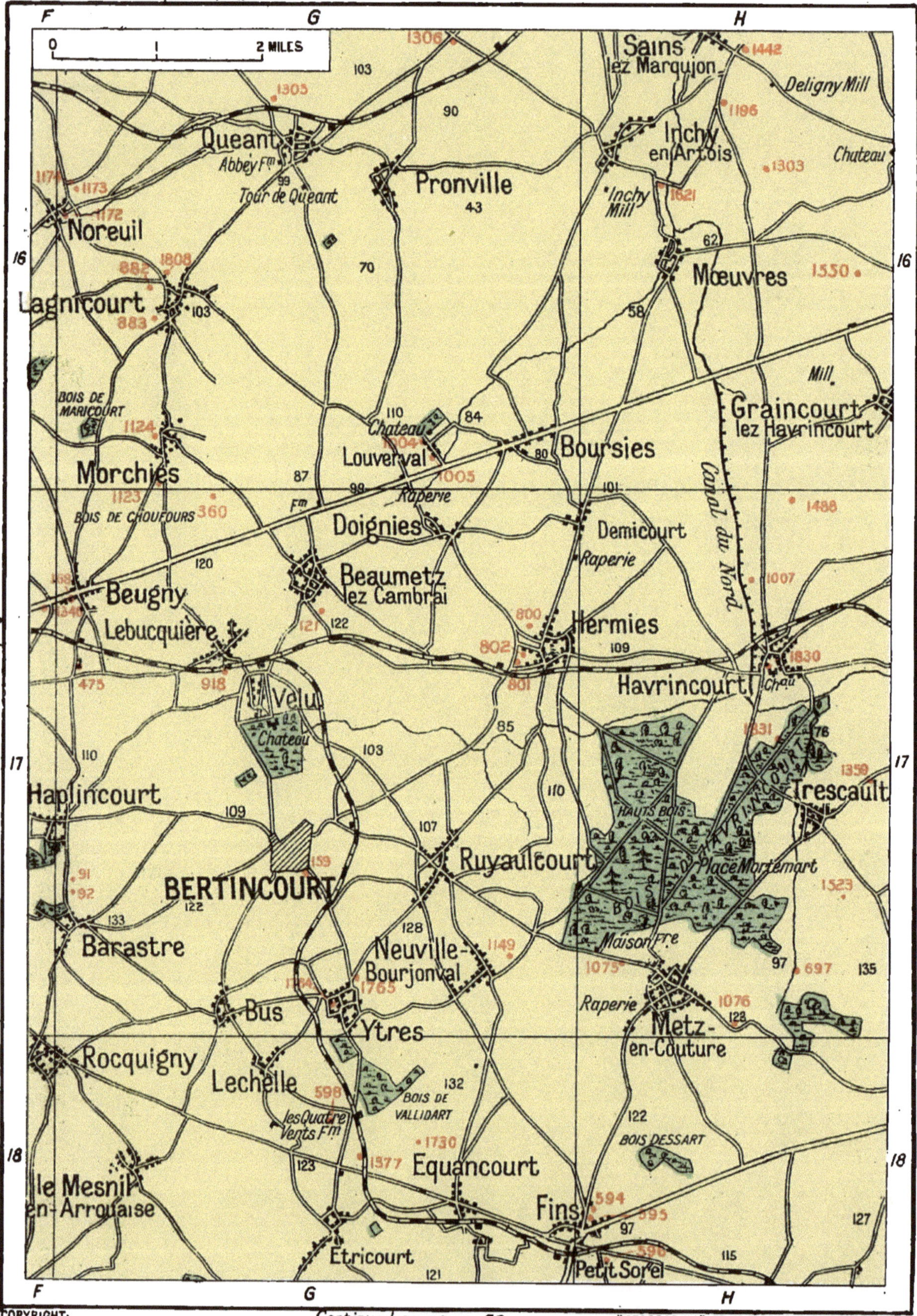


Continued on page 53.



Continued on page 56.

"GEOGRAPHIA" LTD 55 FLEET STREET LONDON. E.C. 4.

Map of the Cambrai area with locations including:

Raillencourt, Sailly, Neuville St Remy, l'Alouette, Coupez Mill, Fbg St Roch, Bourlon, St Olle, Fbg Cantimpré, Petit Fontaine, Chateau, Fontaine Notre Dame, CAMBRAI, Chapelle, Anneux, la Folie, les Vallées, Proville, Fbg St Sepulcre, Rue Ganier, Rue St Lacke, Awoingt, Cantigneul Mill, Fbg St Dreon, Fbg de Paris, la Marlière, Beurre Mill, la Belle Etode, Graincourt lez Havrincourt, Cantaing, Lock, Neave Mill, la Justice, Noyelles sur l'Escaut, Mt sur l'Œuvre, Floi Fm, Niergnies, Forenville, Bois de l'Orival, Raperie, Bois des Neufs, Premy, Chateau Talma, Bance Mill (Ruins), MARCOING, Rumilly, l'Epine, Seranvillers, Flesquieres, Masnières, Ribecourt, les Rues Vertes, Crévecœur sur l'Escaut, R. Esnes, St Waast, Bois de Femy, Mill Couillet, le Bosquet, Bithem, Trou a l'Argent, les Rues des Vignes, Lesdain, le Bosquet Tower, Beaucamp, Bon Vieillard Fm, le Quennet, Bois Lateau, Bel Aise, la Pte Maison, Villers-Plouich, Bonavis, la Vacquerie, le Pavé, Manières Fm, Bois de Gouzeaucourt, Fm, les Baraque, Pont des Voleurs, Bonne Enfance Fm, Farm, Banteux, Chateau, Gonnelieu, Bantouzelle, Geatte par ches Fm, Gouzeaucourt, Quentin Mill, Ravin des Vingt deux, les Catelets, Bonabus R., Montcoaux, Bois Gauche, les Blanches Fontaines, Honnecourt, NobleVille, Bonabus Fm, Villers Guislain, los Montagnes, Bois Maillard, les Tranchees, Bosquet Fm, Lock, la Terriere, Aubencheul

0 1 2 MILES

Continued on page 52.
Continued on page 57.
"GEOGRAPHIA" LTD 55 FLEET STREET LONDON. E.C. 4.

Continued on page 50.

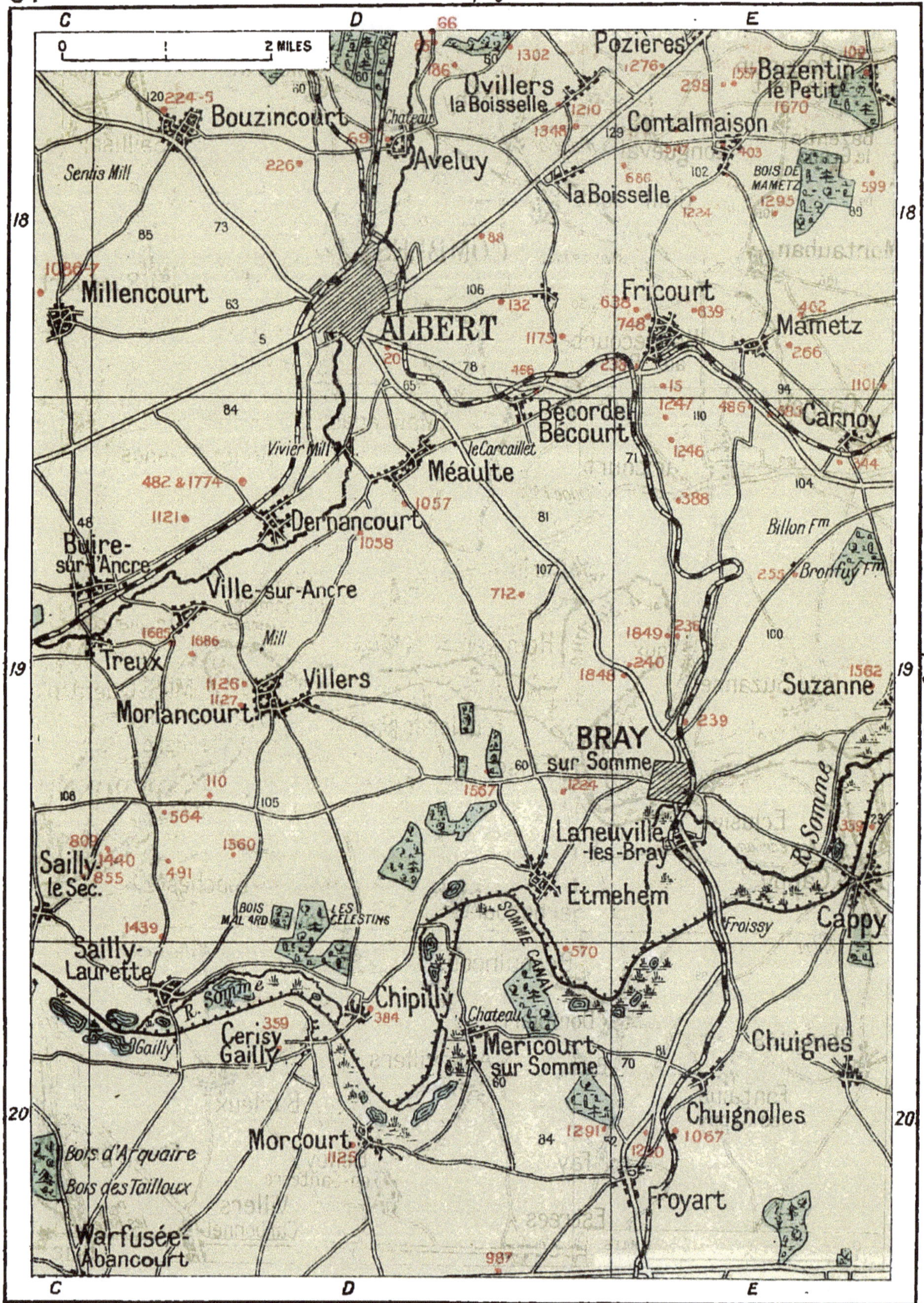


Continued on page 55.

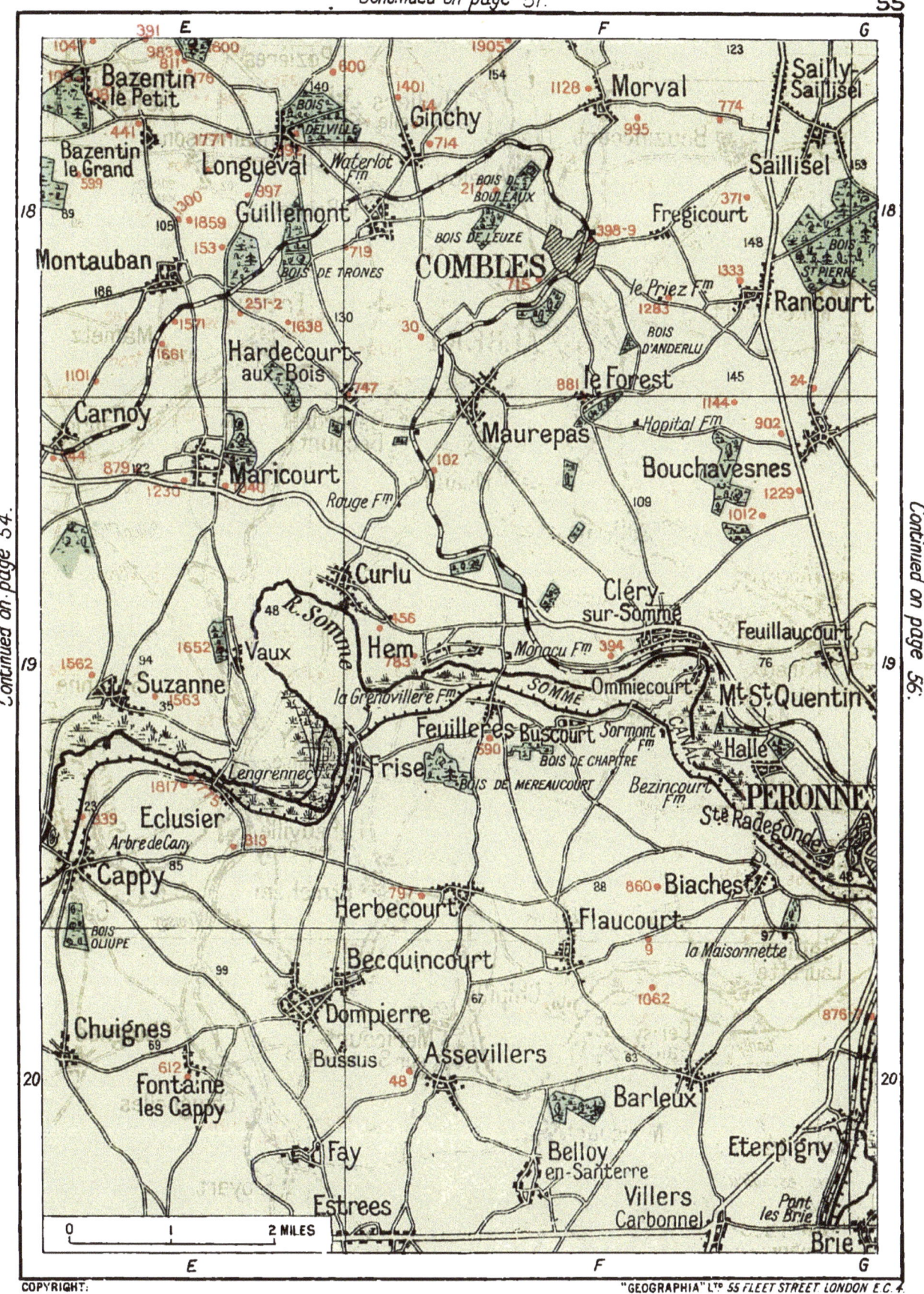

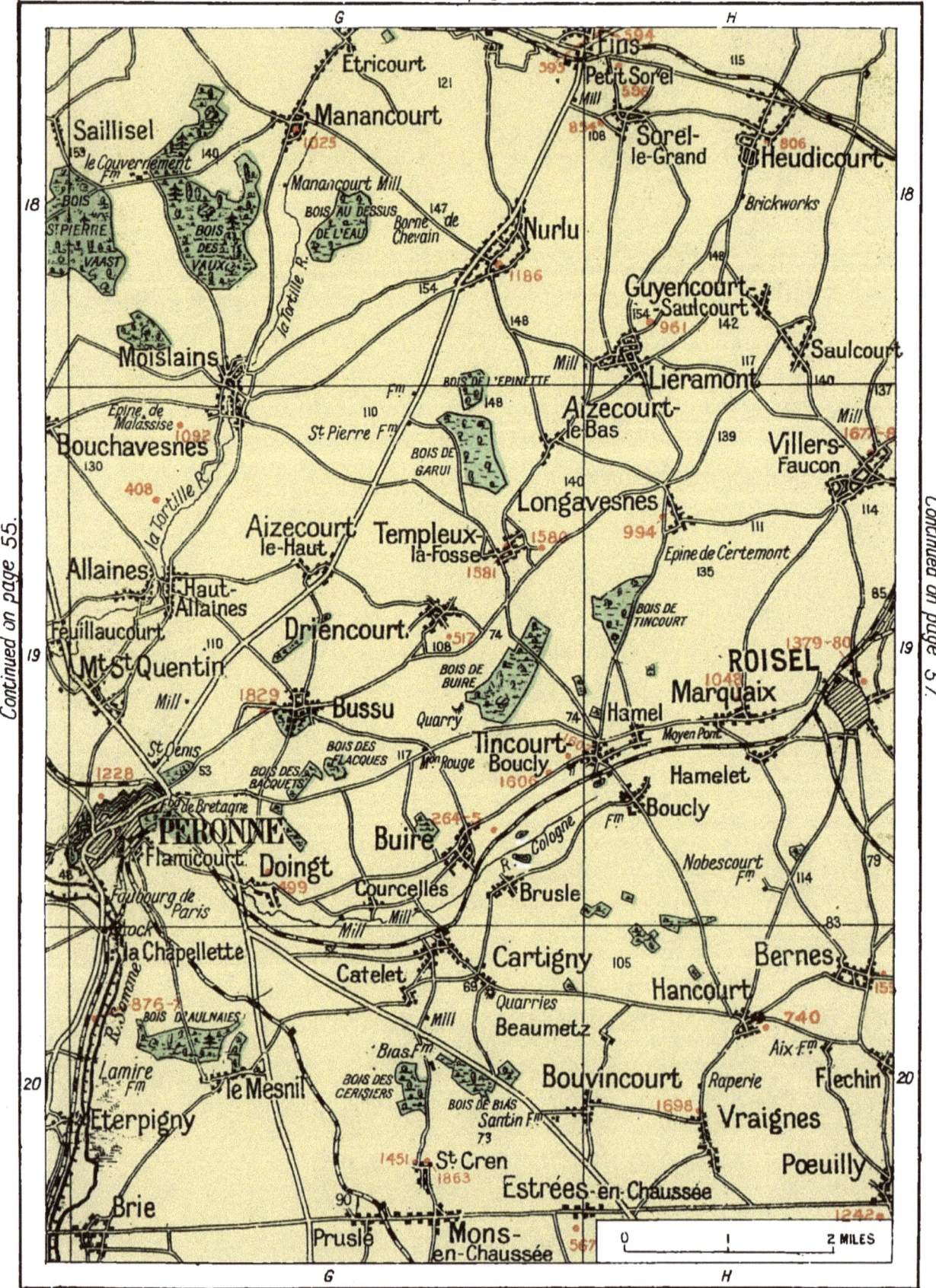

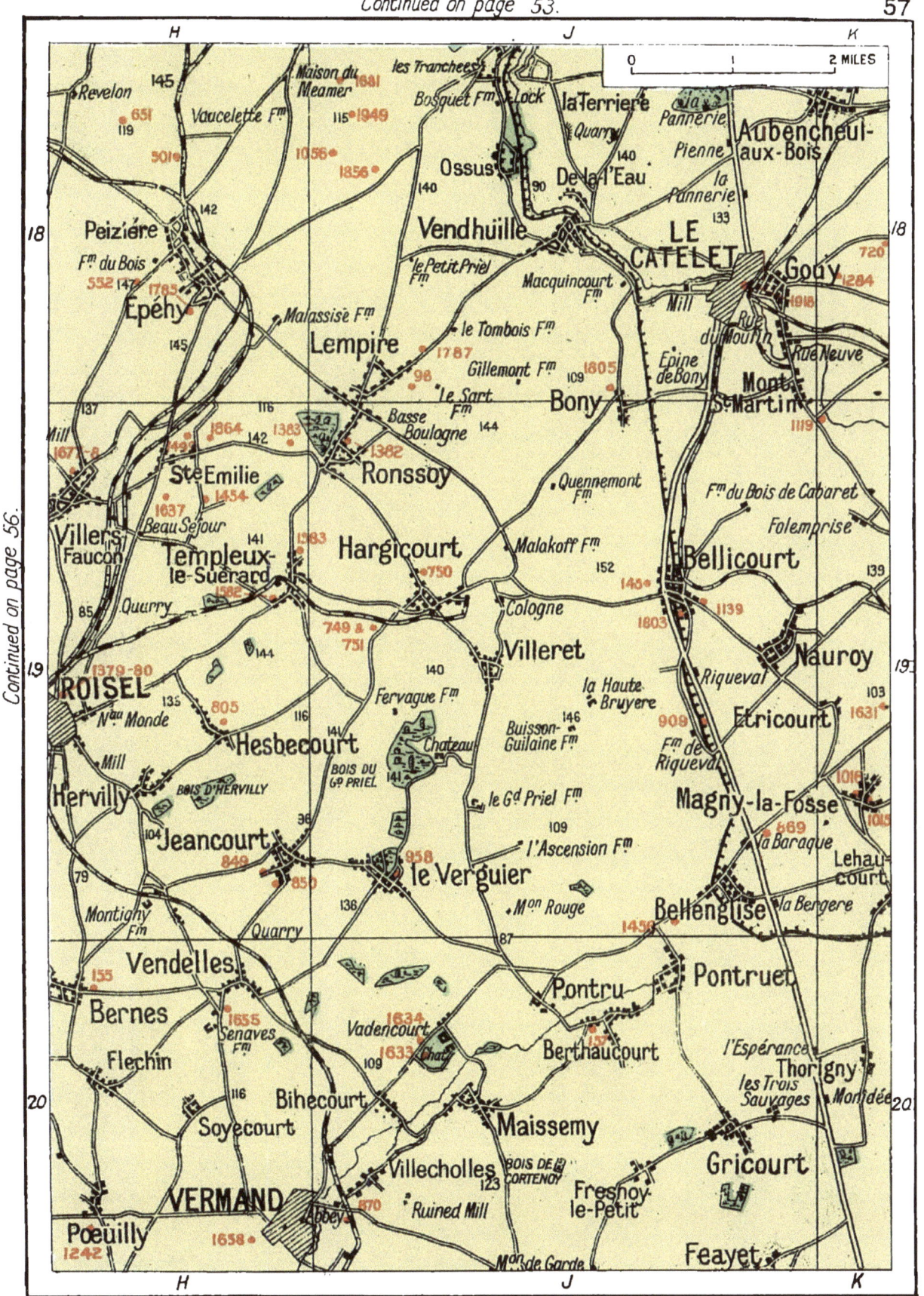

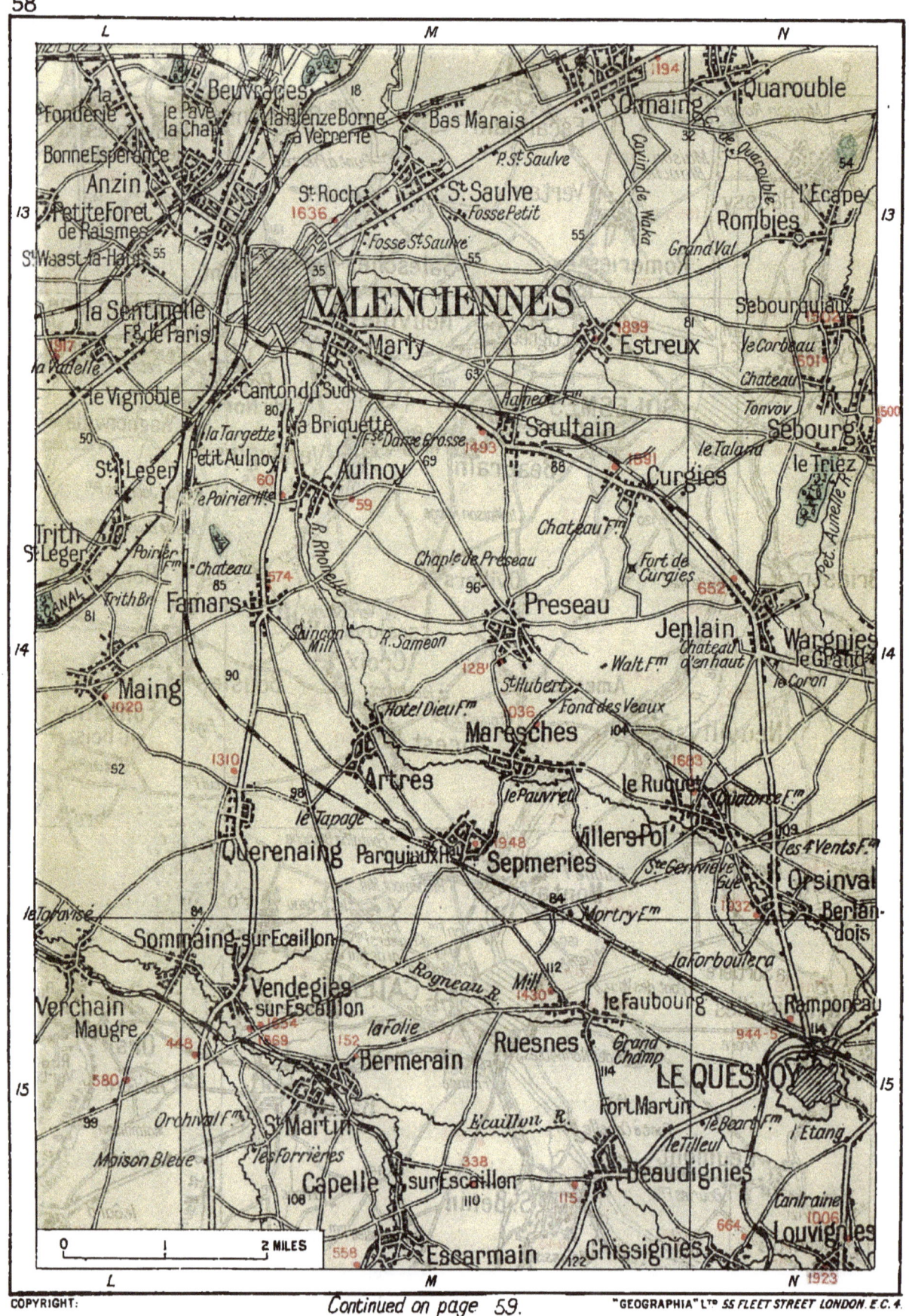

Continued on page 59.

Continued on page 58. 

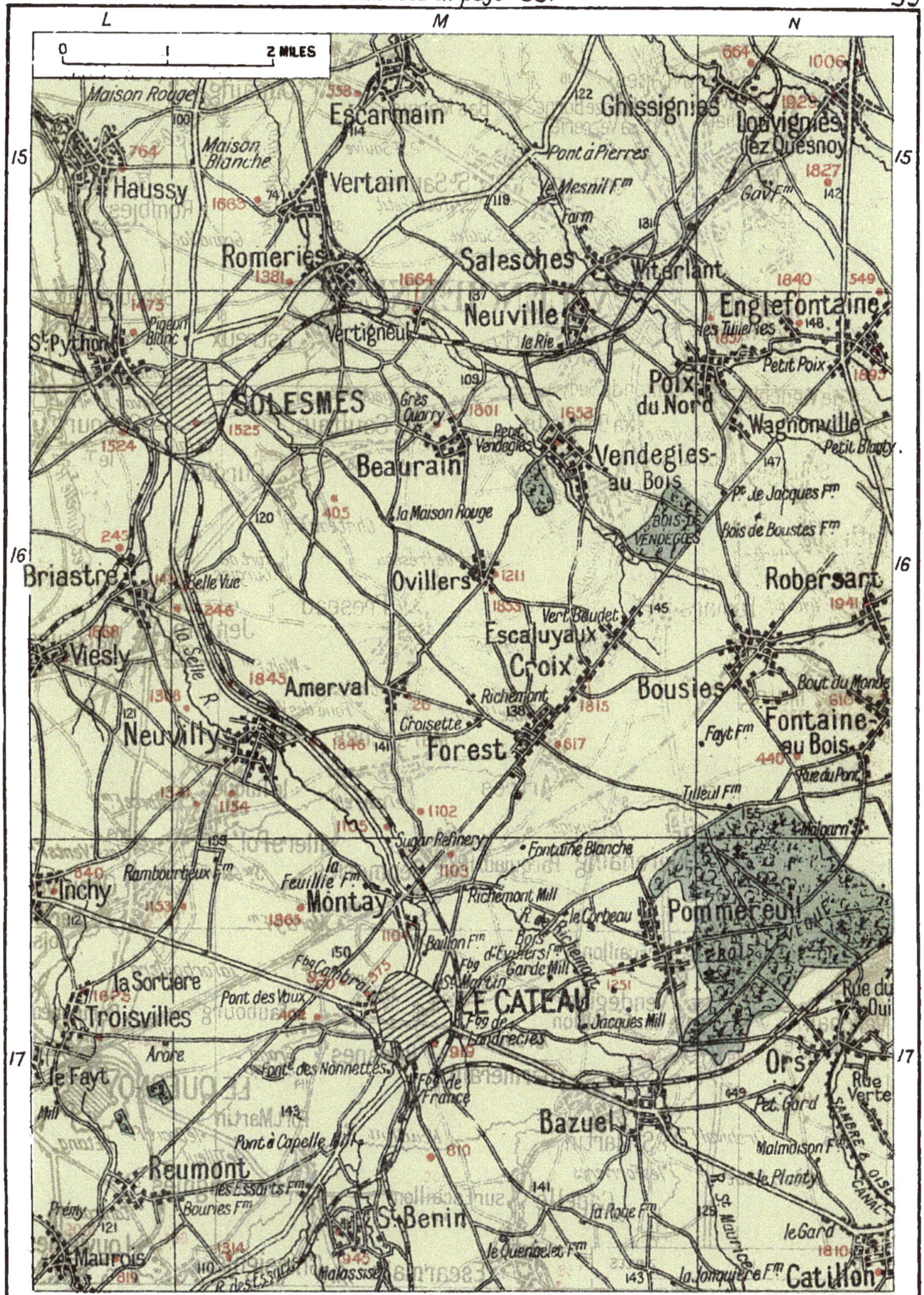


 "GEOGRAPHIA" LTD 55 FLEET STREET LONDON E.C.4.

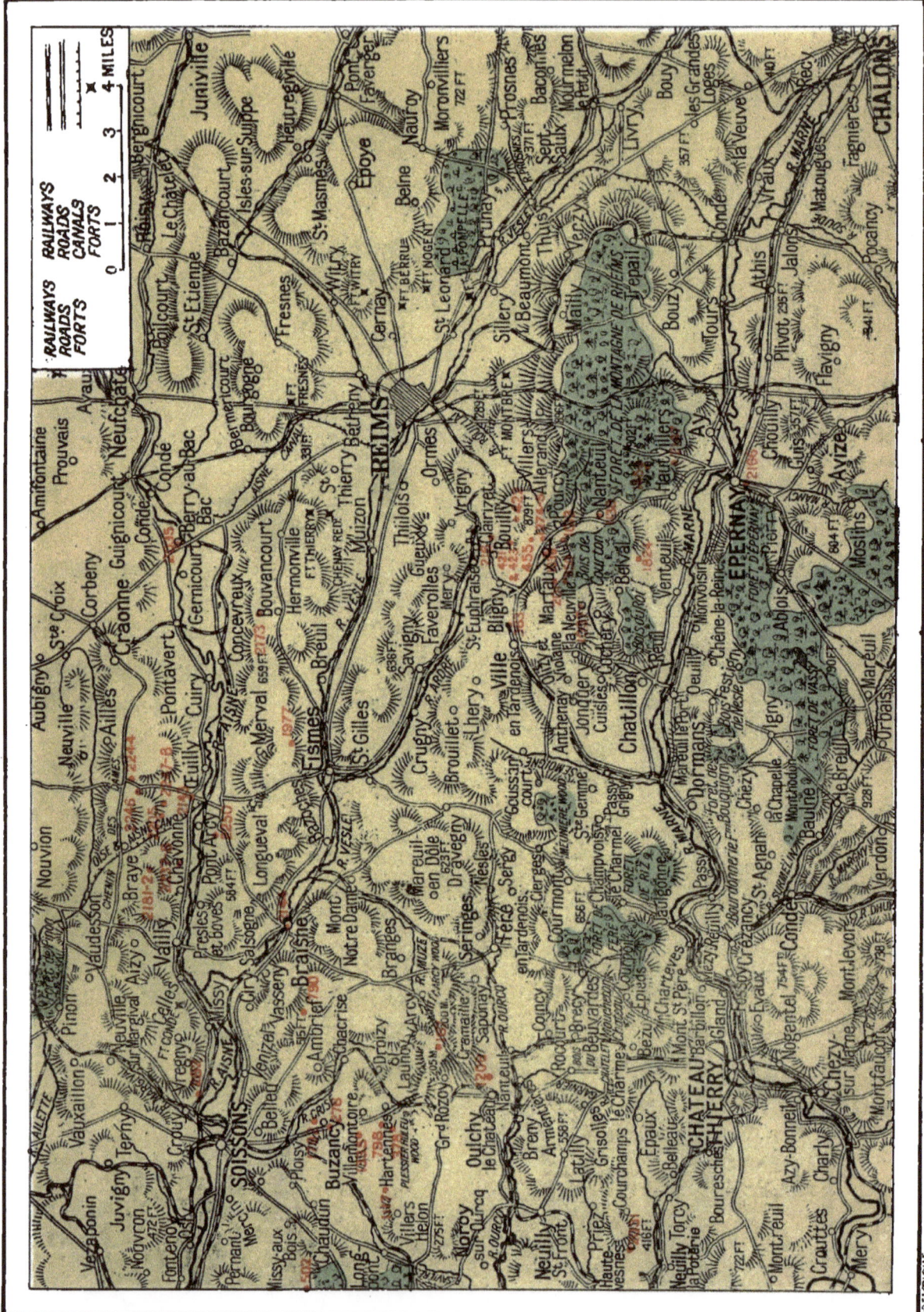

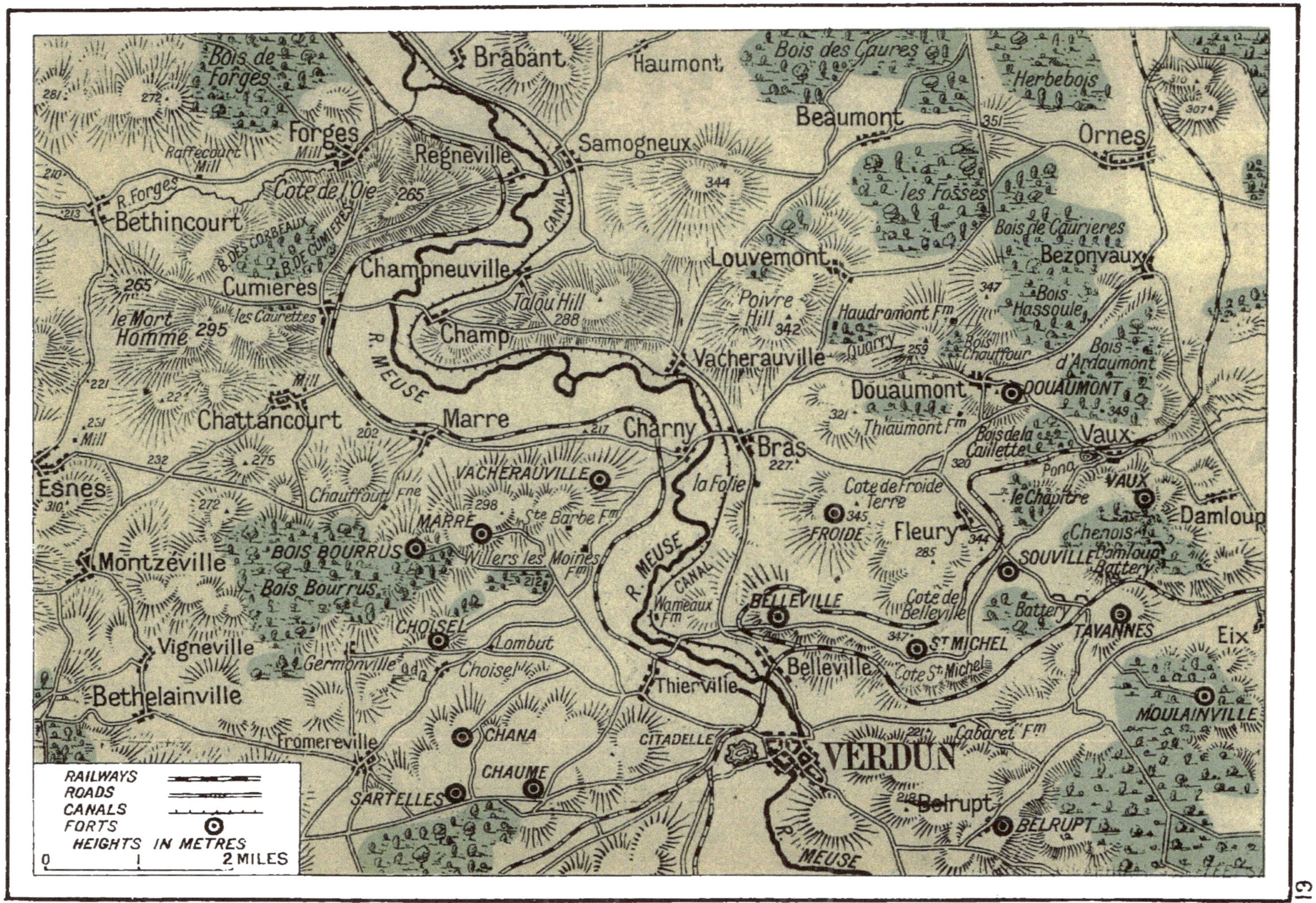




"GEOGRAPHIA" LTD 55 FLEET STREET LONDON E.C. 4

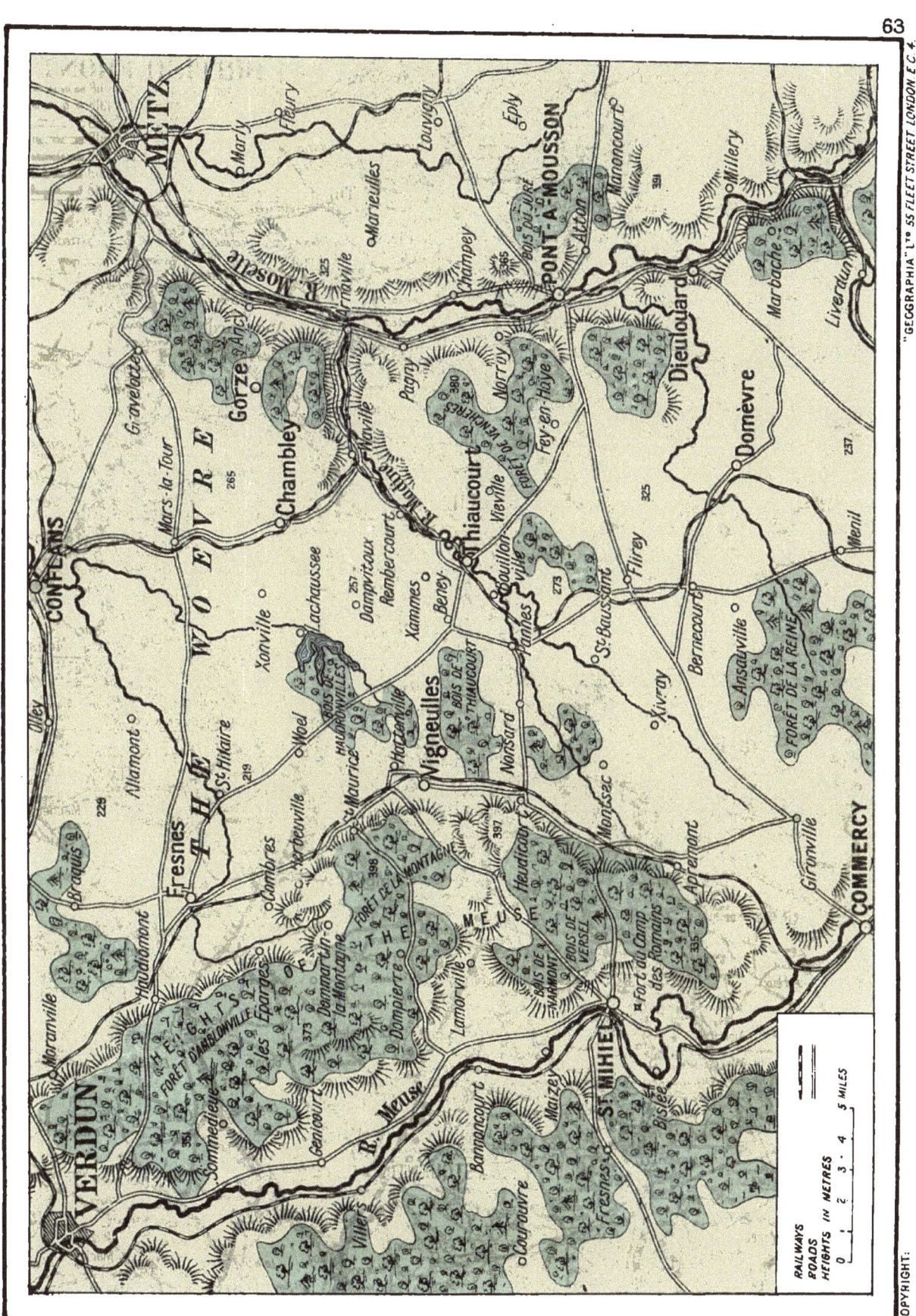

## WESTERN FRONT 1914-1918

THE WHITE CROSS INSURANCE ASSOCIATION LTD.

THE
# WHITE CROSS
## MOTOR POLICIES

FOR

PRIVATE CARS
COMMERCIAL VEHICLES
MOTOR CYCLES

and

EVERY TYPE OF MECHANICALLY PROPELLED VEHICLE.

---

The White Cross Insurance Association Ltd. was one of the first Offices to undertake Motor Insurance. It has specialised in this business for many years and holds the foremost position both as regards volume of business and the organisation it offers to the Motor Owner.

Motor Insurance differs to such an extent from any other class of insurance that an Office devoting special attention to one class is in a much more favourable position to handle the business in an expeditious and satisfactory manner. As some small indication of the extent of the business, the "White Cross" were, prior to the War, dealing with no less than 20,000 claims annually.

# Index to the Towns and Villages mentioned in the Description of the Battlefields (pages 69—109).

| | PAGE | | PAGE |
|---|---|---|---|
| AMIENS | 86 | Courdemange | 104 |
| Avocourt | 108 | Cumières | 106 |
| ALBERT | 89 | Chauny | 91 |
| ARRAS | 84 | Charny | 108 |
| ARMENTIERES | 81 | CHATEAU-THIERRY | 97 |
| Acy | 102 | Catigny | 91 |
| Augers | 103 | | |
| ANTWERP | 72 | Dour | 77 |
| | | Douaumont | 106 |
| Braches | 88 | Damloup | 107 |
| BAPAUME | 90 | DOUAI | 85 |
| Berry-au-Bec | 94 | | |
| Bras | 106 | Esnes | 108 |
| BAR-le-DUC | 104 | Etreux | 78 |
| Beaumont Hamel | 89 | Etrépilly | 102 |
| BRAY | 76 | Ermenonville | 102 |
| Bavai | 77 | Esternay | 103 |
| Betz | 77 | | |
| BAILLEUL | 82 | Fleury | 106 |
| BETHUNE | 82 | Frameries | 77 |
| Bethincourt | 106 | Flavy | 77 |
| Barcy | 102 | Fere-Champenoise | 103 |
| Baron | 102 | | |
| BRABANT-le-ROI | 105 | Gheluvelt | 83 |
| Beauzée | 105 | Gommecourt | 89 |
| BRUGES | 70 | Givenchy | 81 |
| BLANKENBERGHE | 69 | GHENT | 71 |
| BRUSSELS | 73 | | |
| BELFORT | 108 | Ham | 91 |
| | | Hulluch | 82 |
| Courtecon | 94 | Huiron | 104 |
| Chauvoncourt | 105 | | |
| CHANTILLY | 98 | | |
| Chattancourt | 108 | Lens | 82 |
| COULOMMIERS | 100 | LILLE | 79 |
| COURTRAI | 82 | Louvremont | 106 |
| COMBLES | 89 | LOUVAIN | 75 |
| CAMBRAI | 85 | La Fère | 91 |
| Crepy-en-Valois | 77 | LANDRECIES | 78 |
| Carency | 85 | LE CATEAU | 77 |
| Cuinchy | 82 | La Boiselle | 89 |
| CHAMBRY | 102 | Ligny | 78 |
| Crécy-en-Brie | 102 | LA BASSÉE | 81 |
| Chatillon | 103 | LOOS | 81 |
| Charleville | 103 | LAON | 91 |
| CHALONS-sur-MARNE | 103 | Liege | 75 |

## INDEX TO TOWNS AND VILLAGES (continued).

| | PAGE | | PAGE |
|---|---|---|---|
| Marcelcave | 88 | St. Paul | 93 |
| Morisel | 88 | St. Mihiel | 105 |
| Mailly-Raineval | 88 | St. Médard | 93 |
| Morlancourt | 88 | Souville (Forte) | 106 |
| Malancourt | 108 | Samogneux | 108 |
| MEAUX | 100 | SENLIS | 99 |
| Menin | 83 | Serre | 89 |
| Martinpuich | 89 | ST. QUENTIN | 90 |
| Mametz | 89 | Souchez | 85 |
| Montauban | 89 | Sézanne | 103 |
| MONS | 76 | Soummesous | 103 |
| Maroilles | 77 | Sommeilles | 105 |
| Marcilly | 102 | ST. OMER | 78 |
| Montceaux | 103 | | |
| Mondement | 103 | Thiaumont | 107 |
| MONTDIDIER | 91 | Thiepval | 89 |
| Mort Homme | 106 | Trocy | 102 |
| | | | |
| Nesle | 77 | Varennes | 105 |
| NOYON | 96 | Villers-Bretonneux | 88 |
| Nery | 78 | VERDUN | 105 |
| Neuville St. Vaast | 85 | Vauquois | 105 |
| Neuve Chapelle | 81 | Vaux | 107 |
| Normée | 103 | Vacherauville | 108 |
| NIEUPORT | 69 | VITRY-le-FRANÇOIS | 104 |
| | | Villers Cotterets | 77 |
| Ornes | 106 | Voulton | 103 |
| OSTEND | 69 | Villeneuve | 103 |
| | | Vassimont | 103 |
| PERONNE | 90 | Vimy | 108 |
| PROVINS | 101 | | |
| Presles | 77 | Wasmes | 77 |
| | | | |
| RHEIMS | 95 | YPRES | 82 |
| Revigny | 104 | | |
| Rembercourt-aux-Pots | 104 | Zandvoorde | 53 |
| | | Zillebeke | 83 |
| SOISSONS | 92 | | |

THE WHITE CROSS INSURANCE ASSOCIATION LTD.

# PRIVATE CARS.

Many of the present day features of Motor Insurance were inaugurated by the "White Cross" before they became generally adopted by competing Companies.

A most important and unique feature is the system of Authorised Repairers, a great advantage to Policy Holders. A Motorist touring away from Home—meeting with an accident has merely to acquaint the nearest Authorised Repairer, who will collect the damaged Car, and proceed immediately with the repairs, avoiding the loss of time necessitated by the securing and approval of an estimate.

### FEATURES OF THE PRIVATE CAR POLICY

**THIRD PARTY.** Unlimited Indemnity including Liability to Passengers.
Assured Indemnified whilst driving other Cars.
Relatives and Friends indemnified whilst driving insured Car.

**DAMAGE TO CAR.** Up to full insured Value, including Fire and Theft, whilst any person is using the Car.
Damage or loss of Accessories insured whether Car is damaged or stolen at the same time or not.
Value agreed and paid in full for Total Loss.
Immediate Repairs (see above).

RIOT AND CIVIL COMMOTIONS RISK
CONTINENTAL COVER AND TRANSIT RISK
FREE LEGAL DEFENCE    FREE TECHNICAL ADVICE
NO COMPULSORY ARBITRATION

*TRANSFERS FROM OTHER COMPANIES WITHOUT LOSS OF BONUS.*

# DESCRIPTION OF THE BATTLEFIELDS.

## BELGIUM.

OSTEND is one of the most brilliant watering-places in Europe, and is famous alike for its gaiety and for its fashionable and cosmopolitan habitués. Upon this bright little town fell the unhappy fate of being a seaboard fortress on the flank of the German line, and as such, had at times to be subjected to bombardment by British ships, and bombs, too, were frequenting dropped upon it by raiding aeroplanes and seaplanes. The Germans very strongly fortified the seafront with concrete emplacements and heavy naval guns, and on several occasions the shelling of these by British monitors and destroyers involved the destruction of the fine hotels and residences along the Digue. This latter is a stone dyke, about a mile in length and twenty-five feet high, the promenade portion being laid out in terra-cotta brick. The Kursaal, on the sea-front, contains the concert hall, ballroom and an exclusive *salle de jeu*. Beyond the Kursaal is the *châlet* where King Leopold used to spend part of the summer, and two fine parks added to the attractions which in peace time called over 50,000 visitors annually to the town. For one short period, in the early 17th century, Ostend was a pirate city. This was a few years after the famous siege by Spinola (1601-1604), which reduced the town to ruins. Jan Jacobsen, the pirate who sank the pursuing Dutch admiral's flagship and then set match to his own powder-magazine, hailed from Ostend, which has always produced a hardy breed of sailors and fishermen.

BLANKENBERGHE'S fate in the war was very similar to that of its more flourishing neighbour, Ostend. It is a more modest watering-place than the latter resort, but it is just as popular, though with rather a different type of visitor. It also possesses a Kursaal, and (a unique feature on the Belgian coast) a pier in the English style. The Digue rivals that of Ostend.

NIEUPORT, situated about ten miles from Ostend, was at one time a harbour of considerable importance. Bitter struggles were fought out among the dunes in its neighbourhood between German and Belgian troops, and it was often bombarded by long-range guns and bombed by aeroplanes.

Nieuport, like Ostend, had in the late Middle Ages a reputation as a pirate city. In 1600 Prince Maurice of Orange, a son of William the Silent, defeated the Archduke Charles under its walls, and it was also the scene of Turenne's victory in the " Battle of the Dunes " against the Spaniards, in 1658.

BRUGES is half-an-hour's journey by rail inland from Ostend. It is the most typical of all the older Belgian cities. Memling is the artistic genius of the place, and his celebrated " *Châsse de St. Ursula* " is the chief treasure of the Hospital of St. John, which so charmed Thackeray (" Roundabout Papers "). This painter, whose antecedents remain obscure, lived at Bruges for twenty years, dying there in 1495. The " *Châsse* " is a diminutive Gothic chapel, the painted panels of which are a series of exquisite miniatures depicting the life of Saint Ursula. Conspicuous from afar is the graceful spire of the church of Notre Dame, 400 feet high. This church dates from the 13th and 14th centuries. The modern cathedral is of no architectural importance, though the interior decoration is worth attention. Interest chiefly centres in the Market Place, where several historic buildings are grouped together. The famous belfry, which dominates the Place, was begun in 1291. Adjacent is the castle called the " *Lion de Flandre*," where Charles II. lived during his period of exile. On the south of the square stands the Town Hall, which was completed in 1387, and possesses unusually good exterior stone carving. The " Maison de l'Ancien Greffe," which was built in 1537, and retains traces of the gilding which once adorned much of its exterior surface, is near by, as is also the *Palais de Justice,* which contains a remarkable mantelpiece of black marble and oak, with life-sized figures of Charles V., Charles the Bold and Mary of Burgundy, historic personalities whose names occur in the history of the city. Bruges, which is called " Bruges the Dead," has declined greatly from the days when it numbered 200,000 inhabitants and was the central mart of the Hanseatic League. At the outbreak of war its population was about 55,000, and the newly-constructed canals were rapidly reviving its ancient prosperity. This canal system played a very important part in the German submarine warfare. When British monitors and seaplanes made things precarious for undersea craft while in dock at Zeebrugge, the enemy constructed a range of concrete-roofed docks at Bruges, and many submarines were brought there for repair. This brought upon the town frequent bombardments from the air, and although on more than one occasion the submarine docks were struck, damage was inevitably done to several buildings in the city.

GHENT, even more typically Flemish than Bruges, contrasts strongly with that city in its greater animation and commercial activity. In the days of Charles V. it was the largest town in Europe. At the outbreak of the recent war its population was under 170,000. At one time in its history, the period, namely, when Edward I. of England failed before its walls in spite of his powerful army, the Gantois could raise a fighting force of 80,000. In addition to Charles V., it was the birthplace of Van Artevelde (1290-1345), the famous "Dean" of the fifty-three trade-guilds, who attempted the bold and far-sighted policy of forming a federation of the Netherlands, and who, at the time of the Anglo-French wars of that period, assumed and deserved the title of "Guardian of the Public Peace of Flanders." Finally he was assassinated by those who opposed his scheme to have the English Black Prince elected Count of Flanders. Ghent was involved in a century of conflict with the Dukes of Burgundy to achieve its independence. In 1576 the "Pacification of Ghent" united the city with the rest of the Netherlands under William the Silent against the King of Spain. Its importance in the world of art dates from 1419, when the brothers Van Eyck went to live there. The city is full of quaint Mediæval corners. The Cathedral has few exterior beauties, but it is well furnished within by works of art of the highest quality. Near by stands the Belfry, 375 feet high, with the bell on which is inscribed: "My name is Roland; when I toll there is fire; when I ring there is victory in Flanders." The Oudeburg, which was the residence of the Counts of Flanders, the Rabot Gateway, the Hotel-de-Ville and the Grande Bequinage, are all places of interest. Modern halls of amusement are numerous enough.

ANTWERP. The fall of Antwerp in October, 1914, had great bearing upon events on the British front, for by reducing this fortress the Germans were able to liberate great forces just in time to take part in the operations which were developing north of La Bassee. When the Belgian army evacuated Brussels in August, it withdrew within the shelter of the wide fortified area of Antwerp, and in the ensuing weeks was a source of considerable anxiety and damage to the German northern lines of communication. Eventually the numerous and vigorous sallies of the beleagured Belgians enforced upon the Germans the necessity of taking the fortress, and early in October they brought up heavy artillery and began the siege in earnest. It was immediately obvious that the outlying forts were obsolete in the face of the new type of German howitzer, and the problem arose how best to save the city the horrors of bombardment without incidentally imperilling the existence of the hard-pressed garrison —the entire Belgian Army, that is to say. No trained Allied troops were available, except for part of the 7th British Division and a division of British cavalry, and these arrived only to find themselves involved in the confusion which was already becoming apparent owing to the rapid closing in of the encompassing enemy. Nevertheless, reinforcements of some kind to cover the retreat of the exhausted Belgian troops were imperative, and in these circumstances the British Minister of War decided to send out the Marine Brigade of the Royal Naval Division, composed at that time of about one-third first-class veteran marines and two-thirds raw and youthful recruits. On October 3rd this force, numbering about 2,000, arrived at Antwerp, and early next morning found itself occupying forward trenches, in contact with the Germans, who were then inside the outer chain of forts and were assaulting the inner ring. The Marine Brigade held the line for forty-eight hours under heavy shell-fire. Then, however, they were exposed on the flanks by the falling back of the Belgians, and were themselves compelled to retreat to reserve positions nearer the city. The enterprise ended somewhat ingloriously, but the main end was achieved. The Belgian army was enabled to extricate itself. Unfortunately, a large contingent of the retreating marines, striking north, fare. When British monitors and seaplanes made things precarious for undersea craft while in dock at Zeebrugge, the enemy constructed a range of concrete-roofed docks at Bruges, and many submarines were brought there for repair. This brought upon the town frequent bombardments from the air, and although on more than one occasion the submarine docks were struck, damage was inevitably done to several buildings in the city.

GHENT, even more typically Flemish than Bruges, contrasts strongly with that city in its greater animation and commercial activity. In the days of Charles V. it was the largest town in Europe. At the outbreak of the recent war its population was under 170,000. At one time in its history, the period, namely, when Edward I. of England failed before its walls in spite of his powerful army, the Gantois could raise a fighting force of 80,000. In addition to Charles V., it was the birthplace of Van Artevelde (1290-1345), the famous " Dean " of the fifty-three trade-guilds, who attempted the bold and far-sighted policy of forming a federation of the Netherlands, and who, at the time of the Anglo-French wars of that period, assumed and deserved the title of " Guardian of the Public Peace of Flanders." Finally he was assassinated by those who opposed his scheme to have the English Black Prince elected Count of Flanders. Ghent was involved in a century of conflict with the Dukes of Burgundy to achieve its independence. In 1576 the " Pacification of Ghent " united the city with the rest of the Netherlands under William the Silent against the King of Spain. Its importance in the world of art dates from 1419, when the brothers Van Eyck went to live there. The city is full of quaint Mediæval corners. The Cathedral has few exterior beauties, but it is well furnished within by works of art of the highest quality. Near by stands the Belfry, 375 feet high, with the bell on which is inscribed: " My name is Roland; when I toll there is fire; when I ring there is victory in Flanders." The Oudeburg, which was the residence of the Counts of Flanders, the Rabot Gateway, the Hotel-de-Ville and the Grande Bequinage, are all places of interest. Modern halls of amusement are numerous enough.

ANTWERP. The fall of Antwerp in October, 1914, had great bearing upon events on the British front, for by reducing this fortress the Germans were able to liberate great forces just in time to take part in the operations which were developing north of La Bassee. When the Belgian army evacuated Brussels in August, it withdrew within the shelter of the wide fortified area of Antwerp, and in the ensuing weeks was a source of considerable anxiety and damage to the German northern lines of communication. Eventually the numerous and vigorous sallies of the beleagured Belgians enforced upon the Germans the necessity of taking the fortress, and early in October they brought up heavy artillery and began the siege in earnest. It was immediately obvious that the outlying forts were obsolete in the face of the new type of German howitzer, and the problem arose how best to save the city the horrors of bombardment without incidentally imperilling the existence of the hard-pressed garrison —the entire Belgian Army, that is to say. No trained Allied troops were available, except for part of the 7th British Division and a division of British cavalry, and these arrived only to find themselves involved in the confusion which was already becoming apparent owing to the rapid closing in of the encompassing enemy. Nevertheless, reinforcements of some kind to cover the retreat of the exhausted Belgian troops were imperative, and in these circumstances the British Minister of War decided to send out the Marine Brigade of the Royal Naval Division, composed at that time of about one-third first-class veteran marines and two-thirds raw and youthful recruits. On October 3rd this force, numbering about 2,000, arrived at Antwerp, and early next morning found itself occupying forward trenches, in contact with the Germans, who were then inside the outer chain of forts and were assaulting the inner ring. The Marine Brigade held the line for forty-eight hours under heavy shell-fire. Then, however, they were exposed on the flanks by the falling back of the Belgians, and were themselves compelled to retreat to reserve positions nearer the city. The enterprise ended somewhat ingloriously, but the main end was achieved. The Belgian army was enabled to extricate itself. Unfortunately, a large contingent of the retreating marines, striking north, lost their way and wandered into Holland, where they were interned until the end of the war. Other parties were cut off by the pursuing enemy. The greater number managed to reach Ostend and safety. From first to last the total British loss in the Antwerp affair was not far short of 3,000.

Antwerp is by far the largest of the Belgian ports, and with its population of over 300,000, ranks next to Brussels. As seen from the Scheldt it presents a magnificent spectacle. It owed its modern commercial prosperity to Napoleon I., who relied upon it to deal a crushing blow at English trade. It is a veritable storehouse of works of art, and has retained many of the best works of Van Dyck and Rubens, whose lives and fame were so closely allied with the city. There are several fine examples of Ruben's work in the Museum, a handsome building that was formerly a Franciscan convent, near the Avenue du Sud. There, also, are admirable works by Van Dyck, Teniers, Van Eyck, and all the masters of the brilliant Flemish school. The most charming building in Antwerp is the Musée Plantin, so named after the printer, Christopher Plantin. It is no more than the business premises with attached residence of a rich Flemish citizen of the 16th century, and yet it recalls the harmony, beauty and seclusion of a college quadrangle at Oxford. The Cathedral, with its lofty, tapering spire, which has been compared to Mechlin lace, is familiar to all lovers of architectural beauty. A building of vastly different interest is the Steen Museum, which was once the city gaol, on the banks of the Scheldt. Here are to be seen mementoes of the cruelties practised by the infamous Alva and his like, terrifying dungeons and a collection of implements of torture of horrible ingenuity. But the real "sights" of Antwerp are the docks and canals, always, in pre-war days, crowded with shipping, and the great quays which have been built to meet the requirements of the thirty steamship lines which used the port.

BRUSSELS, early in the war, passed into the hands of the Germans. The sudden fall of Namur left the way clear to the enemy's armies, the right wing of which, throwing out containing forces to hold the Belgians within the Antwerp enceinte, swung through Brussels in its first curving swoop through Northern France towards Paris. Thenceforward the

Belgian capital was a captive city, far in the rear of the battle line.

Although its population numbers over half-a-million, Brussels is nevertheless a very compact city, and it is thoroughly up-to-date in all the improvements of modern civilisation, while yet retaining architectural and art treasures of past ages. In the *Bois de la Cambre* it possesses a suburban resort of immense attraction to the citizens. The *Quartier Léopold* is made up chiefly of the handsome residences of wealthy people. Within the last generation Old Brussels has to a large extent disappeared to make room for magnificent modern buildings and boulevards. Brussels is one of the foremost Continental training-grounds for musicians and singers. The *Théâtre de la Monnaie* is renowned as a home of grand opera, and the *Conservatoire* has produced many noted singers and violinists. For students of art the *Musée Wiertz* offers a display of works in which genuine power is curiously combined with eccentricity. Wiertz, who was born in Dinant, had an astonishing career of early adversity and eventual official recognition. The *Musée* was erected during his life-time to give scope to his peculiar talents. There are other art museums, such as that at *Cinquantenaire* and the *Musée du Congo,* which are worth a visit. The *Grande Place* is admittedly the finest square in Europe. The *Hotel-de-Ville* is a very imposing structure, and the *Maison du Roi,* which houses the Communal Museum, is also admirable, while historically, the square has staged some of the most lurid scenes in the history of the Netherlands. The Cathedral of St. Gudule dates back to 1220. A stained glass window commemorates the incident of the supposed theft there of the Sacred Host by Jews, on Good Friday, 1370, which resulted in a local " pogrom." The Verbruggen pulpit is worth a visit. In the Picture Gallery are numerous masterpieces, representative of the galaxy of Flemish painters. Close to the Museum of Old Masters is the Museum of Modern Painters and the Royal Library, which possesses over 300,000 volumes and numbers Phillippe le Bon's celebrated 15th century Burgundian collection of manuscripts among its treasures, including a variety of beautifully illustrated missals.

LOUVAIN, the deliberate, punitive destruction of which astounded and horrified the civilised world in the first month of the war, possesses a university foundation which, in the sixteenth century, when Lipsius drew over 6,000 students to his lectures, ranked first among the universities of the world. At the time of the invasion it still possessed twenty colleges and some 2,000 students, but the university had long since ceased to belong to the state, and had become affiliated to the Roman Catholic Church. Despite the numerous buildings of beauty and architectural value, there was always in Louvain an unusual number of squalid bye-ways for a town of this class. The *Hôtel-de-Ville*, the masterpiece of De Leyens and the pride of the city, was betraying obvious evidence of its 500 years' existence at the time of its complete destruction by German incendiarism. It was held to surpass the town-halls of all the greater Netherland cities, and in its elaborate sculpture and statuary was embodied a history of the country and the city. The library, comprehensive and rich in treasures, was also destroyed. The best of the churches is that of St. Peter, which has escaped complete destruction. In it is a good example of those realistically-carved pulpits which are sometimes met with in old-world Belgian churches.

LIEGE, with which history will hereafter associate the names of Brialmont, the designer of the fortress, and General Leman, who conducted the heroic defence, and was himself rescued from the debris of the last fort to be taken by the Germans, by its resistance in the first days of the war performed a service of inestimable value to the Allies, for by impeding the enemy's advance in the north for a precious week it did much to rob the invasion of its character of a surprise. The Germans lost heavily in two vain attempts to carry the entire position by assault. Eventually, after entering the town, they were obliged to invest and destroy each fort separately. The town is distinguished by its handsome public buildings and pleasant boulevards, while the river Meuse displays itself to full advantage there, and excellent views of it can be obtained from various points in the city, particularly from the citadel and from the bridges. The Cathedral, the University buildings and the church of St.

Jacques are all noteworthy, but still more attractive is the *Palais de Justice,* with its old-world quadrangle. The chief industry is the working of iron and steel, and machinery, particularly locomotive and marine machinery, is manufactured in the suburbs on a huge scale. The chief establishment is that of the Cockerill Company, the founder of which was an Englishman, who introduced steam engines on the Continent, as well as the conversion of steel by English processes. He died in 1840, and a street and a monument testify to the city's gratitude to him for his work.

MONS, whose name had acquired a kind of symbolic significance, and which meant so much of anxiety and afterwards of pride to the British Army, was the capital of the ancient Countdom of Hainaut, whose countess, Philippa, was the wife of Edward III. of England. Known in its early days as "the poor land of a proud people," the city in the 14th century became a market for cloth, and was henceforward prosperous. Its capture and subsequent surrender by Louis of Nassau in 1572 had some bearing upon the outcome of the religious wars. Several times besieged in the 17th and 18th centuries, it was made an open town in 1862. Its only noteworthy buildings are the late-Gothic Cathedral and the Hotel de Ville. Mons was a very flourishing town of some 30,000 inhabitants when the British Expeditionary Force formed up beside it to await the enemy attack. In its vicinity are the old battlefields of Malplaquet and Jemappes.

With this town on its right flank and Bray on its left, giving a front of about 20 miles, the British force, numbering 76,000 infantry, 10,000 cavalry, with 300 guns, met the German advance on the morning of August 23rd. It was a spectacular battle, for neither side had yet rid itself of the old traditions of warfare. The Germans attacked in massed, regular formation, as they had done in '70, and the British met them in trenches as shallow as those dug in the South African war. The enemy was successfully held at bay, though the losses were considerable, but next morning came the news of the defeat of the French 5th Army on the Sambre, whereby the British flank was stripped, and at the same time the real overwhelming preponderance of the enemy's strength became known. On August 24th the memorable retreat from Mons began.

After severe rearguard actions at Dour, Wasmes and Frameries, General Smith-Dorrien's Corps (the 2nd) managed to reach Bavai in good order. General Haig's Corps (the 1st), which had escaped the force of Von Kluck's flanking attack, continued to get off lightly, so far as fighting was concerned. The two corps parted company at Bavai. On August 25th Haig was in sharp contact with the enemy at Landrecies and Maroilles, while at the end of the same day Smith-Dorrien reached the Cambrai-Le Cateau line, where next day he gave battle, withdrawing at night in the direction of St. Quentin. Continuing the march south through Ham, Nesle and Flavy, Smith-Dorrien's corps then crossed the Oise near Noyon. Meanwhile Haig's corps had taken the line of the Aisne, and thus the British Expeditionary Force was spread over all the country between Nery, Crépy-en-Valois and Villers-Cotterets, the 1st Corps being involved in an action at the last-named place. Great exhaustion and confusion of units prevailed, and the two corps did not unite and get into order until Betz, further on the road to Paris, was reached, on September 1st. On September 2nd the British Force, having crossed the Marne, came to a halt near Presles. Of the towns involved in this Homeric retreat there are few that do not figure again, more or less outstandingly, in subsequent operations, but on account of the famous action fought there by a wing of the Expeditionary Force, mention must be made of

LE CATEAU. This is a small, wool-spinning town of about 12,000 inhabitants. In history it is remembered by reason of the treaty signed there between England, France and Spain in 1559. A 17th century church and a Renaissance town hall are its principal buildings, and a communal college is established there. General Smith-Dorrien, when he reached the town, was on the extreme left of the Allied line, which was in process of being rolled up by Von Kluck's torrential flanking advance. He elected to stay and fight a delaying action. It is upon this decision that Viscount French passed such severe censure in his book entitled " 1914." Smith-Dorrien had under him 70,000 men all told, a great part of whom had passed through the ordeal of Mons, and all of whom had shared in the first rigours of the retreat. Upon this force was rapidly massed a German army of at least 170,000, and a huge number of guns. The battle was neither lost nor won. But it served Smith-Dorrien's purpose, for the German advance appreciably slackened. The price paid, however, was very high, and several fine regiments were decimated. Near Le Cateau, north of the village of Ligny, are the quarries which were heroically held by units of the 11th Brigade, and Etreux, further south of the town, was the scene of the practical annihilation of the 2nd Munsters.

LANDRECIES, a small fortress town in the valley of the Sambre, where Haig's corps was in contact with the enemy during the retreat, is well known as the birth-place of Dupleix, the French counterpart of the great Anglo-Indian pioneer, Clive.

NERY, south of Compiegne, is one other place that should not escape notice in connection with the retreat from Mons. It was here that "L" Battery of the Horse Artillery was surprised by a German force with guns, and although all but one gun was put out of action by the first rounds of the enemy, that one gun was worked by a handful of wounded officers and men with such determination that the attacking force was successfully held off until assistance arrived.

## FRENCH FLANDERS.

ST. OMER came into prominence during the war as the seat of General Headquarters of the British Expeditionary Force. Known to the enemy as such, many air raids were made upon it and extensive damage done. Lord Roberts died there in November, 1914. It is built on the canalised Aa, which there joins another canal, connecting with the Lys. The Cathedral (13th to 15th centuries) is impressive, but not remarkable for beauty, although there are interior monuments and decorations of value. There are, indeed, many buildings of early date, each of which has claims of some kind or another, but none of them are of first importance. In addition to the Lycée there are schools of music and art, and diverse industries are carried on in leisurely fashion. In the suburb of Haut Pont is to be found a surviving stock of purely

Flemish land-cultivators, who retain jealously Flemish speech, costume and customs. The land around is very marshy, the reclaimed tracts being intersected by canals. Situated as it was in territory that was always being fought for by French, English, Flemish or Spaniards, the town had a chequered early history, and was often besieged. The feat of Jacqueline Robin, who outwitted the besieging army of the Duke of Marlborough to bring provisions to the citizens who were about to surrender through famine in 1711, is commemorated by a large monument in the city.

LILLE. Situated between the rivers Lys, Escaut and Scarpe, in the centre of the richest coalfields, Lille is the chief industrial town of France. But unlike so many similar industrial centres in England and other countries, Lille has a notable history, which begins as early as the 11th century, and as a frontier town it played a prominent part in the several great wars that were fought out in the plains of Flanders. Louis XIV. gave it a foretaste of trench fighting when he besieged it in 1667, and after its surrender to Marlborough in 1708 it was not restored to France until the Treaty of Utrecht. The citizens of Lille very gallantly resisted the Austrians in the Revolutionary Wars, and to-day, in the Grande Place, the chief feature is the statue of Jeanne Maillotte, who, emulating the Biblical Judith, crossed the enemy's lines during the siege of 1792, and with incredible bravery set fire to the Austrian batteries that were bombarding the town.

Lille remained outside the area of operations during the Franco-German war of 1870, but it was doomed to the hardest fate in the war just past. At the end of September, 1914, German patrols paid a transient visit to the town, from which the garrison had been withdrawn—Lille having long since ceased to rank as a fortress. In the rapid movement northwards of opposing forces which followed the first battle of the Marne, though meanwhile an inadequate garrison had been drafted into the town, Lille was left more or less to her fate, the Allied troops operating along the Yser not being strong enough to open a road to her. After a brief but intense bombardment, the French garrison surrendered on October 12th, 1914, and from then until October 17th, 1918, when the British marched in, Lille remained under German rule, suffering bombardment from her friends, and famine, requisitions, a galling system of passports and espionage, and all the armoury of suppression at the hands of the enemy.

Despite her grime and smoke, Lille has her show places. Not the least of these is the Bourse, which is recognised to be the finest example of 17th century Flemish architecture in France. The shops which now occupy the ground floor conceal the real harmony of the structure, but the upper storeys are a testimony to the quality of those twenty-four merchants who, in 1652, petitioned their then ruler, the King of Spain, for permission to erect a building worthy of their ambitious commerce. In an interior courtyard there is a statue of Napoleon I. of considerable merit, and the quite modern symbolic sculptures in the galleries are worth notice.

The remaining fragment of the Palais de Rihur, once the residence of Philippe le Bon, is perhaps the most interesting monument from the archæological point of view, but the church of St. Maurice, a 15th century building in the flamboyant Gothic style, with its unusual arrangement of five equal and co-lateral naves, has great attractions for students of architecture. This church also possesses several valuable paintings by Van Oost, Van der Burgh, and others of that school. The building was seriously damaged in the bombardment of October, 1914. Indeed, much of the quarter in which the church lies is in ruin. However, Lille churches are not of the first order, though most of them have a value in one respect or another. As something of a curiosity in the way of interior decoration, the sound-board of the pulpit in the church of St. Andre deserves notice. The carving represents a curtain held up by an angel, the massive folds of the curtain being very realistically treated. In the same church is a Rubens.

The pride of artistic Lille is the Museum, which is particularly rich in paintings. Rubens, Paul Veronese and Van Dyck are each worthily represented, and, indeed, the collection affords an excellent opportunity for a comprehensive appreciation of the Flemish, French and Italian masters. The museum is undoubtedly one of the best in provincial France, and before dispersal could count over 1,200 works of art.

The building was frequently struck in successive bombardments, but as it happened, the Germans, from motives perhaps easily inferred, had packed off most of the treasures to Brussels and elsewhere. The famous "Wax Head of a Girl," once the subject of universal discussion among connoisseurs, was concealed from the invaders by a trick, but subsequently came very near to being destroyed in its underground hiding-place.

With the Paris Gate and Vauban's celebrated Citadelle, which is said to be the masterpiece of that genius of military fortification (and which, since the Armistice, was involved in a serious fire), the objects of historical value are practically exhausted; but there are many ornate modern buildings, notably the Prefecture and the Palais des Beaux Arts, of which the Museum is a part.

Probably, however, for many a year to come the most engrossing sight of all will be the wide areas of ruin and destruction, which form strange vistas in the city. In this respect Lille suffered exceedingly, the blowing up of the German ammunition depot in the huge underground vaults in the ramparts called the "*Dix-huit Ponts*" being the worst, but not the only calamity of its kind.

ARMENTIERES, an industrial (linen) town of 28,000 population, was first occupied by the British in October, 1914, and subsequently became a "rest town" for units occupied in the trenches. The town came conspicuously into the war news in October, 1914, when the main British forces moved up from the Aisne to the extreme left of the Allied line, and entered upon the manœuvre which was intended to outflank the Germans at La Bassee and relieve Lille. The attempt brought the British troops to within half-a-mile of La Bassee, but the counter-manœuvres of the enemy turned what was begun as a flank attack into a frontal attack against superior numbers, and at the end of a week's fighting the battle-line was fluctuating further west, among the villages of Givenchy, Neuve Chapelle and others, south of Armentieres—fighting in which the Indian Corps took an active part.

LOOS, a town of no historical interest, with a population of about 10,000, can show no buildings of note. A very fierce battle there in 1915, on the British front, left a salient very similar to that at Ypres, and the fighting in the Loos salient in February, 1916, was characterised by extraordinary mining activity, in which mines were counter-mined and huge subterranean explosions were of daily occurrence. A poison gas attack of a particularly deadly nature was made just south of Hulluch in that month, in which the Irish Division lost 1,500 men.

BAILLEUL, a quaint little town, characteristically Flemish and picturesque, is chiefly noted for its beautiful hand-made lace. It did not suffer to any considerable extent from bombardment until the warfare opened somewhat, in 1918, when street fighting occurred there, as it had done also in 1914, and the town hall was destroyed. It was for more than three years in British hands, and was used as one of the places of rest behind the line.

BETHUNE was another behind-the-line refuge endeared to the memories of many of our fighting forces. It lies in the centre of the industrial area of France and makes, with Lens and La Bassee, the triangle containing such towns and villages as Cuinchy, Hulluch and Loos, each of which has given its name to one or more hard-fought battles. Bethune suffered badly in the German break-through in 1918.

YPRES was in former times considered as the capital of Flanders. It had prior to the war a population of nearly 20,000, and is situated on the Yperlee, a small canalised river which flows into the Yser, about 35 miles from Ostend. In its great days in the Middle Ages it numbered nearly 200,000 inhabitants, and rivalled Bruges and Ghent. The city is now laid waste. It possessed a 13th century Cathedral, in which Jensen, who was bishop of this diocese, was buried, and a Butchers Hall, built in the 15th century, was a memorial of great value and beauty. But its finest building—and it was one of the finest of its sort in existence—was the famous Halles, or Cloth Hall, which had a façade 150 yards in length. The Halles, begun in 1201, was completed a hundred years later.

A cavalry training school of the Belgian army was established in the town, whose citizens were proud of the part their ancestors played in the important battle of Courtrai, in

1302, when they decided the issue. It was a thriving butter-market, and had a prosperous linen and lace trade.

The town, which in its former aspect resembled a survival in these times of an unspoiled city of the Middle Ages, is now one of the most stupendous testimonies to the horror and destruction incidental to modern war. Its ruin is far more absolute than in the case of Louvain. Indeed, hardly a house remains standing, and most of the streets have been utterly obliterated by the ceaseless rain of shells and bombs that fell upon the place during more than four years of war. Ypres was the Verdun of the British front.

Of the two battles which go by the name of this town, the brunt of the first was borne by the 7th Division, under General Rawlinson, eventually reinforced by Haig's corps, which was in process of being transferred from the Aisne when the battle began. At its climax in the last days of October, 1914, the battle front extended over twelve miles, from the fateful Ypres-Menin road, through Zandvoorde, to Messines, and after a concentration of attack on Zandvoorde, it developed into a deadly action in and around the village of Gheluvelt, and the British line became worn so thin that but for the timely arrival of French reinforcements on October 31st, it is difficult to see how disaster could have been averted. The main battle lasted ten days, and it is admitted that had the enemy been able to throw in one more attack of an impetus and strength equal to the many that had gone before, Ypres would undoubtedly have been lost, and with it Calais, and, perhaps, the command of the English Channel. Until winter brought it to an end, fighting for positions continued, notably at Zillebeke, but with the repulse of the Prussian Guard at Polygon Wood the enemy strove no more for a time, and contented himself with the bombardment of the town he had failed to capture.

The second Battle of Ypres opened on March 16th, 1915, with a terrible gas attack which took the Canadian defenders of the salient quite by surprise. A panic among some Zouave troops on the flank spread temporary confusion, and resulted in the loss of valuable positions; but despite the gas the Canadians held on and checked the first furious German advance. Eventually the arrival of reinforcements brought about a definite repulse of the enemy, with grievous losses, although he succeeded in narrowing the salient, and was able to maintain several of the positions he nad gained. In the course of this battle the civilian population was evacuated from Ypres, which was constantly and heavily shelled. Fighting continued on a large scale until May 17th, 1915, but even when the battle proper came to an end there was rarely a day's quietness on the salient, though there was no more heavy and continuous warfare involving large forces until the August of 1917. All the villages in the wide arc are historic on account of the conflicts waged for their possession, and all of them have been devastated.

ARRAS formed a forward base for Haig's great Vimy offensive in the spring of 1917, which was one of the most carefully planned and prepared operations ever undertaken by the British, and which was backed by artillery support for the first time commensurate with, if it was not actually superior to, that of the enemy. In ancient days Arras was the chief city of the Gallic tribe of that region. It became noted for its cloth manufacture as early as the 4th century, and the tapestries woven there in the Middle Ages have ever since been renowned. In later days it prospered chiefly on its trade in grain, and it numbered more than 25,000 inhabitants on the outbreak of war. After the Battle of Agincourt, the treaty of peace between the French and English was signed there. It was twice occupied by the Germans in the course of the war just ended, first in September, 1914, and afterwards in 1918—in each case for a short period. But it spent most of the intervening time within range of German heavy artillery. Nevertheless most of the citizens remained, and the city was a boon to men released for a few days' rest from trench fighting. The plucky little newspaper which from time to time was printed and issued there reflected the spirit with which the civilian population faced the situation. Arras suffered severely from bombardment, and of the several buildings of great worth and historical interest it is unfortunately necessary to speak as though they no longer existed. The late-Gothic Town Hall had been finely restored in the last century, and the Cathedral, a modern building, possessed interior decoration of much beauty. A street of quaint

Spanish houses served to remind the citizens of the extent of Spain's domination and influence in the 17th century.

Between Arras and Lens, in the neighbourhood of Neuville St. Vaast, was situated the celebrated German " Labyrinth," a complex system of field fortifications guarding the flank of the Vimy Ridge. Tremendous fighting occurred hereabouts between the French and Germans, as also at Souchez and CARENCY—villages further north. The ruins of Carency have been engulfed in the craters of the huge mines exploded there.

DOUAI, situated in a marshy plain on the banks of the Scarpe, 20 miles south of Lille, has a normal population of 33,000. The principal building is the 15th century Town Hall, which possesses an unusually lofty belfry. The church of Notre Dame dates from the 12th to the 14th centuries, and has a celebrated altar-piece of a later date. It is the seat of various educational institutions. In the 16th century many English and Scottish religious and collegiate foundations were established there, and it has given its name to an English translation of the Bible known as the " Douai Version." It was not definitely annexed to France until the Treaty of Utrecht, in 1713. The museum contains paintings of value.

CAMBRAI. A handsome and interesting town of about 27,000 inhabitants, situated on the Scheldt, 37 miles south east of Lille. First fortified by Charlemagne, it achieved fame on account of the League of Cambrai (1508), and the Peace of Cambrai, or the " Ladies' Peace " (1529), so called because it was signed by Louise of Savoy, mother of Francis I., and Margaret of Austria, aunt of Charles V., in the name of these monarchs. Among the monuments in the 19th century Cathedral of Notre Dame is that of Fenelon, who was Archbishop of Cambrai from 1695 to 1715. The ancient fortifications of the town have been demolished in great part, but there remains the square citadelle in the east of the town, called the Castle of Selles, an immense example of 13th century military construction.

Cambrai has given its name to the startling attack which General Byng delivered in that sector in November, 1917. The town was then an important enemy depôt, and it appeared to be impregnably shielded by the hitherto impenetrable Hindenburg Line. Moreover, the time of the year and the unfavourable weather conditions left the world unexpectant of any momentous activity on the Western front just then. However, affairs in Italy demanded a diversion, and this operation was the outcome.

In it tanks made their debut as a real arm, with results so far-reaching as actually to have imperilled, in the long run, the success of the venture. The Hindenburg Line was badly breached, and a deep salient thrust into the German positions. No less dramatic was the German counter-attack. Massing an overwhelming force with astonishing rapidity, the enemy burst upon the extended and poorly-supported British line, which was rather badly broken and thrown back, with considerable loss in men and material, to its original position. Despite the momentary depression which followed the elation of victory, something was gained, namely, the knowledge that the Hindenburg Line was not invulnerable, and that tanks were irresistible.

## THE SOMME AREA.

AMIENS. This historic city, built at the juncture of the Somme, Avre and Selle, the radiating centre of nine railways, took on something of the character of a war capital or centre of operations from the time hostilities in the West became definitely restricted to the northern regions of France. Its normal population was over 90,000, and, physically, the city divides itself into three sections, namely, the South, or new, town which comprises the chief boulevards and residential districts; the Centre, the business part, where most of the public and historical buildings are situated, and the Lower Town, Old Amiens, where, amid quaint old-world streets, are the workshops and factories of modern industry.

On the whole 15th and 16th century architecture is best represented in the numerous buildings of historical or archæological interest. An exception is the Theatre, the oldest playhouse in France, which has a Louis XVI. façade of considerable artistic value, though now much damaged by a German shell. An example of Renaissance domiciliary architecture in its purest form is to be found in the Maison du Sagittaire (" The Archer's House "). The Ancien Bailliage ("Old Bailiwick") is an interesting survival of the 16th century. The church of St. Germain (much damaged by a bomb), and that of St. Leu, in the Old Town, are 15th century, and are not to any great extent spoilt by restoration. The ancient and delapidated Hotel Morgan de Belloy (1493), and the Citadelle are the chief of the remaining monumental features of the city, but of modern buildings the Museum, which was in part ruined by an aerial torpedo, is noteworthy on account of the collection of the paintings of that very individual artist, Puvis de Chavannes. These large mural decorations, which had happily been removed to a place of safety before the Museum was struck, represent the dawn of humanity, and the scenes are rendered with a breadth and imaginative vagueness that is in curious accord with scientific conceptions of the life of mankind in its earliest stages. The corners of the city that are most favoured by lovers of the quaint and the picturesque are the Place des Huchers, where a group of ancient wooden houses are to be seen, and, in the same neighbourhood, the very curious "Hortillonnages," the islet kitchen-gardens, the produce of which is carried for sale to the "market of boats," or the "floating market," at the Place Parmentier.

But as so often is the case in the ancient towns of France, Amiens is dominated by its Cathedral, which is of almost unrivalled fame as the largest church in France, and the structure in which the magnificent possibilities of Gothic architecture came very near to complete realisation. Begun in 1220, it is also unique in that, having been finished in about fifty years, it was reared in the closest conformity to the plans of the architect, Robert de Luzarches. A marvel of strength and adjustment, nevertheless, with such refinement of art was it planned, an effect is produced of aerial, insubstantial grace in all its aspects. The vault of the nave, 140 feet high, is the second highest of its kind in France.

Sculpture contributes greatly to the beauty of the building, the triple doorway of the west façade being particularly fine, while among the interior decorations the works of a Picardy sculptor of genius, Nicolas Blasset (d. 1659) are noteworthy. The paintings in the Cathedral are of no great significance, the altar screen in the south transept, by Francken, being considered the best of them. But the oak stalls of the choir, the flamboyant Gothic masterpieces of local woodcutters in the early 15th century, are unsurpassed. They excel in every respect, in the comprehensiveness and the human interest of the subjects chosen for representation, in detail and perfection of finish. This incomparable church suffered to some extent from bombardment, but though it was struck by nine shells in all, damage was confined to chapels on the south of the nave. Its escape from severer damage was, however, often miraculous, as neighbouring ruins testify.

Amiens made a very early acquaintance with the enemy, who occupied it on August 31, 1914, in the course of his first rush towards Paris, but he was obliged to evacuate the city as one of the results of the first Battle of the Marne, and Amiens ever after remained inviolate, so far as armed enemy forces were concerned. It experienced days of acute peril, however, in the spring of 1918, when Ludendorff launched his desperate offensive, and made Amiens, which had become the hinge of the Allied front, his chief objective. The German attack was then extremely fierce and sustained, and after the check which followed on its first partial success, was again renewed with the utmost determination. The enemy reached the village of MARCELCAVE in the first onrush, and in their second attempt, on April 4th, succeeded in crossing the Avre and reaching MORISEL and MAILLY-RAINEVAL. The attack was finally brought to an end on April 26th, when French and British, fighting together, definitely repulsed the enemy at VILLERS-BRETONNEUX. In the ensuing two months the city suffered its severest series of bombardments, but already, in the second week of April, the civilian population had been withdrawn. The final relief dates from the combined French and British attack of August 8th-9th, on the line BRACHES-MORLANCOURT, to which attack the Germans offered only a half-hearted resistance, and were soon driven to a distance that made Amiens quite safe from their guns.

Throughout the city extensive destruction has been wrought, and most of the finest buildings were hit at least once. The roof of the Prefecture, for instance, was partially demolished, the church of St. Remy and the St. Roch railway station were also damaged, the latter very badly, while in some parts whole sections of streets have been levelled.

ALBERT. This considerable industrial town and numerous outlying villages such as Thiepval, Gommecourt, Martinpuich, recall episodes in the sanguinary Somme Battle, which opened on July 1st, 1916. Thiepval saw the extinction of the heroic 8th Division, which moved out to an attack on the German trenches and never returned, a few hundred wounded and stragglers being all that were ever recovered. Martinpuich was the scene of a dashing advance by the 15th Division, consisting of Scottish regiments. It may be taken for granted that all the villages that are mentioned in connection with this battle are now in ruins.

The Battle of the Somme a conjoint effort by French and British was a mixture of victory and repulse. As at Thiepval, the 10th Corps suffered a bloody reverse, so the 7th Corps failed before Gommecourt, and the 8th were checked with heavy losses at Serre and Beaumont Hamel. But La Boisselle, Mametz and Montauban were the scenes of brilliant successes of British arms, while south of this last-named village, where the French attack joined, on a scale not quite so large as the British, the battle went steadily in favour of the Allies. On a battle-front of twenty-two miles the British could claim victory over seven miles. Combles, which was one of the chief objectives, was entered in conjunction with the French on September 25th. On July 1st, the first terrible day of the battle which was only brought to a close by the total break-up of the weather in October, it is estimated that the combined losses, Allied and German, was more than 100,000 in less than twenty-four hours' fighting, and at the end of the day nearly 10,000 prisoners remained in the hands of the French and British.

Prior to the war, Albert was known to the pious on account of the popular pilgrimage to its chief church, Notre Dame de Brebières. From the summit of the steeple of this church hung precariously the statue of the Virgin, which had been partially dislodged by a shell. This hanging statue became a land-mark of no very happy significance to troops on their way to the marshy trenches of this area, and a prophecy became attached to it that when it fell the war would end.

The statue was eventually brought to the ground in the final stage of the fighting. Albert has been utterly devastated by the continuous bombardment to which it was subjected, and which became especially severe during the operations of 1918.

BAPAUME, which was of military importance in the defence of Amiens, was, in 1871, the scene of a memorable secondary battle in the Franco-German War, when the French gallantly thrust back the Germans beyond the Somme. In the recent war fighting first occurred there on August 27th, 1914. On that occasion two French divisions, thrown forward to oppose the German advance, were driven in, and Amiens was temporarily lost. Bapaume lay behind the German line until March, 1917, when the British captured it on Hindenburg's extensive withdrawal movement. A year later it was lost by the 5th British Army in the course of Ludendorff's general offensive.

PERONNE, the fate of which had also a bearing upon the safety of Amiens, shared Bapaume's vicissitudes. It is a small town, with a normal population of about 4,500. It is, however, of ancient origin, for it is recorded that St. Fursy, an Irish monk, founded a monastery there as far back as the year 600. Practically the only object of historic interest is the cell in which Charles the Simple is said to have lain until he starved to death. Peronne was a fortress in 1815, when the Duke of Wellington took it. After its capture by the Germans in the first weeks of the war, it remained an enemy headquarters until the British took it in 1917. An important series of conflicts was fought in the vicinity in September, 1914, after the first Marne battle, until the front line became stabilised. In Ludendorff's drive in the early spring of 1918 it passed into his hands for a short period.

ST. QUENTIN, after coming into prominence on account of an action which was fought there in the first weeks of the war, subsequently gave its name to a sector of the British line, based along the Crozat Canal, which was held chiefly by London troops when the enemy made it one of his points of attack in his tremendous and final offensive. The town, which existed before the days of the Roman conquest, rises from the right bank of the Somme, at the juncture of the

St. Quentin and Crozat canals. It was engaged largely in the woollens industry, and had a population of about 50,000. It is mentioned in English history as being part of the dowry of Mary, Queen of Scots. The French Northern Army was defeated there in 1871. The church of St. Quentin dates from the 12th to the 15th centuries. Otherwise, besides the Town Hall, the chief building is the extensive municipal edifice called the Palais de Fervoques, which contains the Courts of Justice, the Library and the Gallery of Paintings.

In the St. Quentin sector La Fère, Chauny, Ham and many other villages suffered severely in the course of the German attempt to break through. Ham, which was of some military consequence to the Allies, is chiefly noted as the prison of Napoleon III., and its show-place is the donjon from which the future emperor made his escape in 1846.

MONTDIDIER, 23 miles south-east of Amiens, has a population of some 5,000. It marks the limit of the German advance—or perhaps the village of Cantigny—in 1918. During the fighting then, when it passed into the enemy's hands for a short time, it was very severely damaged, chiefly by the batteries of the Allies. Its church of St. Pierre (15th century) has an exceptionally beautiful porch, and in the church of St. Sepulchre there is to be seen the well-known 16th century representation named the " Holy Sepulchre." The town is said to owe its name to the Lombard king Didier, whom Charlemagne imprisoned there. Historically it is proud of its resistance to a Spanish army in 1636. A statue in the town commemorates the birth there of Parmentier, who introduced the cultivation of the potato into France.

## THE AISNE AREA.

LAON is a fortress town guarding the " Trouee de l'Oise," and it forms with La Fere and Rheims a fortified triangle protecting the roads to Paris from the East. It is of ancient origin, and owing to its strategic situation has often been the bone of contention between rival armies. The population numbers about 17,000. Although in the centre of the war area in the recent war, and although it more than once changed hands, and was an objective in offensives, it has not suffered damage to the same degree as Rheims. It is situated on an isolated ridge, down the sides of which many of its roads run in zig-zag fashion, while from the railway station to the gates of the town a stairway of several hundred steps has proved necessary. Three of its 13th century gates have been preserved. The Cathedral (12th-13th centuries) is cruciform in design, and has no apse, the choir ending abruptly in a straight wall. There are six towers flanking the façades, and a square central tower. Its west front rivals hat of Notre Dame of Paris in beauty and elaboration. There are several other ecclesiastical buildings of worth, not omitting the 12th century Templars' Chapel. Napoleon suffered one of his few defeats in the vicinity of Laon in 1814. In 1870 a French sapper put a match to a powder-magazine in the citadel at the moment the Germans were entering the town, and as a result many lives were lost, and the Cathedral and the episcopal palace were damaged.

SOISSONS, on the left bank of the Aisne, with suburbs on the right bank, was an unfortified town on the outbreak of war. It is identified with the Noviodunum of the days of Cæsar. Its heyday was in the Dark Ages, and its eventful history conjures up some of the most glowing figures of that part of the history of France which is blended with legend. Clovis was married there, and Peppin the Short was proclaimed king and crowned there, while it was at the Synod of Soissons in 1121 that Abelard's teachings were condemned. In the religious wars round about 1560 the city passed from hand to hand, and was once sacked.

A description of Soissons as it is to-day resolves itself into an enumeration of ruins. Of the Cathedral all but the choir, apse and transepts have been wholly or in part demolished. The nave is a complete ruin, a huge gap at the western end separating it from the shattered tower. It was never one of the primary churches of France, but it has, or had, some good 13th and 14th century characteristics, while the southern arm of the transept, happily quite intact, is an example of 12th century Primitive Gothic in which the severity and simplicity of that period of architecture is shown in its noblest form. Among the other chief buildings which display evidence of merciless bombardment are the Bishop's Palace, with its 13th century tower, the Theatre and other edifices in the Grand Place, and the College. Of the church of St. Leger, a 12th century abbey church much transformed by restoration, the tower has been destroyed, and the nave greatly damaged. Luckily the crypt has escaped injury, but that cannot be said of the fine early cloister. The Hotel-de-Ville, which houses the Museum, a large modern structure in good style, was shelled, and there are, or were until recently, trenches in the garden to bear witness how near the fight had come. Beyond fairly valuable specimens of 12th and 13th century sculpture, there is little of note in the museum. The ruin called the Abbey of St. Jean-des-Vignes is the remnant of what was one of the greatest monasteries of the Middle Ages. The main front, with its towers each nearly 240 feet tall, was preserved on the appeal of the inhabitants against the vandalism of officials, who were using the stones of the abbey in the work of restoring the cathedral. Even this ruin received the attentions of the German gunners.

In the environs of Soissons, at the Chateau de Saint Crépin-en-Chaye (now a mass of debris) the field fortifications begin; and there were trenches the whole length of the Mail, the promenade beside the Aisne which used to hold a high place among the public gardens of France. The Pont-Neuf, a bridge of reinforced concrete built in 1903, was blown up by the British in their memorable retreat after Mons. The whole suburban area on this side was a net-work of field-fortifications. Across the Aisne, about half-a-mile from the Pont-Neuf, is the ruined distillery which figured largely in the accounts of the fighting around Soissons, and confronting it, at Vauxrot, is the glass-works which formed an important post in the German line. There are examples hereabouts of every conceivable subterfuge and device for cover and observation in trench warfare. At Pasly are the caves which were first fortified by the Germans and afterwards became a place of refuge for the inhabitants of the village.

Another interesting point in the French line at Soissons was the fortified hamlet of St. Paul, which formed the apex of a German salient; and the military features are repeated at St. Médard, further south. This latter is a very historic faubourg, which has associations as early as the Merovingian kings, and is named after the saint over whose ashes a monastery was raised which became the venue of a famous pilgrimage. Indeed, it is on record that on one occasion, in the great days before the religious wars destroyed the monastery, a procession of upwards of 300,000 pilgrims marched to the shrine. The 9th century crypt is the sole remnant of this former importance, and it is one of the most ancient in France. The suburb and church of St. Waast (the church is modern and ordinary) is an area of ruins and military works. The bridge there is called the Pont-des-Anglais, having been rebuilt by British engineers late in 1914.

The city, on account of its situation on the line of invasion towards Paris from the east, and by virtue of its command of the juncture of several military roads, has always been regarded as an outpost of the capital, and its history records several sieges. It was an industrial centre of some importance, with a population of 14,500 before the war, being notable chiefly for its refineries and distilleries. In the course of the war it was twice occupied, the first occupation, in 1914, lasting only from the 2nd to the 13th of September. But it remained practically in the front line and within easy artillery range from that time until March, 1917, when, after the re-adjustment of the German line, bombardments became less frequent and less severe. Nowhere better than at Soissons can an idea be formed of what trench warfare meant. An extraordinary feature of what was for more than two years in a very real sense a siege was the manner in which a percentage of the inhabitants elected to remain in the town and continue their ordinary civilian occupations. This was only rendered possible by a system of trench communication in the streets and recourse to cellars during bombardments. After the surprise attack at Chemin-des-Dames (May 29th to August 2nd, 1918) which was of such perilous moment to the Allies, the enemy captured and pillaged the town, and when, at the end of August, he was once more driven out, there followed that final and intensive bombardment which proved so utterly ruinous.

It is of interest to note that the section from Courtecon to Berry-au-Bec on the Chemin-des-Dames, prior to that attack, was the furthest point south held by British troops after the fluctuations of the first few weeks of warfare.

RHEIMS, the ancient capital of the Remi, and of importance even under the Romans, is an archbishopric, and has always been a great religious centre, particularly in the 10th and 11th centuries, when several Councils of the Church were held there. Its early history is a chequered one. The Vandals captured it. Attila took it and put it to the sword. After Clovis was baptised and crowned there it became the special desire of all subsequent French Kings to hold their coronation ceremony in Rheims Cathedral, possibly on account of the sacred phial of holy unguents preserved there, which, according to the superstition of those times, was brought down from heaven by a dove for use at the crowning of King Clovis. The prerogative of the archbishops of Rheims to crown kings was, of course, an enviable one.

The city is built on the right bank of the Vesle, on a plain which is enclosed on the south and west by vine-clad hills. It formed part of a defence scheme for Paris. In addition to its woollen manufactures, it is a centre of the champagne industry, and one of the sights of the place is the system of wine cellars. In recent times most of its picturesque aspects were sacrificed for the sake of new boulevards on the Parisian plan, but it remains one of the most interesting, historically, of French towns, and, before the war, was undoubtedly one of the most beautiful. The monument of earliest date is the Mars Gate, a triple arch 43 feet in height, which was probably built in the 3rd century. Near by an extensive Roman mosaic, depicting gladiators and animals, has been discovered, and preserved in the museum is the sarcophagus of the Roman consul Jovinus. The archiepiscopal palace, built about 1500, was the place of residence of kings during coronation festivities. Its "Salle du Tau," where the royal banquets were held, contained, until the outbreak of war, the portraits of the fourteen kings crowned at Rheims. In this palace are hung the well-known Perpersack tapestries. The abbey church of St. Remi is the equal of many cathedrals, and reveals examples of Gothic architecture from the 11th to the 15th centuries. The Romanesque nave and transepts are the earliest portions of the building. This church was pillaged of its interior decoration during the Revolution, but some rare 12th century glass windows remain.

The glory of Rheims is, or was, the Cathedral of Notre Dame. Unfortunately, although it is still possible to distinguish its beauties, the wonderful structure has been shattered beyond repair by the enemy's guns. One of the finest examples of Early Gothic extant, it was begun in 1210, and having been completed with exceptional expedition, possesses a singular unity and cohesion of design. It was the Middle Ages in epitome. The highest praise was for centuries lavished upon this, of its kind, almost perfect structure, which was magnificent even as regards size, the nave being 455 feet long, 99 feet wide, and 125 feet in height, while its towers were over 260 feet. Interiorly it preserved in the highest degree that aspect of simplicity which was the crowning virtue of Early Gothic architecture. One of the two bells which used to hang in the south tower weighed eleven tons. The tapestries, the Mediæval organ in its flamboyant Gothic case, the quaint clock in the choir with its mechanical figures, and the surpassing rose window over the main portal were all a source of delight and admiration, and there were also several valuable paintings, among them a Tintoretto and a Nicolas Poussin. Endeavours were made to protect the more precious parts of the building by sand-bags and other defences, but the German gunners, during the years in which Rheims was in range, made a target of the building, and reduced it to a crumbling ruin. Its doom was sealed very early in the war, for the worst destruction was wrought on September 20th, 1914, during the Battle of the Aisne. All the buildings in the town shared much the same fate, a misfortune which was due chiefly to the peculiarities of the site and the terrain, which are such as to have caused Rheims, in 1874, to be selected as one of the chief defences of Paris. Surrounded by the ridge of St. Thierry and the hills of Arnay, its eminent suitability to the requirements of defence in modern war forced upon Rheims the onus of defending, primarily the Laon railway, and incidently a road to Paris.

NOYON, which was involved in the German 1918 offensive after being freed a year before, is a small cathedral town built at the foot and on the slopes of a hill, and traversed by the Verse, a small tributary of the Oise. It is of ancient origin, and was christianised by St. Quentin in the 3rd century. Peppin the Short and Charlemagne were crowned there; it was plundered by the Normans in 859, and ravaged by the English and Burgundians in the Hundred Years War, while in the wars of the 16th century it was taken and retaken. It is the birth-place of John Calvin. The Cathedral is chiefly interesting as displaying the transition of architecture from Romanesque to Gothic, the windows of the aisles and clerestory, and the arches of the triforium being of the round type, though in the lower gallery of the latter the pointed arches of Gothic appear. Time and the vicissitudes of wars and revolutions had already shorn the building of much of its sculpture and decoration, and bombardment recently has sadly damaged the main structure. The fine cloister, which dates from 1230, was also demolished in places. In the Bishop's Palace, the Canon's Library and the Town Hall various styles of architecture are exemplified, while on the outskirts of the town traces remain of the ancient Roman wall.

CHATEAU-THIERRY, 59 miles from Paris, is built on rising ground on the right bank of the Marne, with a suburb on the left bank. La Fontaine, the fabulist, was born there in 1621, and there is a statue to him on the quay, while his house is preserved in a street named after him. On a hill are the ruins of a castle which is said to have been built by Charlemagne to imprison Thierry, a king of the Franks; and this would seem to have been the origin of the town. The traditional skill of the inhabitants in the manufacture of the finer sort of mathematical and other delicate instruments kept that industry in a flourishing condition. Chateau-Thierry has had a troublous history. The English captured it in 1421, it was taken by Charles V. in 1544, and taken and sacked by the Spaniards in 1591. It was again pillaged during the Fronde, in 1692, and it met with disaster once more in the campaign of 1814, in which year Napoleon I. defeated a Russo-Prussian army close by.

In the recent war British troops were in action in the neighbourhood on re-crossing the Marne after the Mons retreat, to take part in the victorious counter-offensive. It marked the southern limit reached by the enemy in his great attack upon the Allied front between Soissons and Rheims in May, 1918. Finally it was the scene of the American army's noteworthy achievement when it crossed the Marne and re-took the town in the final phase of the war. Chateau-Thierry now lies in utter ruin and desolation.

## BATTLES OF THE MARNE.

A quadrilateral figure described on the points Chantilly, Châlons, Provins and Vitry-le-François encloses, very roughly, the country over which the two battles of the Marne were fought, and perhaps the country lying between Vitry and Bar-le-Duc should also be reckoned as within the area of these particular operations. It is one of the most beautiful and fruitful regions of France, much of it being devoted to the cultivation of the vine.

CHANTILLY is to Paris what Epsom is to London, although in the case of the French horse-racing centre, a very fine flavour of romance and history attaches to the name. The town is merely a modern parasitic growth upon the castle, a part of it, indeed, having been built, in the post-Revolutionary epoch, upon the pleasure grounds. Chantilly Castle was the home of the powerful Montmorency family, and in the time of Henri IV. had reached such a pitch of magnificence as to arouse the envy of the King himself. Cardinal Richelieu, in the course of his policy of humbling the nobility, confiscated the domain for the benefit of Louis XIII., but eventually it came back to the Montmorencys, in the person of the " Great Condé," who expended a considerable part of his wealth upon the castle and grounds, which were frequently the scene of extravagant festivities at the time of Louis XIV. Succeeding members of the semi-royal house followed Condé's example, and just prior to the Revolution the subsidiary Castle of Enghien was raised within the grounds. In more recent times, Henry of Orleans, while in exile in England, commenced the collection of art treasures, which now includes works of Raphael, Philippino Lippi, and other objects of fabulous value.

The records and traditions of Chantilly read like a romance of Dumas. The lodge known as "Sylvie's House," for instance, perpetuates the story of a relationship between a poet, Théophile de Viau, and the youthful mistress of the castle in 1625; while in the Hamlet of Chantilly we find one of those make-believe villages by means of which an enervated aristocracy, under the influence of Jean Jacques Rousseau, played with the fashionable idea of "a return to nature."

The Germans entered the town and took possession of the Castle, in which they quartered men, on September 3rd, 1914. They were only permitted to remain a few days, however, and in their second attempt on Paris they did not reach nearly so far. In the town a large residence called "Joffre's House" is pointed out, where, until the end of 1916, the imperturbable French marshal had his headquarters.

SENLIS. Nestled amid the beautiful forests of Chantilly and Ermenonville, this little town has the air of having retired from modern life. Its ancient ramparts, a Gallic-Roman wall, remains in astonishingly good preservation, and the spectacle is presented of buildings of priceless archæological value being used for the prosaic purposes of everyday life. An instance of this is a carpenter's shop in the ruins of the ancient church of St. Frambourg, while the church of St. Pierre, which is an object lesson in the development of Gothic, is in use as a market. Other buildings which, in a city less rich in such relics, would be carefully guarded, serve as barns, etc. The Castle was a favourite resort of kings, from Clovis to Henry IV.; with the latter monarch the city, which was the first to espouse his cause, remained always an object of affection. Several notable treaties were signed at Senlis. The Cathedral, which reveals all the stages of Gothic from the 12th to the 16th century, is chiefly remarkable for its exceptionally fine 13th century spire. The galleries are also much admired, while in the Chapter House the true spirit of the Middle Ages is discernible in a series of caricatures of monks which form the decoration of one of the capitals. Fifty or sixty years ago a 3rd century Roman arena was excavated, and in the region of the city known as the "Roman Enclosure" other vestiges of Roman civilisation are to be seen, including two well-preserved towers.

Senlis, whose population numbers only about 8,000, had an unfortunate experience in the early days of the war. The Germans, who entered it in September, 1914, shot the mayor, M. Odent, as a supposedly punitive measure, and during the time of their occupation a part of the town was set on fire. The Cathedral and other buildings suffered some damage from shell-fire.

MEAUX, which has now a population of some 14,000, is a bishopric which dates from the 4th century. The chief glory of its ecclesiastical history is the renown of its bishop Bossuet, " The Eagle of Meaux," whose tomb is prominent in the Cathedral of St. Stephen. This latter building was commenced in the 12th century, finished in the 16th, and has since been completely restored. It is chiefly noteworthy on account of its rich interior decoration. The pulpit contains some of the panels of Bossuet's original pulpit, and the tomb of the great preacher attracts attention by the excellence of the sculptured figures of Marshal Turenne and that famous Mlle. de la Vallière, the mistress of Louis XIV., whose love story and subsequent penitence forms such an intriguing romance. The King's Room in the Archiepiscopal Palace was occupied by Louis XVI. and Marie Antoinette on a stage of the memorable return journey from Varennes, and Napoleon I. spent a night there on his way back to Paris after the Russian disaster. The town was also the scene of the famous historical episode called " The Enterprise of Meaux," in which the Huguenots attempted the kidnapping of Charles IX. and his sinister mother, Catherine de Medici—an enterprise which many historians believe to have been one of the immediate causes of the St. Bartholomew Day Massacre. The inhabitants, who are mostly engaged in the marketing of grain and other agricultural produce, were never in direct contact with the enemy, who, except for a stray patrol or two, never actually reached the city.

COULOMMIERS, the ancient Castrum Columbarium (" Camp of the Doves ") of the Romans, was in English hands for some time in Plantagenet days. It had an enforced acquaintance with Russian invaders in 1814, and was obliged to receive the Germans in 1870. During their brief occupation in September, 1914, the enemy pillaged the town to some extent.

PROVINS, like Senlis, has numerous remains of its great days in the Middle Ages, when, it is recorded, the population of the town, which is now no more than 7,000, was no less than sixty or seventy thousand. The Plague started the decline of Provins, and the Hundred Years' War all but completed its ruin. The town has certain English associations. In the 15th century it was held by the English, who, during their occupation, strengthened the building known as the King's (or Cæsar's) Tower, with masonry which remains to this day, and the name of St. Edmund, Archbishop of Canterbury, is connected with the city. In the Cistercian monastery, to which Provins owed so much in the 10th century, Abelard found refuge from the uncles of Heloïse. The poet, Moreau, and Pierre Lebrun lived at Provins. Physically the town is divisible into two parts, the Ville-haut and the Ville-basse, the latter being the less ancient portion. As might be expected, its churches are full of interest, but they have not been too well treated in the course of successive restorations. That of St. Ayoul (restored 14th and 16th century Gothic) has unspoiled features, as has also the church of Sainte-Croix. In the ancient Cloister Hospital, where some very fine 14th century timber-work is to be found, is the tomb of Thibault, the founder of the hospital, containing his heart and that of his wife Isobel, a daughter of St. Louis of France. The ramparts of Provins, which are complete with the original gates and turrets, make the days of chivalry live again before the eyes. In the Grange-aux-Dimes, an 11th century building, the purpose of which is not certain, is housed a museum, and beneath is preserved a good crypt. In the suburbs is pointed out a melancholy-looking building, the last occupant of which was Sanson, who assisted his brother, the official executioner in the days of the Terror, to guillotine Louis XVI. It is called the Executioner's House.

Provins, called from one of its chief industries, the " City of Roses " marks the southern extremity reached in the first Marne operations in the sector which has become known as the Saint-Gond Battlefield.

## TOWNS AND VILLAGES OF THE MARNE AREA.

No more than passing comment can be made of the numerous small towns and villages which were affected by the two extensive Marne operations. In both cases the tide of battle ebbed and flowed with great rapidity, the fighting being very open, and very seldom stagnating into fixed trench warfare. The countryside bears witness to this. Roads and woods are not to any great extent damaged, and except here and there, on a plateau or hill-side of tactical importance, there are few of the usual traces of war. But it was village-to-village warfare, and amid the unspoiled, familiar beauty of the landscape there lie broken and desolate many a township, whose inhabitants, now for the most part dispersed, had cultivated and were sustained by the fruits of these rich corn and vine lands.

At CHAMBRY, where some of the fiercest fighting in the Ourcq Battlefield took place, the cemetery has become the venue of a pilgrimage. It was used alternately by the French and the enemy as a fortress, and many dead are buried thereabouts. The village was bombarded heavily. BARCY, MARCILLY and ACY (the latter has a good 12th-13th century church) were all three the scene of fighting, and show traces of the fluctuating conflicts that were fought out among their houses. ETREPILLY has an imposing memorial to those who fell heroically in the succession of encounters there, and outside TROCY, on a plateau which was fiercely contested, traces of heavy shell-fire are to be seen. CRECY-en-BRIE escaped lightly. It is a small township of 1,000 inhabitants, remarkable for its ancient fortifications, and for the picturesque views it affords of the river Morin, which has become known as the "Artists' River." There is here a beautiful 13th century church. At BARON, between Senlis and Nanteuil, occurred an episode very typical of French spirit—the defence of his house by the poet Albéric Magnard against the invaders. Magnard was quite alone when the Germans arrived in 1914, but armed only with a revolver, he kept the enemy at bay until they set fire to the villa, and even then, rather than submit, he took his own life. Baron church has memories of Joan of Arc, while at ERMENONVILLE, near by, is the tomb of Jean Jacques Rousseau, who died there.

The first Marne Battle proved most fatal to many of the villages around PROVINS and SEZANNE. The 12th century church at VOULTON, however, escaped, but at AUGERS the church, of no historical importance, was destroyed, and MONTCEAUX church was much damaged. Hostilities at ESTERNAY and CHATILLON developed on a large scale, and the latter village was completely gutted, while at CHARLEVILLE the church was badly damaged, and at LA VILLENEUVE both church and village were wrecked. SEZANNE is notable for its 15th century church and ancient fortifications.

MONDEMENT was the centre of fierce indecisive fighting in the marshes of St. Gond. Its ruined castle has become famous through the heroism the French displayed there, as also in the fighting in and around the wrecked farm. Here also the local church was damaged.

In the beautiful country between SEZANNE and CHALON-sur-MARNE, where rapid movement to and fro characterised the hostilities which occurred from September 5th to 14th, 1914, several villages were devastated, notably SOUMMESOUS, VASSIMONT AND NORMEE.

FERE-CHAMPENOISE was the French pivot in their defence of the important plain which the German armies were obliged to cross after forcing the passage of the Somme (Soude) river.

CHALONS-sur-MARNE, 107 miles east of Paris, is situated on the right bank of the Marne, and is traversed by branches of the Marne Canal and by small streams. Its streets are narrow, but it is surrounded by good avenues in the modern style, and in the Jard it owns an unusually attractive park. Its churches are of interest. The Cathedral of St. Etienne, founded in the 10th century and three times destroyed by fire, was slowly rebuilt during the 15th, 16th and 17th centuries, and shows a not too pleasing combination of Gothic and Renaissance styles. Four Romanesque towers distinguish the church of Notre Dame, that of St. Jchn (11th century) is the most ancient, and in St. Alpin's is to be seen a good window depicting the circumstances of that saint's interview with Attila, which procured the safety of the town, just prior to the defeat of the Huns in the vicinity in 451. The seat of a bishop and the headquarters of an army corps, Chalons, with its population of some 30,000, finds prosperity in various industries, the chief of which is brewing, and it possesses an extensive system of galleries cut out in the limestone hill and served by a railroad for the storage of beer. In history, apart from the decisive battle which saved Western Europe from the Huns in 451, it figures in the two sieges it withstood against the English in 1430 and 1434. Napoleon III.'s famous Camp of Chalons was formed a few miles outside the town in 1856, and it was the Army of Chalons mobilised there by Marshal MacMahon that was eventually surrounded and forced to capitulate at Sedan by the Germans in 1870. At L'Epine, five miles away, is the beautiful 16th century church to which pilgrimages are made in honour of a venerated statue of the Virgin.

VITRY-le-FRANCOIS. The area here represents another of the fields of operations into which the wide-spreading Marne battles were divisible, and the villages show sad vestiges of the fighting. HUIRON was completely destroyed, and COURDEMANGE is in little better plight. Vitry, a town of over 8,000 population, dates from the 16th century only, and possesses a church, that of Notre Dame, which is of interest on account of its interior decoration.

BAR-le-DUC, a town of 17,000 inhabitants, forms the centre of a semi-circle within which, to the destruction of several villages, battles were waged in the most eastern of the Marne operations. The German advance, however, was brought to a halt within a few hours' march of its gates. It was of little importance until it appears as a fortified place in the 10th century. In 1652 it suffered a famous siege by Turenne. The town is rather curiously built, its lower, more modern, half extending along the valley of the Ornain, which is crossed by a series of small bridges. The ancient portion is on a height that is reached by steep winding causeways and staircases. Here is situated the 16th century castle of the Dukes of Bar, who played leading parts in the early French wars. The 14th century church of St. Pierre possesses a curiosity in the shape of a realistically carved figure of a human skeleton, done in whitened stone to imitate human bone, by Richier, a pupil of Michael Angelo.

BRABANT-le-ROI and REVIGNY both were shattered by bombardment, and while in the enemy's hands were partly burnt down. At the latter place a Zeppelin was destroyed.

SOMMEILLES was also subjected to artillery fire. Here, and indeed, in several of the villages hereabout, the buildings are of considerable size and often of architectural value. At REMBERCOURT-aux-POTS a fine 15th century church, classed as a historical monument, was fortunately only partially damaged amid the general ruin, but the similar building at BEAUZEE was not spared.

It is interesting to note that the small railway line from Bar-le-Duc through Beauzee was the one on which the defenders of Verdun depended entirely during the great battle.

### THE ENTRENCHED CAMP OF VERDUN.

VERDUN ranks as a fortress of the first class. For a long time before the outbreak of war it had become the centre of the modern system of defence known as an " entrenched camp," and as such rivalled the great German fortress of Metz. Although the town itself lies in a hollow, a circle of wooded and vine-clad hills gives it great natural advantages for defence, and in comparatively recent years this natural strength has been immensely augmented by sixteen main forts and twenty-two lesser military works, contained within a perimeter of nearly 30 miles.

At the time of the Roman conquest it was known as Verodunum, and was a place of considerable importance even at this early entry into history. It was destroyed at the time of the barbarian invasions, but was rebuilt, and in the 10th century was annexed to Germany until 1552.

When, in September, 1914, the opposing armies settled down to trench warfare, the Germans were firmly planted on a wide semi-circle stretching from Vauquios, near Varennes, to Chauvoncourt, a village on the left bank of the Meuse, in front of St. Mihiel. Intermittent localised fighting proceeded throughout 1915, but on February 21st, 1916, the battle began which is generally recognised to have been the greatest and most bloody engagement in history to which the term " battle " can be properly applied. Fighting on a gigantic scale raged uninterruptedly until October of that year, but on account of the nature of the locale and the relative positions into which the opposing forces fell, hostilities never broadened out; it was the Battle of Verdun until the end.

Undertaken by the German High Command to forestall an Allied offensive further north, for which vast preparations were nearing completion, the enemy, making the fullest use of his elaborate railway system, massed an unprecedented quantity of artillery for the attack, and, in mid-winter, hurled no less than seven army corps upon what was undoubtedly the strongest position on the Allied front. It was an amazing gamble, and although it seemed at one time that the Germans had a chance of success, recent information proves that he never, in fact, even reached the real core of French resistance. The enemy plan was for a break-through between Bras and Douaumont, and after the first tremendous rush had carried him over the outermost positions, each succeeding day brought him some advance, though always at great sacrifice. A huge and wasteful effort on the third day of the battle gave the enemy Hill 344, Fosses Wood, Chaume Wood, and the village of Ornes. There followed the French troops' heroic defence of Talou Hill and Louvremont village; but the Germans, rushing Vauche Wood, carried Douaumont Fort by surprise, and from that time the eyes of all the world were fixed upon the fluctuating battle.

By the 10th of March the enemy, using five army corps, had reached, but had not taken, Fort Vaux, and checked on the line Béthincourt—Mort Homme—Cumières, the offensive, in its character of an attack in mass, came for a time to an end. The German High Command had learnt one more bitter lesson, and henceforth the fight was limited to local battles for position—local, but by no means insignificant, for the fate of the positions assaulted had great bearing on the general battle. Mort Homme then became a name of terrible significance, and Douaumont Fort, now a heap of debris, was taken and re-taken with terrific slaughter. Not until the 3rd of June did Fort Vaux fall, and then the German attack culminated in a general assault of great magnitude and intensity, which gave them Thiaumont Redoubt and brought them into the village of Fleury and to the gates of Fort Souville, but at a price which left them exhausted in human material. The attack on

Verdun had failed. Fierce and continuous warfare continued until October 24th, but then General Mangin initiated the French counter-offensive which entirely retrieved the whole situation. In a preliminary attack which had in it some of the elements of surprise, the French recovered Damloup, Thiaumont and Douaumont, and compelled the enemy to abandon Vaux. Following an interval of intensive preparation the main French attack was then delivered, and within a few days the Germans had lost all the ground they had paid so dearly to win during five months of effort and sacrifice. The final deliverance of Verdun came with the American offensive of September, 1918. For the part it played Verdun received the distinction of being " decorated," each of the Allied nations presenting to the city a high military decoration, in handing which to the mayor the President, M. Poincare, uttered the world's estimate of the victory when he said that before the walls of Verdun the supreme hope of German imperialism had been extinguished. The city itself has not very many features of striking interest. The Chaussée Gate is officially classed as a historical monument, and part of it is 14th century work, while the most interesting fact about the Hotel-de-Ville is the tradition that it once gave refuge to Marie de Médicis. The Cathedral, which was heavily battered by shell-fire, dates, for the most part, from the mid-eighteenth century, it having been much remodelled then after a fire which destroyed the greater part of the original 13th century structure. Its architecture is curious rather than impressive, as it has two transepts, two apses, and consequently two choirs. Preserved in the crypt and elsewhere are fragments of ancient Roman stone-carvings. According to an unusually positive legend, the Citadelle is built on a site which was the haunt of a dragon that was tamed by the local abbot St. Vanne, in the days of King Clovis. Vauban, who constructed this Citadelle, incorporated in it the remains of the ancient abbey, a tower of which still stands. The vaults proved invaluable to the defenders in the recent war, but viewing them it is easy to understand how intolerable were the hardships endured by the poilus who were sometimes crowded there in thousands. On the Faubourg Pavé, not far from the Chaussée Gate, is one of the largest military cemeteries in the war area.

A survey of the region comprising the fortified area reveals a spectacle of ruined villages, the debris of villages which are no longer recognisable as such, and hills and valleys torn and tunnelled by shell-holes and trenches. Vaux Fort and Douaumont Fort are but hillocks of broken stone and concrete. The villages of Vaux and Chattancourt have been literally obliterated, while Fleury and Louvremont are levelled, and, except for a few walls and a roof or two, the same is true of Vacherauville, Samogneux, Cumières, Esnes, and several other villages. Charny, which ranks as a town rather than a village, also suffered gravely. In addition to Mort Homme, which can never be forgotten, two other localities mark especially memorable incidents; Avocourt, the scene of a French attack to the beat of a drum, and Malancourt Wood, which saw the introduction of the terrible weapon of liquid fire into warfare.

BELFORT is the town of a first-class fortress guarding the passes between the Vosges and the Jura mountains. It is a flourishing industrial centre whose population had grown to nearly 35,000 before the war. It has frequently paid the penalty of its status as a fortress in former wars, but in the recent struggle it was not fated to withstand a German siege, and beyond occasional bombardment from the air it suffered little material damage. It has few buildings of historical worth, the finest sight it has to offer the visitor being Bartholdi's colossal monument " The Lion of Belfort," which stands in front of the Citadel.

VIMY. This considerable village gives its name to the great bleak ridge which dominates the plain of Douai and the Lens coalfields. Vimy Ridge was regarded as a key position, and two great battles had already been fought for its possession since the end of 1914, when it was at last wrested from the enemy in the course of the magnificently organised British offensive, which opened on a front stretching from Lens to St. Quentin, on April 9th, 1917. The Ridge was not captured until the 13th, the fifth day of the battle, and the feat ranks among the finest achievements of the Canadian Division. The Ridge protected the northern end of the Hindenburg Line, and its defensive system included such strongholds as the famous Labyrinth at Neuville St. Vaast, and the elaborately fortified post called Telegraph Hill, on the Ridge itself. The enemy succeeded in repulsing the first attacks, but eventually, after a heavy and sustained bombardment, the Canadians rushed the position, capturing the greater part of the surviving garrison. Although heavy snowstorms hampered operations, in the month's fighting which centred round Vimy, and in which Bullecourt figured largely towards the end, the enemy lost 166 guns and more than 13,000 prisoners.

THE WHITE CROSS INSURANCE ASSOCIATION LTD.

# WHITE CROSS
### REPAIR FACILITIES.

PRIVATE CAR AND COMMERCIAL VEHICLE INSURANCES.

The Association have arrangements with over 1,000 of the leading Firms of Repairers—including the Manufacturers—in nearly every town of importance in the United Kingdom, whereby in the event of accident Repairs may be commenced immediately irrespective of the amount involved.

A List of these Repairers and a " Repair Permit," together with other useful information, is supplied with the Policy. The Assured is not required to obtain an Estimate, but simply to produce the Repairs Permit.

There is no obligation upon the Assured to take his Vehicle to any Authorised Repairer. The " White Cross " arrangements with these Firms are solely for the convenience of Owners, and avoid the delay necessitated by the preparation and approval of an Estimate.

# INDEX

## TO THE

# WAR GRAVES

## OF THE

# WESTERN FRONT.

The number in the second column shows the page on which the Cemetery will be found; the number in the third column indicates the map square in which the Cemetery is situated; the number in the fourth column corresponds with the number on the map marking the position of the Cemetery.

| Name of Cemetery. | Page. | Map Square. | No. on Map. |
|---|---|---|---|
| Abancourt Communal Cemetery Extension.. | 11 | H 5 | 1794 |
| Abbeville Communal Cemetery and Extension | 9 | E 5 | 2128 |
| Abbey Grounds, La Boutillerie, Fleurbaix | 45 | F 10 | 1 |
| Abbey Wall Cemetery, La Boutillerie, Fleurbaix .. | 45 | F 10 | 2 |
| Abeele Aerodrome Military Cemetery, Watou | 40 | D 7 | 3 |
| Ablain St. Nazaire Military Cemetery | 46 | D 13 | 4 |
| Acheux British Cemetery | 11 | G 5 | 1770 |
| Acheville Road Cemetery, Vimy | 47 | F 13 | 5 |
| Achicourt Churchyard Extension | 48 | E 15 | 6 |
| Achicourt Road British Cemetery | 48 | E 15 | 7 |
| Achiet le Grand Communal Cemetery Extension | 51 | E 16 | 8 |
| Achiet le Petit Communal Cemetery Extension | 50 | E 17 | 1795 |
| Achille British Cemetery, Flaucourt.. | 55 | F 20 | 9 |
| Adelaide Military Cemetery, Villers Bretonneux | 21 | G 6 | 10 |
| Adinkerke British Cemetery, Furnes | 3 | G 2 | 11 |
| Adinkerke Churchyard Military Extension.. | 3 | G 2 | 12 |
| Admiral's British Cemetery, Boesinghe | 41 | F 6 | 13 |
| Advanced Dressing Station, Ginchy .. | 55 | F 18 | 14 |
| Aeroplane Cemetery, Fricourt | 54 | E 18 | 15 |
| Aeroplane Cemetery, Ypres .. | 41 | F 6 | 16 |
| Agny Military Cemetery | 48 | E 15 | 17 |
| Agny Railway Arch .. | 48 | E 15 | 18 |
| Ailly-sur-Noye Communal Cemetery | 20 | G 6 | 1967 |
| Aire Communal Cemetery | 10 | G 3 | 1791 |
| Aix-Noulette Communal Cemetery Extension | 46 | D 12 | 19 |
| Albert Communal Cemetery Extension | 54 | D 18 | 20 |
| Albert Road Cemetery, Richebourg l'Avoue | 44 | E 10 | 21 |

( 111 )

| Name of Cemetery. | Page. | Map Square. | No. on Map. |
|---|---|---|---|
| Albuera Cemetery, Bailleul-sire-Berthoult | 49 | F 14 | 23 |
| Aldershot Military Cemetery, Bouchavesnes | 55 | F 18 | 24 |
| Allery Communal Cemetery | 9 | E 6 | 1968 |
| Allonville Communal Cemetery | 10 | G 6 | 25 |
| Amerval Communal Cemetery Extension, Solesmes | 59 | M 16 | 26 |
| Ancre British Cemetery, Beaumont-Hamel | 50 | D 17 | 27 |
| Ancre River Cemetery, Beaumont-Hamel | 50 | D 17 | 28 |
| Andigny-les-Fermes British Cemetery, Vaux Andigny | 12 | J 5 | 29 |
| Angle Wood Cemetery, Ginchy | 55 | F 18 | 30 |
| Angreau Communal Cemetery | 12 | K 4 | 2129 |
| Angres Churchyard | 46 | E 13 | 32 |
| Angres Road Cemetery, Givenchy-en-Gohelle | 47 | E 13 | 33 |
| Anneux British Cemetery, Anneux | 53 | H 16 | 35 |
| Annezin Communal Cemetery Extension, Annezin-les-Bethune | 44 | D 11 | 36 |
| Annois Communal Cemetery | 21 | H 6 | 1969 |
| Antheit Communal Cemetery | 14 | N 3 | 1070 |
| Anzac Cemetery, Sailly-sur-la-Lys | 42 | E 9 | 37 |
| Anzin St. Aubin British Cemetery | 48 | E 14 | 38 |
| Aqueduct Road British Cemetery, Pys | 51 | E 17 | 39 |
| Argyle Road Cemetery, Beaucamp, Villers-Plouich | 53 | H 17 | 40 |
| Arneke British Cemetery | 3 | G 2 | 42 |
| Artillery Wood Cemetery, Boesinghe | 41 | F 6 | 45 |
| Arvillers Communal Cemetery | 21 | G 6 | 1870 |
| Ascq Communal Cemetery | 11 | H 3 | 47 |
| Asquillies Churchyard | 12 | K 4 | 1971 |
| Assevillers Military Cemetery | 55 | F 20 | 48 |
| Asylum, The, Ypres | 41 | F 7 | 1590 |
| Ath Communal Cemetery | 12 | K 3 | 2130 |
| Athies (l'Abbayette) Military Cemetery | 49 | F 14 | 51 |
| Auberchicourt British Cemetery | 11 | H 4 | 52 |
| Aubigny British Cemetery | 11 | G 6 | 54 |
| Aubigny Communal Cemetery | 21 | G 6 | 1871 |
| Aubigny Communal Cemetery Extension | 46 | C 14 | 53 |
| Auchonvillers Communal Cemetery | 50 | D 17 | 55 |
| Auchonvillers Military Cemetery | 50 | D 17 | 56 |
| Auckland Cemetery (Stinking Farm), Ploegsteert | 43 | F 8 | 57 |
| Audencourt Cemetery | 12 | J 5 | 58 |
| Audregnies Churchyard Cemetery | 12 | K 4 | 1972 |
| Audrehem Churchyard | 2 | F 3 | 1973 |
| Audruicq Churchyard | 2 | F 4 | 1974 |
| Aulnoy British Cemetery | 58 | M 14 | 59 |
| Aulnoy Communal Cemetery | 58 | M 14 | 60 |
| Aulnoye Communal Cemetery Extension | 12 | K 5 | 2131 |
| Australian Cemetery, Bapaume | 51 | F 17 | 64 |
| A.I.F. Burial Ground, Grass Lane, Gueudecourt | 51 | F 18 | 63 |
| Authuille Communal Cemetery Extension | 50 | D 18 | 65 |
| Authuille French Military Cemetery | 50 | D 18 | — |
| Authuille Military Cemetery | 50 | D 18 | 66 |
| Autre Eglise Churchyard | 13 | M 3 | 1975 |
| Aux Rietz Military Cemetery, Neuville St. Vaast | 48 | E 14 | 67 |
| Aval Wood Military Cemetery, Vieux Berquin | 11 | G 3 | 68 |
| Aveluy Communal Cemetery Extension | 54 | D 18 | 69 |
| Aveluy Military Cemetery | 54 | D 18 | — |
| Aveluy Wood Cemetery (Lancashire Dump), Mesnil-Martinsart | 50 | D 18 | 70 |
| Avesnelles British Cemetery | 12 | K 5 | 2132 |
| Avesnes-le-Comte Communal Cemetery Extension | 11 | G 4 | 72 |
| Avesnes-les-Aubert Communal Cemetery | 11 | J 5 | 74 |
| Avesnes-le-Sec Communal Cemetery Extension | 11 | J 5 | 73 |
| Avin Communal Cemetery | 13 | N 3 | 2012 |
| Avion British Cemetery | 47 | E 13 | 75 |
| Awoingt British Cemetery | 11 | J 5 | 76 |
| Ayette British Cemetery | 50 | E 16 | 77 |
| Ayette Indian and Chinese Cemetery | 50 | E 16 | 1797 |
| Aywaille Churchyard | 14 | O 4 | 1976 |

| Name of Cemetery. | Page. | Map. Square. | No. on Map. |
|---|---|---|---|
| Bac du Sud British Cemetery, Bailleulval | 11 | G 5 | 78 |
| Bagneux British Cemetery, Gezaincourt | 10 | F 5 | 79 |
| Bailleul Communal Cemetery | 42 | E 8 | 81 |
| Bailleul Communal Cemetery Extension | 42 | E 8 | 82 |
| Bailleulmont Communal Cemetery | 11 | G 5 | 83 |
| Bailleul Road German Cemetery | 49 | E 14 | 1798 |
| Bailleul Road Military Cemetery, East, St. Laurent-Blangy | 49 | E 14 | 84 |
| Bailleul Road Military Cemetery, West, St. Laurent-Blangy | 48 | E 14 | 85 |
| Bailleulval Communal Cemetery | 48 | D 15 | 1874 |
| Baisieux Communal Cemetery | 12 | K 4 | 1873 |
| Bajus Churchyard | 10 | G 4 | 1872 |
| Baluchi Road Cemetery, Neuve Chapelle | 45 | E 10 | 86 |
| Bancourt British Cemetery | 51 | F 17 | 1799 |
| Bapaume Australian Cemetery | 51 | F 17 | — |
| Bapaume Communal Cemetery | 51 | F 17 | 87 |
| Bapaume Post Military Cemetery, near Albert | 54 | D 18 | 88 |
| Baraile British Cemetery | 11 | H 5 | 90 |
| Barastre Communal Cemetery | 52 | G 17 | 91 |
| Barastre German Cemetery | 52 | G 17 | 92 |
| Bard Cottage, Boesinghe | 41 | F 6 | 93 |
| Barlin Communal Cemetery Extension | 46 | D 12 | 94 |
| Barly Military Cemetery | 11 | G 5 | 95 |
| Barracks, The, Ypres | 41 | F 7 | 96 |
| Bart's Alley Cemetery, near Vermelles | 46 | E 11 | 97 |
| Basilieux Military Cemetery, Chemin des Dames | 60 | — | 1977 |
| Basse Boulogne British Cemetery, Lempire | 57 | J 18 | 98 |
| Bastian Cemetery, Fonquevillers | 50 | D 16 | 100 |
| Battery Copse Military Cemetery, Curlu | 55 | F 19 | 102 |
| Bavaria House Cemetery, Ypres | 41 | F 6 | 103 |
| Bavay Communal Cemetery | 12 | K 4 | 2133 |
| Baveliccourt Communal Cemetery | 10 | G 6 | 105 |
| Bavincourt Communal Cemetery | 11 | G 5 | 1875 |
| Bayenghem-lez-Eperlecques Churchyard | 3 | F 3 | 1978 |
| Bayenghem-lez-Seninghem Churchyard | 2 | F 3 | 1979 |
| Bayonvillers British Cemetery | 21 | G 6 | 106 |
| Bayonvillers German Cemetery | 21 | G 6 | 107 |
| Bazentin-le-Petit Communal Cemetery Extension | 55 | E 18 | 108 |
| Bazentin-le-Petit Military Cemetery | 55 | E 18 | 109 |
| Beacon British Cemetery, Sailly Laurette | 54 | D 19 | 110 |
| Beaucamps German Cemetery, Beaucamps | 45 | F 10 | 111 |
| Beaucourt British Cem. (V. Corps Cem. No. 13), Beaucourt-sur-Ancre | 50 | D 17 | 114 |
| Beaucourt Churchyard, Beaucourt-en-Santerre | 21 | G 6 | 112 |
| Beaudignies Communal Cemetery | 58 | M 15 | 115 |
| Beaufort British Cemetery | 21 | G 6 | 116 |
| Beaulencourt British Cemetery, Ligny-Thilloy | 51 | F 17 | 117 |
| Beaulencourt German Cemetery | 51 | F 17 | 118 |
| Beaulencourt Road Cemetery | 51 | F 17 | 119 |
| Beaumetz Communal Cemetery, Beaumetz-les-Loges | 48 | D 15 | 120 |
| Beaumetz Cross Roads Military Cemetery, Beaumetz-les-Cambrai | 52 | G 17 | 121 |
| Beaumont Communal Cemetery | 12 | J 5 | 122 |
| Beaumont-Hamel British Cemetery (V. Corps Cemetery No. 23) | 50 | D 17 | 123 |
| Beaumont-Hamel Ravine Cemetery | 50 | D 17 | 124 |
| Beauquesne Communal Cemetery | 10 | G 5 | 1876 |
| Beaurain British Cemetery | 59 | M 16 | 1801 |
| Beaurains Road British Cemetery | 48 | E 15 | 125 |
| Beaurains Road British Cemetery No. 2, Neuville Vitasse | 48 | E 15 | 126 |
| Beaurevoir British Cemetery | 11 | J 5 | 127 |
| Beaurevoir Communal Cemetery Extension | 11 | J 5 | 128 |
| Beaussart British Cemetery | 50 | C 17 | 1802 |

| Name of Cemetery. | Page. | Map Square. | No. on Map. |
|---|---|---|---|
| Beaussart Communal Cemetery Extension, Mailly-Maillet | 11 | G 5 | 129 |
| Beauvais Communal Cemetery (Oise) | 20 | F 7 | 2134 |
| Beauval Communal Cemetery | 10 | F 5 | 130 |
| Beauvois Communal Cemetery, Beauvois en Cambrésis | 12 | J 5 | 131 |
| Becourt Military Cemetery | 54 | D 18 | 132 |
| Bedford House Cemetery, Zillebeke, Enclosure No. 1 | 41 | F 7 | 133 |
| Bedford House Cemetery, Zillebeke, Enclosure No. 2 | 41 | F 7 | 134 |
| Bedford House Cemetery, Zillebeke, Enclosure No. 3 | 41 | F 7 | 135 |
| Bedford House Cemetery, Zillebeke, Enclosure No. 4 | 41 | F 7 | 136 |
| Bedford House Cemetery, Zillebeke, Enclosure No. 5 | 41 | F 7 | 137 |
| Beehive Cemetery, Willerval | 47 | F 13 | 138 |
| Bel-Aise Farm Cemetery, Crèvecour-sur-l'Escaut | 53 | J 17 | 139 |
| Belgian Battery Corner Military Cemetery, Ypres | 41 | F 7 | 140 |
| Belgian Chateau, Kruistraat, near Vlamertinghe | 41 | F 7 | 141 |
| Belgrade Communal Cemetery | 13 | M 4 | 1980 |
| Bellacourt Military Cemetery, Rivière | 48 | D 15 | 142 |
| Bellevue Farm Cemetery, Briastre | 59 | M 16 | 143 |
| Bell Farm Cemetery, Wytschaete | 41 | F 8 | 144 |
| Bellicourt British Cemetery | 57 | J 19 | 145 |
| Bellicourt German Cemetery | 57 | J 19 | 1803 |
| Berguette Churchyard | 10 | G 3 | 1878 |
| Berks Cemetery Extension, Ploegsteert Wood | 43 | F 8 | 147 |
| Berlaimont Communal Cemetery Extension | 12 | K 5 | 2135 |
| Berles-au-Bois Churchyard Extension | 11 | G 5 | 149 |
| Berles-au-Bois New Military Cemetery | 11 | G 5 | 150 |
| Berles Position | 50 | D 16 | 151 |
| Bermerain Communal Cemetery | 58 | M 15 | 152 |
| Bernafay Wood British Cemetery, Montauban | 55 | E 18 | 153 |
| Bernes Communal Cemetery, Bernes-Fléchin | 57 | H 20 | 155 |
| Berneville Communal Cemetery | 48 | D 15 | 1877 |
| Bertenacre French Military Cemetery, Flêtre | 3 | G 3 | 156 |
| Bertheaucourt Communal Cemetery, Pontru | 57 | J 20 | 157 |
| Berthen Churchyard | 40 | D 8 | 158 |
| Bertincourt Communal Cemetery, German Extension | 52 | G 17 | 159 |
| Bertrancourt Military Cemetery | 11 | G 5 | 160 |
| Bertry Communal Cemetery | 12 | J 5 | 161 |
| Bethencourt Communal Cemetery | 12 | J 5 | 162 |
| Bethléem Farm (East) Military Cemetery, Messines | 43 | F 8 | 163 |
| Bethléem Farm (West) Military Cemetery, Messines | 43 | F 8 | 164 |
| Béthune Town Cemetery | 44 | D 11 | 165 |
| Bettencourt Rivière Churchyard | 10 | F 5 | 2136 |
| Bettrechies Communal Cemetery | 12 | K 4 | 2137 |
| Beugneux British Cemetery | 60 | — | 167 |
| Beugny Churchyard | 52 | G 17 | 168 |
| Beussent Churchyard | 9 | E 4 | 1981 |
| Beuvry Communal Cemetery | 44 | D 11 | 170 |
| Beuvry Communal Cemetery Extension | 44 | D 11 | 169 |
| Bévillers | 12 | J 5 | 1879 |
| Bienvillers Military Cemetery | 50 | D 16 | 171 |
| Biganos Communal Cemetery, 25 m. S.W. of Bordeaux | — | — | — |
| Birr Cross Roads Cemetery No. 1, Zillebeke | 41 | F 7 | 172 |
| Bisseghem Civil Cemetery, Bisseghem | 4 | J 3 | 174 |
| Black Watch Cemetery, High Wood | 55 | E 18 | 176 |
| Black Watch Cemetery, Ledeghem | 4 | H 2 | 175 |
| Blaindain Churchyard | 11 | J 3 | 177 |
| Blairville Orchard British Cemetery | 48 | E 15 | 178 |
| Blangy Cabaret British Cemetery | 20 | G 6 | 179 |
| Blangy Cross Roads, St. Laurent Blangy | 48 | E 14 | 180 |
| Blangy Military Cemetery, near Arras | 48 | E 14 | 181 |
| Blangy Tronville Communal Cemetery | 20 | G 6 | 182 |
| Blangy Tronville French Military Cemetery | 20 | G 6 | — |
| Blargies Communal Cemetery Extension | 20 | E 7 | 2138 |
| Blauwepoortbeek Cemetery, Wytschaete | 41 | F 8 | 183 |
| Blauwepoort Farm, near Zillebeke | 41 | F 7 | 184 |

| Name of Cemetery. | Page. | Map Square. | No. on Map. |
|---|---|---|---|
| Bleue Maison, Eperlecques | 3 | F 3 | 2139 |
| Bleuet Farm British Cemetery, Elverdinghe | 41 | E 6 | 185 |
| Blighty Valley, Authuille Wood | 50 | D 18 | 186 |
| Bluff Cemetery, Authuille | 50 | D 18 | 187 |
| Boeschèpe Communal Cemetery | 40 | D 7 | 188 |
| Boeschèpe Military Cemetery | 40 | D 7 | 1804 |
| Boesinghe Chateau British Cemetery | 41 | F 6 | 189 |
| Bohain British Cemetery | 12 | J 5 | 191 |
| Bohain Station British Cemtery | 12 | J 5 | 192 |
| Boiry St. Rictrude British Cemetery | 48 | E 16 | 193 |
| Bois Carré Cemetery, Thelus | 47 | E 13 | 194 |
| Bois Carré Military Cemetery, near Haisnes | 47 | E 12 | 195 |
| Bois de Gentelles Cemetery, Gentelles | 20 | G 6 | 200 |
| Bois de l'Aulnay British Cemetery, Chaumuzy | 60 | — | 201 |
| Bois de Montigny German Cemetery | 11 | H 4 | 202 |
| Bois de Noulette New Cemetery, Aix Noulette | 46 | D 13 | 196 |
| Bois de Noulette Road Cemetery, Aix Noulette | 46 | D 13 | 197 |
| Bois des Angles British Cemetery, Crèvecœur sur l'Escaut | 11 | J 5 | 203 |
| Bois des Montagnes British Cemetery, Vaudricourt | 44 | D 11 | 198 |
| Bois du Sart British Cemetery, Pelves | 49 | F 14 | 204 |
| Bois du Vert British Cemetery | 49 | F 15 | 205 |
| Bois Grenier Communal Cemetery | 43 | F 9 | 199 |
| Boisguillaume Communal Cemetery and Extension, Rouen | 19 | D 7 | 2140 |
| Boisleux-St. Marc Military Cemetery | 48 | E 15 | 206 |
| Bollezeele Communal Cemetery | 3 | F 2 | 1880 |
| Bomy Churchyard | 10 | F 3 | 1983 |
| Bon Fermier Gully, Messines | 43 | F 8 | 207 |
| Bonnay Communal Cemetery Extension | 11 | G 6 | 208 |
| Bonningues Communal Cemetery | 2 | F 3 | 1984 |
| Bony American Cemetery | 57 | J 18 | 1805 |
| Bootham Cemetery, Héninel | 49 | F 15 | 209 |
| Borre British Cemetery | 3 | G 3 | 210 |
| Borre Churchyard | 3 | G 3 | 211 |
| Bossaert Farm Cemetery, Langemarck | 41 | F 6 | 212 |
| Bouchain Communal Cemetery Extension (German Portion) | 11 | J 6 | 214 |
| Bouchoir British Cemetery | 21 | G 6 | 215 |
| Bouilly (Marne) Cross Roads Military Cemetery | 60 | — | 216 |
| Bouleaux Wood Cemetery, Combles | 55 | F 18 | 217 |
| Boulogne Eastern Cemetery | 2 | E 3 | 2141 |
| Bourdon Chinese Cemetery | 10 | F 6 | 2142 |
| Bourg Communal Cemetery | 60 | — | 2143 |
| Bourlon Wood British Cemetery, Bourlon | 53 | H 16 | 219 |
| Bousbecque German Cemetery | 4 | G 3 | 1806 |
| Boussu Bois Communal Cemetery | 12 | K 4 | 1986 |
| Boussu Communal Cemetery | 12 | K 4 | 1985 |
| Bousval Communal Cemetery | 13 | L 3 | 1987 |
| Bout-de-Ville, German Cemetery, Richebourg St. Vaast | 44 | E 10 | 220 |
| Bout-de-Ville, Richebourg St. Vaast | 44 | E 10 | 221 |
| Bouvigny-Boyeffles Military Cemetery | 46 | D 13 | 222 |
| Bouzincourt Communal Cemetery | 11 | G 6 | 223 |
| Bouzincourt Communal Cemetery Extension | 54 | D 18 | 224 |
| Bouzincourt Ridge British Cemetery, Albert | 54 | D 18 | 225 |
| Bouzincourt French Cemetery, Hamel | 54 | D 18 | 226 |
| Boves Military Cemetery | 20 | G 6 | 227 |
| Boves West Communal Cemetery | 20 | G 6 | 229 |
| Boves West Communal Cemetery Extension | 20 | G 6 | 228 |
| Boyelles Communal Cemetery Extension | 49 | E 15 | 230 |
| Braine Communal Cemetery | 60 | — | 2144 |
| Braine l'Alleud Communal Cemetery | 5 | L 3 | 1988 |
| Braine le Comte Communal Cemetery | 12 | L 3 | 1989 |
| Brancourt Communal Cemetery, Brancourt-le-Grand | 12 | J 6 | 231 |
| Brandhoek Military Cemetery, Vlamertinghe | 40 | E 7 | 232 |

| Name of Cemetery. | Page. | Map Square. | No. on Map. |
|---|---|---|---|
| Brandhoek New Military Cemetery, Vlamertinghe | 40 | E 7 | 233 |
| Brandhoek New Military Cemetery No. 3, Vlamertinghe | 40 | E 7 | 234 |
| Brasserie Military Cemetery, Le Fermont, Rivière | 48 | E 15 | 235 |
| Bray Hill British Cemetery, Bray-sur-Somme | 54 | E 19 | 236 |
| Bray Military Cemetery, Mont St. Eloy | 48 | D 14 | 237 |
| Bray Road Cemetery, Fricourt | 54 | E 18 | 238 |
| Bray-sur-Somme Military Cemetery | 54 | E 19 | 239 |
| Bray Vale British Cemetery, Bray-sur-Somme | 54 | E 19 | 240 |
| Bréblères British Cemetery | 11 | H 4 | 241 |
| Bresle Communal Cemetery | 11 | G 6 | 1881 |
| Bresle Wood British Cemetery | 11 | G 5 | 242 |
| Bretencourt French Military Cemetery, Rivière | 48 | D 15 | 243 |
| Brewery Orchard, Bois Grenier | 43 | F 9 | 244 |
| Briastre Communal Cemetery Extension | 59 | L 16 | 245 |
| Briastre-Solesmes Road Military Cemetery, Briastre | 59 | M 16 | 246 |
| Brickfields British Cemetery, Aire | 10 | G 3 | 247 |
| Bridge House, Langemarck | 41 | F 6 | 248 |
| Brie British Cemetery | 21 | H 6 | 249 |
| Brielen Military Cemetery | 41 | F 6 | 250 |
| Briqueterie Graves, Carnoy | 55 | E 18 | — |
| Briqueterie Cemetery, Montauban | 55 | E 18 | 251 |
| Briqueterie East Cemetery, Montauban | 55 | E 18 | 252 |
| Brissein House Cemetery, Bixschoote | 41 | F 6 | 253 |
| Bristol Castle Military Cemetery, Messines | 43 | F 8 | 254 |
| British Cemetery No. 2, Bray-sur-Somme | 54 | E 19 | 1848 |
| British Cemetery No. 3, Bray-sur-Somme | 54 | E 19 | 1849 |
| Bronfay Farm Military Cemetery, Bray-sur-Somme | 54 | E 19 | 255 |
| Brouchy Churchyard Cemetery | 21 | H 6 | 1990 |
| Brown Line British Cemetery, St. Laurent-Blangy | 48 | E 14 | 257 |
| Brown's Copse British Cemetery, Fampoux | 49 | F 14 | 256 |
| Brown's Road Military Cemetery, Festubert | 44 | E 11 | 258 |
| Broxeele Churchyard | 3 | F 3 | 1882 |
| Bruay Communal Cemetery Extension | 11 | G 4 | 259 |
| Bucks Cemetery, Ploegsteert Wood | 43 | F 8 | 260 |
| Bucquoy Communal Cemetery and Extension | 50 | E 16 | 261 |
| Bucquoy Road British Cemetery, Ficheux | 48 | E 15 | 262 |
| Bucy-le-Long British Cemetery, Aisne | 60 | — | 282 |
| Buffs Road Cemetery, St. Jean | 41 | F 6 | 263 |
| Buire British Cemetery | 56 | G 19 | 264 |
| Buire Communal Cemetery | 56 | G 19 | 265 |
| Bulgar Alley British Cemetery, Mametz | 54 | E 18 | 266 |
| Bulls Road Military Cemetery, Flers | 51 | F 18 | 267 |
| Bully Communal Cemetery Extension | 46 | D 12 | 268 |
| Bunyans British Cemetery, Tilloy-les-Mafflaines | 49 | E 15 | 269 |
| Burbure Communal Cemetery | 10 | G 4 | 1883 |
| Bushes British Cemetery, Boisleux St. Marc | 48 | E 15 | 270 |
| Bus German Cemetery, Lagnicourt | 52 | G 16 | 1808 |
| Bus House Cemetery, Voormezeele | 41 | F 7 | 271 |
| Busigny Communal Cemetery | 12 | J 5 | 273 |
| Busigny Communal Cemetery Extension | 12 | J 5 | 272 |
| Busnes Communal Cemetery | 11 | G 3 | 1884 |
| Bussy-les-Daours | 10 | G 6 | 274 |
| Butte Cemetery, Polygone Wood, Zonnebeke | 41 | G 6 | 275 |
| Buysscheure Churchyard | 3 | F 3 | 1885 |
| Buzancy Military Cemetery | 60 | — | 276 |
| Cabaret Rouge British Cemetery, Souchez | 46 | E 13 | 277 |
| Cabin Hill Cemetery, Wytschaete | 41 | F 8 | 278 |
| Cachy British Cemetery | 21 | G 6 | 279 |
| Caestre Communal Cemetery | 3 | G 3 | 280 |
| Caestre Military Cemetery | 3 | G 3 | 281 |
| Cagnicourt British Cemetery | 11 | H 5 | 283 |
| Cagnoncles Communal Cemetery | 11 | J 5 | 284 |
| Cagny Communal Cemetery Extension | 20 | F 6 | 1886 |
| Caix British Cemetery | 21 | G 6 | 285 |

| Name of Cemetery. | Page. | Map Square. | No. on Map. |
|---|---|---|---|
| Calais Northern Cemetery | 2 | E 2 | 2145 |
| Calais Southern Cemetery | 2 | E 2 | 2146 |
| Caldron Military Cemetery (Red Mill), Liévin | 47 | E 13 | 286 |
| Calvaire (Essex) Military Cemetery, Ploegsteert | 43 | F 8 | 287 |
| Cambrai (East) British Cemetery | 53 | J 16 | 289 |
| Cambrai (East) German Cemetery | 53 | J 16 | 288 |
| Cambrin Churchyard | 44 | E 11 | 290 |
| Cambrin Churchyard Extension | 44 | E 11 | 291 |
| Cambrin Military Cemetery (behind Mayor's house) | 44 | E 11 | 292 |
| Cameron British Cemetery, Tilloy | 11 | H 5 | 293 |
| Camon Communal Cemetery | 20 | G 6 | 1887 |
| Camouflage British Cemetery, Rouvroy-en-Santerre | 21 | G 6 | 294 |
| Campagne Churchyard | 3 | F 3 | 1888 |
| Campagne-les-Boulonnais Churchyard | 9 | F 3 | 1991 |
| Canada Cemetery, Tilloy | 11 | H 5 | 295 |
| Canada Farm British Cemetery, Elverdinghe | 40 | E 6 | 296 |
| Canadian Cemetery C.D. 24, Givenchy-en-Gohelle | 46 | E 13 | 317 |
| Canadian Cemetery, Givenchy-en-Gohelle | 46 | E 13 | 297 |
| Canadian Cemetery, Givenchy Road, Neuville St. Vaast | 46 | E 13 | 311 |
| Canadian Cemetery, near Gunners' Crater, Givenchy-en-Gohelle | 46 | E 13 | 305 |
| Canadian Cemetery No. 1, Loos-en-Gohelle | 47 | E 12 | 303 |
| Canadian Cemetery No. 2, Loos-en-Gohelle | 47 | E 12 | 304 |
| Canadian Cemetery No. 3, Neuville St. Vaast | 48 | E 14 | 313 |
| Canadian Cemetery, Sailly-sur-la-Lys | 42 | E 9 | 314 |
| Canadian Cemetery, Strand, Ploegsteert | 43 | F 8 | 315 |
| Canadian (2nd) Cemetery, Sunken Road, Contalmaison | 54 | E 18 | 298 |
| Canadian (8th) Cemetery, Lens | 47 | E 12 | 299 |
| Canadian (25th) Cemetery, Lens | 47 | E 12 | 300 |
| Canadian (38th) Cemetery, Vimy | 47 | E 13 | 301 |
| Canadian (46th) Cemetery, Liévin | 46 | E 13 | 302 |
| Canadian Grave C.A. 4, Thelus | 48 | E 14 | 320 |
| Canadian Grave C.A. 40, Thelus | 48 | E 14 | 321 |
| Canadian Grave C.B. 1 | 47 | E 13 | 306 |
| Canadian Grave C.B. 2A, Thelus | 47 | E 13 | 322 |
| Canadian Grave C.B. 3A | 47 | E 13 | 307 |
| Canadian Grave C.B. 8, Thelus | 47 | E 13 | 323 |
| Canadian Grave C.C. 2 (Petit Vimy British Cemetery) | 47 | E 13 | 327 |
| Canadian Grave C.D. 7, Vimy | 47 | E 13 | 310 |
| Canadian Military Graves, Avion | 47 | E 13 | 318 |
| Canal Bank Cemetery, Boesinghe | 41 | F 6 | 335 |
| Cane Post Cemetery, St. Jean | 41 | F 6 | 336 |
| Cannes Farm Cemetery, Langemarck | 41 | F 6 | 334 |
| Canopus Trench Cemetery, Langemarck | 41 | F 6 | 337 |
| Capelle-Beaudignies Road Military Cemetery, Capelle-sur-Escaillon | 58 | M 15 | 338 |
| Cappy North Communal Cemetery Extension, Cappy | 55 | E 19 | 339 |
| Captain's Farm Cemetery, Langemarck | 41 | F 6 | 340 |
| Card Copse British Cemetery, Marcelcave | 21 | G 6 | 341 |
| Carency Military Cemetery | 46 | D 13 | 342 |
| Carnières Communal Cemetery Extension | 11 | J 5 | 343 |
| Carnoy Military Cemetery | 54 | E 19 | 344 |
| Carriers British Cemetery | 22 | K 7 | 1902 |
| Cartignies Communal Cemetery | 12 | K 5 | 1993 |
| Carvin Communal Cemetery | 11 | H 4 | 1809 |
| Casualty Corner Cemetery, Contalmaison | 54 | E 18 | 347 |
| Caterpillar Valley Cemetery, Longueval | 55 | E 18 | 1771 |
| Catillon Communal Cemetery | 59 | N 17 | 1810 |
| Caudry Communal Cemetery | 12 | J 5 | 351 |
| Caudry German Military Cemetery | 12 | J 5 | 352 |
| Caudry Municipal Cemetery | 12 | J 5 | — |
| Cayeux-en-Santerre Chateau Cemetery | 21 | G 6 | 354 |

| Name of Cemetery. | Page. | Map Square. | No. on Map. |
|---|---|---|---|
| Cayeux French Military Cemetery, Cayeux-en-Santerre | 21 | G 6 | 353 |
| Cellar Farm, Fromelles | 43 | F 10 | 355 |
| Cement House, Langemarck | 41 | F 6 | 356 |
| Cemetery near the Church, St. Jean | 41 | F 6 | 357 |
| Cemetery Post Station, Pozières | 50 | D 18 | 358 |
| Cérisy-Gailly New French Military Cemetery | 54 | D 20 | 359 |
| Chalk Lane Cemetery, Villers Bretonneux | 21 | G 6 | 362 |
| Chambrecy British Cemetery | 60 | — | 363 |
| Champillon British Cemetery | 60 | — | 2147 |
| Chaos Communal Cemetery, Templeuve | 11 | J 3 | 364 |
| Chapel Corner British Cemetery, Sauchy l'Estrée | 11 | H 5 | 365 |
| Chapel Farm British Cemetery, Fleurbaix | 43 | F 9 | 366 |
| Chapelle British Cemetery, Holnon | 21 | J 6 | 1811 |
| Chapelle d'Armentières Communal Cemetery | 43 | F 9 | 368 |
| Chapelle d'Armentières New Military Cemetery | 43 | F 9 | 369 |
| Chapelle d'Armentières Old Military Cemetery | 43 | F 9 | 370 |
| Charing Cross Cemetery, Sailly-Saillisel | 55 | F 18 | 371 |
| Charleroi Communal Cemetery | 13 | L 4 | 1994 |
| Charmes Military Cemetery (Vosges) | 33 | Q 11 | 2148 |
| Chasseur Farm British Cemetery, Boesinghe | 41 | F 6 | 372 |
| Chateau du Flandre, Beaucamps | 42 | E 9 | 373 |
| Chateau Grounds, La Motte, Morbecque | 11 | G 3 | 374 |
| Chateau Seydoux British Cemetery, Le Cateau | 59 | M 17 | 375 |
| Chaufours Wood British Cemetery, Morchies | 52 | G 17 | 360 |
| Chauny Communal Cemetery, Military Extension | 21 | J 7 | 1995 |
| Cheriots, The, Rue du Bois, Richebourg l'Avoue | 44 | E 11 | 376 |
| Cherisy Road East Cemetery, Héninel | 49 | F 15 | 377 |
| Cheshire British Cemetery, Parcy-Tigny | 60 | — | 378 |
| Chester Farm Military Cemetery, Zillebeke | 51 | F 17 | 379 |
| Cheyne Walk, Givenchy-lez-La Bassée | 44 | E 11 | 380 |
| Chili Trench British Cemetery, Gavrelle | 49 | F 14 | 381 |
| Chinese Cemetery, Reninghelst | 40 | E 7 | 382 |
| Chinese General Hospital Cemetery, Noyelles | 9 | E 5 | 2149 |
| Chinook Cemetery, Vimy | 47 | E 13 | 383 |
| Chipilly Communal Cemetery Extension | 54 | D 20 | 384 |
| Chocques Military Cemetery | 11 | G 4 | 385 |
| Churchyard, St. Jean | 41 | F 6 | 386 |
| Cimitière des Gonards, Versailles | 28 | F 10 | 2150 |
| Cinq Rues British Cemetery, Hazebrouck | 3 | G 3 | 387 |
| Citadel Military Cemetery (Point 71), near Fricourt | 54 | E 19 | 388 |
| Cité Bonjean Military Cemetery, Armentières | 43 | F 9 | 389 |
| Cité Calonne Military Cemetery, Lievin | 46 | E 12 | 390 |
| City of Paris Cemetery, Bagneux | 28 | F 10 | 2151 |
| City of Paris Cemetery, Pantin | 28 | G 9 | 2152 |
| Clark's Dump, High Wood, Bazentin | 51 | E 18 | 391 |
| Clary German Cemetery | 12 | J 5 | 392 |
| Clastres New French Military Cemetery | 21 | J 6 | 393 |
| Clery British Cemetery | 55 | F 19 | 394 |
| Cloudy Trench Cemetery No. 2, Gueudecourt | 51 | F 18 | — |
| Clump British Cemetery, Rosières-en-Santerre | 21 | G 6 | 395 |
| Cojeul British Cemetery, St. Martin-sur-Cojeul | 49 | F 15 | 396 |
| Coine Valley Cemetery, Boesinghe | 41 | F 6 | 397 |
| Combles Communal Cemetery | 55 | F 18 | 399 |
| Combles Communal Cemetery Extension | 55 | F 18 | 398 |
| Comedy Farm Cemetery, Langemarck | 41 | F 6 | 400 |
| Conches Communal Cemetery, 33 m. S. of Rouen | — | — | — |
| Connaught British Cemetery, Le Cateau | 59 | M 17 | 402 |
| Connaught Cemetery, Thiepval | 50 | D 18 | 401 |
| Contalmaison Chateau Cemetery | 54 | E 18 | 403 |
| Contay British Cemetery | 10 | G 5 | 404 |
| Contour British Cemetery, Solesmes | 59 | M 16 | 405 |
| Convent Villa, La Boutillerie, Fleurbaix | 43 | F 10 | 406 |
| Copse Corner British Cemetery, Vauvillers | 21 | G 6 | 407 |
| Copse Trench British Cemetery, Allaines | 56 | G 19 | 408 |

| Name of Cemetery. | Page. | Map Square. | No. on Map. |
|---|---|---|---|
| Corbehem Communal Cemetery | 11 | H 4 | 1813 |
| Corbie Communal Cemetery | 11 | G 6 | 409 |
| Corbie Communal Cemetery Extension | 11 | G 6 | 410 |
| Corkscrew British Cemetery, Lievin | 47 | E 12 | 411 |
| Cornwall Cemetery (Stinking Farm), Messines | 43 | F 8 | 412 |
| Cottage Garden, St. Jean | 41 | F 6 | 413 |
| Cottenchy Communal Cemetery | 20 | G 6 | 414 |
| Couin British Cemetery | 11 | G 5 | 415 |
| Couin New British Cemetery | 11 | G 5 | 416 |
| Coulomby Churchyard | 2 | F 3 | 1996 |
| Courcelette British Cemetery | 50 | E 18 | 420 |
| Courcelles-au-Bois Communal Cemetery Extension | 50 | C 17 | 417 |
| Courcelles Communal Cemetery, Courcelles-lez-Lens | 11 | H 4 | 418 |
| Courcelles-le-Comte German Military Cemetery | 51 | E 16 | 419 |
| Courmas Chateau British Cemetery | 60 | — | 421 |
| Courmas Cross Roads British Cemetery, Marfaux | 60 | — | 422 |
| Courmas Village British Cemetery, Courmas | 60 | — | 423 |
| Courrières Communal Cemetery | 11 | H 4 | 424 |
| Courte Dreve Farm, Ploegsteert | 43 | F 8 | 425 |
| Courtrai British Military Cemetery | 4 | J 3 | 426 |
| Cousolre Communal Cemetery | 12 | L 4 | 1998 |
| Coutiches | 11 | H 4 | 1890 |
| Couturelle Communal Cemetery Extension | 11 | G 5 | 427 |
| Couture St. Germain | 13 | L 3 | 1997 |
| Coxyde Military Cemetery | 3 | G 2 | 428 |
| Coyghem Communal Cemetery | 4 | J 3 | 1999 |
| Crest British Cemetery, Fontaine-Notre-Dame | 53 | J 16 | 429 |
| Crèvecœur Churchyard, Crèvecœur-sur-l'Escaut | 53 | J 17 | 430 |
| Crèvecœur Courtyard Cemetery, Crèvecœur-sur-l'Escaut | 53 | J 17 | 431 |
| Croisilles British Cemetery | 49 | F 15 | 432 |
| Croisilles Communal Cemetery Extension | 49 | F 16 | 433 |
| Croisilles Railway Military Cemetery | 49 | F 16 | 434 |
| Croisilles Road Cemetery, Héninel | 49 | F 15 | 435 |
| Croix-Blanche British Cemetery, Fleurbaix | 43 | F 10 | 436 |
| Croix Churchyard | 59 | M 16 | 1815 |
| Croix-du-Bac British Cemetery, Steenwerck | 42 | E 9 | 437 |
| Croix-Maréchal Military Cemetery, Fleurbaix | 43 | F 10 | 438 |
| Croix Rouge Military Cemetery, Quaedypre | 3 | G 2 | 1773 |
| Croonaert Chapel Cemetery, Wytschaete | 41 | F 7 | 439 |
| Cross Roads British Cemetery, Fontaine-au-Bois | 59 | N 16 | 440 |
| Cross Roads Cemetery, Bazentin | 55 | E 18 | 441 |
| Cross Roads Cemetery, Boisleux-St. Marc | 48 | E 15 | 442 |
| Cross Roads Cemetery, Masnières | 53 | J 17 | 443 |
| Cross Roads, St. Jean | 41 | F 6 | 445 |
| Crouy British Cemetery | 10 | F 5 | 2154 |
| Croydon Military Cemetery, Gilsy | 20 | G 6 | 447 |
| Crucifix British Cemetery, Vendegies-sur-Ecaillon | 58 | M 15 | 448 |
| Crucifix Corner British Cemetery, Villers Bretonneux | 21 | G 6 | 449 |
| Crump Trench British Cemetery, Fampoux | 49 | F 14 | 452 |
| Cuckoo Passage, Héninel | 49 | F 15 | 451 |
| Cugny British Cemetery | 21 | H 6 | 2155 |
| Cuinchy Municipal Cemetery | 44 | E 11 | 454 |
| Cuitron British Cemetery, Marfaux | 60 | — | 455 |
| Curgies Communal Cemetery | 58 | M 14 | 1891 |
| Curlu French Military Cemetery | 55 | F 19 | 456 |
| Cuthbert Farm Cemetery, Rue Tilleloy, Neuve Chapelle | 45 | E 10 | 457 |
| Dadizeele Communal Cemetery | 4 | H 2 | 458 |
| Dainville British Cemetery | 48 | D 14 | 459 |
| Dainville Communal Cemetery | 48 | E 14 | 460 |
| Dallon German Military Cemetery | 21 | J 6 | 1816 |
| Damery British Cemetery, Parvillers | 24 | G 6 | 461 |
| Dantzig Alley British Cemetery, near Mametz | 54 | E 18 | 462 |
| Danube Post Military Cemetery, Thiepval | 50 | D 18 | 463 |

| Name of Cemetery. | Page. | Map Square. | No. on Map. |
|---|---|---|---|
| Daours Communal Cemetery Extension | 10 | G 6 | 464 |
| Darcy German Cemetery, Hénin Liétard | 11 | H 4 | 465 |
| Dartmoor Cemetery, near Becordel | 54 | D 18 | 466 |
| D.C.L.I. Cemetery, Avion | 47 | E 13 | 468 |
| D.C.L.I. Cemetery, The Bluff, Zillebeke | 41 | F 7 | 467 |
| Dechy Communal Cemetery | 11 | H 4 | 469 |
| De Cusine Ravine British Cemetery, Basseux | 48 | D 15 | 470 |
| Deerlyck Churchyard | 4 | J 2 | 2156 |
| De la Madeleine Cemetery, Courtrai | 4 | J 3 | 2157 |
| Delette Communal Cemetery | 10 | F 3 | 2000 |
| Delmadge British Cemetery, Fontaine-Notre-Dame | 53 | J 16 | 474 |
| Delsaux Farm British Cemetery, Beugny | 52 | G 17 | 475 |
| De Luce British Cemetery, Caix | 21 | G 6 | 476 |
| Delville Wood Cemetery | 55 | E 18 | — |
| Demuin British Cemetery | 21 | G 6 | 477 |
| Denain British Cemetery | 12 | J 4 | 478 |
| Denain Communal Cemetery and Extension | 12 | J 4 | 1892 |
| Denain German Cemetery | 12 | J 4 | 479 |
| De Nieuwe Kruiseecke Cabaret Cemetery, Gheluvelt | 4 | H 2 | 480 |
| De Pierre British Cemetery, Crèvecœur-sur-l'Escaut | 11 | J 5 | 481 |
| Dernancourt Communal Cemetery | 54 | D 19 | 1774 |
| Dernancourt Communal Cemetery Extension | 54 | D 19 | 482 |
| Derry House Cemetery, No. 2, Wytschaete | 41 | F 8 | 483 |
| Despierre Farm, Ploegsteert | 43 | F 8 | 484 |
| Desplanque Farm British Cemetery | 43 | F 9 | 1893 |
| Desplanque Farm, Chapelle d'Armentières | 43 | F 9 | 485 |
| Desvres Communal Cemetery | 9 | E 3 | 2001 |
| Devonshire Cemetery, Mametz | 54 | E 19 | 486 |
| Dickebusch Churchyard Extension | 40 | E 7 | 487 |
| Dickebusch New Military Cemetery | 40 | E 7 | 488 |
| Dickebusch New Military Cemetery Extension | 40 | E 7 | 489 |
| Dickebusch Old Military Cemetery | 40 | E 7 | 490 |
| Dinant Communal Cemetery | 13 | M 4 | 2002 |
| Dive Copse British Cemetery, Sailly-le-Sec | 54 | D 19 | 491 |
| Divion Communal Cemetery | 11 | G 4 | 492 |
| Divion Road British Cemetery No. 1, Thiepval | 50 | D 17 | 493 |
| Divion Road British Cemetery No. 2, Thiepval | 50 | D 17 | 494 |
| Divion Road British Cemetery No. 3, Thiepval | 50 | D 17 | 495 |
| Divisional Cemetery, Dickebusch Road, Vlamertinghe | 41 | F 7 | 496 |
| Divisional Cemetery (32nd), Hébuterne | 50 | D 17 | 497 |
| Divisional Collecting Post Cemetery, St. Jean | 41 | F 6 | 498 |
| Doingt Communal Cemetery Extension | 56 | G 19 | 499 |
| Dominion British Cemetery, Hendecourt-lez-Cagnicourt | 49 | G 15 | 500 |
| Domino British Cemetery, Epéhy | 57 | H 18 | 501 |
| Dommiers (Aisne) British Cemetery | 60 | — | 502 |
| Don Communal Cemetery, Annoeullin | 45 | F 11 | 503 |
| Dottignies Communal Cemetery Extension | 4 | J 3 | 2158 |
| Douai British Cemetery, Cuinchy | 11 | H 4 | 505 |
| Douai Communal Cemetery | 11 | H 4 | 506 |
| Douai German Cemetery | 11 | H 4 | — |
| Douane, Neuve Eglise | 42 | E 8 | 507 |
| Douchy Communal Cemetery Extension | 12 | J 4 | 508 |
| Douchy-les-Ayette British Cemetery | 50 | E 16 | 509 |
| Douilly Communal Cemetery | 21 | H 6 | 1894 |
| Doullens Communal Cemetery Extension | 10 | G 5 | 510 |
| Dour Communal Cemetery | 12 | K 4 | 2159 |
| Dourges Communal Cemetery, German Extension | 11 | H 4 | 511 |
| Dourlers Communal Cemetery | 12 | K 5 | 2160 |
| Dozinghem British Cemetery, Westvleteren | 40 | D 6 | 513 |
| Dragoon Camp Cemetery, Boesinghe | 41 | F 6 | 514 |
| Dranoutre Churchyard | 42 | E 8 | 515 |
| Dranoutre Military Cemetery | 42 | E 8 | 516 |
| Driencourt British Cemetery | 56 | G 19 | 517 |
| Drummond British Cemetery, Raillencourt | 53 | J 16 | 518 |

| Name of Cemetery. | Page. | Map Square. | No. on Map. |
|---|---|---|---|
| Dud Corner, Loos | 47 | E 12 | 519 |
| Duhallow A.D.S. Cemetery, Ypres | 41 | F 6 | 520 |
| Duisans British Cemetery, Etrun | 48 | D 14 | 521 |
| Dunkerque (Dunkirk) Town Cemetery and Extension | 3 | G 2 | 522 |
| Dury Crucifix British Cemetery | 11 | H 5 | 523 |
| Dury Mill British Cemetery | 11 | H 5 | 524 |
| Ebblinghem British Cemetery | 3 | G 3 | 526 |
| Ebenezer Farm, near Laventie | 45 | E 10 | 527 |
| Eclusier Communal Cemetery, Cappy | 55 | E 19 | 1775 |
| Eclusier Military Cemetery, Cappy | 55 | E 19 | 1817 |
| Ecoivres Military Cemetery, near Mont St. Eloy | 48 | D 14 | 528 |
| Ecole de Bienfaisance, Ypres | 41 | F 7 | — |
| Ecoust Military Cemetery, Ecoust St. Mein | 51 | F 16 | 530 |
| Ecoust St. Mein Communal Cemetery Extension | 51 | F 16 | 529 |
| Ecuelin Churchyard | 12 | K 5 | 2003 |
| Edgware Road British Cemetery, Neuve Chapelle | 44 | E 11 | 532 |
| Edward Road No. 1 Cemetery, Richebourg l'Avoue | 44 | E 10 | 533 |
| Edward Road No. 2 Cemetery, Richebourg l'Avoue | 44 | E 10 | 534 |
| Edward Road No. 3 (Windy Corner) Cemetery, Richebourg l'Avoue | 44 | E 10 | 535 |
| Edward Road No. 4 (Factory Trench) Cemetery, Richebourg l'Avoue | 44 | E 10 | 536 |
| Edward Road No. 5 Cemetery, Richebourg l'Avoue | 44 | E 10 | 537 |
| Effie Trench British Cemetery, Athies | 49 | F 14 | 538 |
| Eikhof Farm, Voormezeele | 41 | F 7 | 540 |
| Elouges Communal Cemetery | 12 | K 4 | 2161 |
| Elzenwalle Brasserie, near Voormezeele | 41 | F 7 | 542 |
| Elzenwalle Brasserie West Cemetery, near Voormezeele | 41 | F 7 | 543 |
| Elzenwalle Chateau Cemetery, Voormezeele | 41 | F 7 | 544 |
| Emerchicourt Churchyard | 11 | J 4 | 546 |
| Engis Communal Cemetery | 14 | N 3 | 2004 |
| Englebelmer Communal Cemetery | 50 | D 18 | 548 |
| Englebelmer Communal Cemetery Extension | 50 | D 18 | 547 |
| Englefontaine British Cemetery | 59 | N 15 | 549 |
| Englefontaine Churchyard | 59 | N 16 | 1895 |
| English Farm, Bixschoote | 41 | F 6 | 550 |
| Epéhy Wood Farm British Cemetery, Epéhy | 57 | H 18 | 552 |
| Eperlecques Churchyard | 3 | F 3 | 2005 |
| Epinoy Chapel British Cemetery, Epinoy | 11 | H 5 | 553 |
| Epinoy Churchyard | 11 | H 5 | 1897 |
| Epinoy Road British Cemetery | 11 | H 5 | 554 |
| Epinoy Sucrerie British Cemetery | 11 | H 5 | 1896 |
| Eppeville Communal Cemetery | 21 | H 6 | 1898 |
| Equarrisage British Cemetery, St. Nicolas, Arras | 48 | E 14 | 531 |
| Erquelinnes Communal Cemetery | 12 | L 4 | 2006 |
| Erquennes Communal Cemetery | 12 | K 4 | 2007 |
| Erquinghem-Lys Churchyard | 43 | F 9 | 555 |
| Erquinghem-Lys Churchyard Extension | 43 | F 9 | 556 |
| Erviliers German Military Cemetery | 51 | E 16 | 557 |
| Escarmain Communal Cemetery Extension | 59 | M 15 | 558 |
| Escaudouvres Convent Cemetery | 11 | J 5 | 559 |
| Esnes Communal Cemetery, German Extension | 11 | J 5 | 560 |
| Escoeuilles Churchyard | 2 | F 3 | 2008 |
| Espierres Communal Cemetery | 4 | J 3 | 2009 |
| Esplechin Communal Cemetery | 11 | J 3 | 561 |
| Esquelbecq Military Cemetery | 3 | G 2 | 562 |
| Esquelmes Communal Cemetery | 12 | J 3 | 2010 |
| Esquerdes Churchyard | 3 | F 3 | 2011 |
| Essex British Cemetery, Sailly-le-Sec | 54 | D 19 | 564 |
| Essex Cemetery, Eterpigny | 49 | G 15 | 563 |
| Essex Farm, Boesinghe | 41 | F 6 | 565 |
| Estaires Communal Cemetery | 42 | E 9 | 551 |
| Estaires Communal Cemetery Extension | 42 | E 9 | 566 |
| Estaires German Cemetery | 42 | D 9 | 1821 |

| Name of Cemetery. | Page. | Map Square. | No. on Map. |
|---|---|---|---|
| Estrées British Cemetery, Estrées-en-Chaussée | 56 | H 10 | 567 |
| Estreux Churchyard | 58 | M 13 | 1899 |
| Eswars German Cemetery | 11 | J 5 | 1776 |
| Etaples Military Cemetery | 9 | E 4 | 2162 |
| Eterpigny British Cemetery | 49 | G 15 | 568 |
| Eth British Cemetery | 12 | J 4 | 569 |
| Etinehem Communal Cemetery | 54 | D 20 | 570 |
| Etretat Churchyard and Extension | 18 | B 6 | 2163 |
| Euston Post, near Laventie, Richebourg l' Avoue | 44 | E 10 | 571 |
| Euston Road British Cemetery, Colincamps | 50 | D 17 | 572 |
| Factory Enclosure, Rue du Bois | 44 | E 11 | 573 |
| Famars Communal Cemetery Extension | 58 | M 14 | 574 |
| Faubourg d'Amiens Cemetery, Arras | 48 | E 14 | 575 |
| Faubourg d'Amiens Military Cemetery | 48 | E 14 | — |
| Faubourg St. Martin Military Cemetery Extension | 21 | J 6 | 1823 |
| Fauquembergues Communal Cemetery | 10 | F 3 | 2013 |
| Fauquissart Military Cemetery, Laventie | 42 | E 10 | 576 |
| Favreuil British Cemetery | 51 | F 17 | 577 |
| Fayt-le-Franc Churchyard | 12 | K 4 | 2014 |
| Fécamp Communal Cemetery | 18 | B 6 | 2015 |
| Ferdinand Farm Cemetery, Langemarck | 41 | F 6 | 578 |
| Ferme de la Buterne Military Cemetery, Houplines | 43 | F 9 | 579 |
| Ferme Cannone British Military Cemetery, Vendegies-sur-Escaillon | 58 | L 15 | 580 |
| Ferme Deloux-Bouquet, Nouveau Monde, La Gorgue | 42 | E 9 | 581 |
| Ferme du Biez, Chapelle d'Armentiéres | 43 | F 9 | 582 |
| Ferme Godezonne, Kemmel | 41 | F 7 | 583 |
| Ferme Olivier, Elverdinghe | 40 | E 6 | 584 |
| Ferme Phillipeaux British Cemetery | 43 | F 9 | — |
| Ferme Phillipeaux, Houplines | 43 | F 9 | 585 |
| Ferrière-la-Petite Communal Cemetery | 12 | K 5 | 2016 |
| Feuchy British Cemetery | 49 | F 14 | 587 |
| Feuchy Chapel British Cemetery, Monchy-le-Preux | 49 | F 15 | 588 |
| Feuchy Chapel Quarry Cemetery, Feuchy | 49 | F 15 | 589 |
| Feuillères British Cemetery | 55 | F 19 | 590 |
| Fienvillers British Cemetery | 10 | F 5 | 2164 |
| Fifteen Ravine British Cemetery, Villers Plouich | 53 | H 17 | 592 |
| Fifty-first Divisional Cemetery (No Man's Cot), Boesinghe | 41 | F 6 | 593 |
| Fillièvres British Cemetery | 10 | F 4 | 2165 |
| Fins British Cemetery | 52 | H 18 | 594 |
| Fins Churchyard Extension | 52 | G 18 | 595 |
| Fins New British Cemetery, Sorel | 52 | H 18 | 596 |
| First Corps Grave "A. 19," Angres | 46 | E 13 | 597 |
| Five Points British Cemetery, Lechelle | 52 | G 18 | 598 |
| Flatiron Copse British Cemetery, near Bazentin | 55 | E 18 | 599 |
| Flaumont Churchyard | 12 | K 5 | 2017 |
| Flers Dressing Station Cemetery, Ginchy | 51 | F 18 | 600 |
| Flers Road Cemetery, Flers | 51 | E 18 | 601 |
| Flesquières Chateau Cemetery | 53 | H 17 | 602 |
| Flesquières Hill British Cemetery | 53 | H 17 | 603 |
| Flêtre Churchyard | 42 | D 8 | 604 |
| Fleurbaix Churchyard | 43 | E 9 | 606 |
| Fleury la Rivière Communal Cemetery (French Military Extension) | 60 | — | 1824 |
| Floursies Churchyard | 12 | K 5 | 2018 |
| Floursies Communal Cemetery | 12 | K 5 | 2019 |
| Folies Communal Cemetery Extension | 21 | G 6 | 607 |
| Fond de Vase Cemetery, Marœuil | 48 | E 14 | 608 |
| Fond de Vase Cemetery No. 2, Marœuil | 48 | E 14 | 609 |
| Fonquevillers Military Cemetery and Extension | 50 | D 16 | 614 |
| Fontaine-au-Bois Communal Cemetery | 59 | N 16 | 610 |
| Fontaine-au-Pire Communal Cemetery | 12 | J 5 | 611 |
| Fontaine-les-Cappy Churchyard Extension | 55 | E 20 | 612 |
| Fontaine Road (Shaft Trench) Cemetery, Héninel | 49 | F 15 | 613 |

| Name of Cemetery. | Page. | Map Square. | No. on Map. |
|---|---|---|---|
| Forceville Communal Cemetery Extension.. | 11 | G 5 | 615 |
| Forenville Communal Cemetery Extension.. | 53 | K 16 | 616 |
| Forest Communal Cemetery | 59 | M 16 | 617 |
| Foreste Communal Cemetery.. | 21 | H 6 | 618 |
| Fort Glatz Cemetery, Loos | 47 | E 12 | 619 |
| Fortrie Farm, Romarin | 43 | E 8 | 620 |
| Forville Churchyard | 13 | M 3 | 2020 |
| Fosse No. 7 Military Cemetery (Quality Street), Mazingarbe | 46 | E 12 | 621 |
| Fosse 10 Communal Cemetery, Sains-en-Gohelle .. | 46 | D 12 | 622 |
| Fosse 10 Communal Cemetery Extension, Sains-en-Gohelle | 46 | D 12 | 623 |
| Fouilloy Communal Cemetery | 11 | G 6 | 624 |
| Fouquereuil Communal Cemetery | 44 | C 11 | 1901 |
| Fouquières Churchyard | 44 | C 11 | 625 |
| Fouquières Churchyard Extension .. | 44 | D 11 | 626 |
| Frameries Communal Cemetery | 12 | K 4 | 2021 |
| Framerville British Cemetery.. | 21 | G 6 | 627 |
| François Farm, Langemarck .. | 41 | F 6 | 628 |
| Frankfurt Trench (V Corps Cemetery No. 11), Beaucourt-sur-Ancre | 50 | D 17 | 629 |
| Franvillers Communal Cemetery Extension | 11 | G 6 | 630 |
| Frasnoy Communal Cemetery and Extension | 12 | J 4 | 631 |
| Frechencourt Communal Cemetery | 10 | G 6 | 632 |
| Fremicourt Communal Cemetery Extension | 51 | F 17 | 633 |
| Fremicourt German Cemetery | 51 | F 17 | 1825 |
| Frenchman's Farm, Wulverghem | 41 | F 8 | 634 |
| French Military Cemetery, Hôpital Auban Moet, Epernay | 60 | — | 2166 |
| French Military Cemetery, Senlis (Oise) | 21 | G 8 | 2167 |
| Fresnoy British Cemetery, Fresnoy-en-Chaussée | 21 | G 6 | 635 |
| Fresnoy-en-Chaussée Churchyard Cemetery.. | 21 | G 6 | 1902 |
| Fresnoy-le-Grand Communal Cemetery Extension.. | 12 | J 6 | 636 |
| Fressenville Military Cemetery | 9 | E 5 | 2168 |
| Fretin Communal Cemetery .. | 11 | H 3 | 637 |
| Fricourt New Military Cemetery | 54 | E 18 | 638 |
| Fricourt Wood Cemetery | 54 | E 18 | 639 |
| Froidmont Communal Cemetery | 11 | J 3 | 1777 |
| Furnes Road British Cemetery, Coxyde | 3 | G 2 | 640 |
| Fusilier Farm Road Cemetery, Boesinghe .. | 41 | F 6 | 641 |
| Fusiliers' Cemetery, Bailleul-sire-Berthoult.. | 59 | F 14 | 643 |
| Garden at Wulverghem Cross Roads.. | 43 | F 8 | 645 |
| Garden of " Y " Farm, Bois Grenier.. | 43 | F 10 | 646 |
| Garter Point Cemetery, Zonnebeke .. | 41 | G 8 | 647 |
| Gauche Wood Cemetery, Villers Guislain | 57 | H 18 | 648 |
| Gaudiempre Military Cemetery | 11 | G 5 | 649 |
| Gavrelle Road Cemetery, Fampoux .. | 49 | F 14 | 650 |
| Gembloux Communal Cemetery | 13 | M 3 | 2024 |
| Genappe Communal Cemetery | 13 | L 3 | 2023 |
| Genin Well Copse Cemetery, Heudecourt | 57 | H 18 | 651 |
| German Cemetery, Heesteert | 4 | J 3 | 2025 |
| German Cemetery, Loos | 47 | E 12 | 653 |
| German Cemetery, St. Symphorien | 12 | K 4 | 2169 |
| German Cemetery, Sorel le Grand | 56 | G 18 | 654 |
| German Military Cemetery, Heule, Courtrai | 4 | J 2 | 2170 |
| German Military Cemetery, Ledeghem | 4 | H 2 | 657 |
| German Military Cemetery, Marcke.. | 4 | J 3 | 658 |
| German Military Cemetery, near Cross Roads, Terhand, Gheluwe | 4 | H 2 | 659 |
| German Military Cemetery, near Waterdamhoek, Moorslede.. | 4 | H 2 | 660 |
| German Military Cemetery, Wervicq | 4 | H 3 | 661 |
| Gezaincourt Communal Cemetery | 10 | F 5 | 662 |
| Gezaincourt Communal Cemetery Extension | 10 | F 5 | 663 |
| Ghent Communal Cemetery, German Plot .. | 4 | K 2 | 2171 |

| Name of Cemetery. | Page. | Map Square. | No. on Map. |
|---|---|---|---|
| Ghissignies British Cemetery | 58 | N 15 | 664 |
| Givenchy-en-Gohelle Military Graves | 47 | E 13 | — |
| Glimpse Cottage Cemetery, Boesinghe | 41 | F 6 | 666 |
| Glisy Communal Cemetery | 20 | G 6 | 1903 |
| Godewaersvelde British Cemetery | 40 | D 7 | 667 |
| Gomiecourt South British Cemetery | 51 | E 16 | 668 |
| Gommecourt Cemetery No. 2, Hébuterne | 50 | D 17 | 670 |
| Gommecourt Chateau Cemetery | 50 | D 16 | 673 |
| Gommecourt Wood Cemetery No. 1, Fonquevillers | 50 | D 16 | 674 |
| Gommecourt Wood Cemetery No. 2, Fonquevillers | 50 | D 16 | 675 |
| Gommecourt Wood Cemetery No. 3, Fonquevillers | 50 | D 16 | 676 |
| Gommecourt Wood Cemetery No. 4, Fonquevillers | 50 | D 16 | 677 |
| Gommecourt Wood Cemetery No. 5, Fonquevillers | 50 | D 16 | 678 |
| Gommecourt Wood Cemetery No. 6, Gommecourt | 50 | D 16 | 679 |
| Gommecourt Wood Cemetery No. 8, Fonquevillers | 50 | D 16 | 680 |
| Gommegnies Communal Cemetery | 12 | K 4 | 2026 |
| Gonnehem British Cemetery | 11 | G 3 | 681 |
| Gonnehem Churchyard | 11 | G 3 | 682 |
| Gordon Castle British Cemetery, Authuille | 50 | D 18 | 683 |
| Gordon Cemetery, Kemmel | 41 | F 7 | 684 |
| Gordon Cemetery, near Mametz | 54 | E 19 | 685 |
| Gordon Dump Cemetery, Ovillers-la-Boisselle | 54 | E 18 | 686 |
| Gordon Farm, Zillebeke | 41 | F 7 | 687 |
| Gorre British Cemetery, near Beuvry | 44 | D 11 | 690 |
| Gorre Indian Cemetery, near Beuvry | 44 | D 11 | 691 |
| Gosnay Communal Cemetery | 44 | D 11 | 1778 |
| Gosselies Communal Cemetery | 13 | L 4 | 2027 |
| Gourock Trench Military Cemetery, Tilloy-les-Mafflaines | 48 | E 14 | 692 |
| Gouy-en-Artois Communal Cemetery Extension | 11 | G 5 | 693 |
| Gouy-Servins Communal Cemetery and Extension | 46 | D 13 | 694 |
| Gouzeaucourt German Cemetery | 53 | H 17 | 1826 |
| Gouzeaucourt Wood British Cemetery, Metz-en-Couture | 52 | H 17 | 697 |
| Grandcourt Road Cemetery, Grandcourt | 50 | E 17 | 699 |
| Grande Flamengrie Farm, Bois Grenier | 43 | F 9 | 700 |
| Grande Gay Farm, Louvignies-les-Quesnoy | 59 | N 15 | 1827 |
| Grande Porte-Egal Farm, Houplines | 43 | F 9 | 701 |
| Grande Ravine British Cemetery, Havrincourt | 52 | H 17 | — |
| Grand Fleet Street Trench Cemetery, Zillebeke | 41 | F 7 | — |
| Grand Seraucourt Communal Cemetery Extension | 21 | J 6 | 702 |
| Green Dump British Cemetery, Beaumont-Hamel | 50 | D 17 | 703 |
| Green Dump Cemetery, Longueval | 55 | E 18 | 704 |
| Green Hunter Cemetery, Vlamertinghe | 41 | F 7 | 705 |
| Grenadier Guards' Cemetery, St. Leger | 51 | F 16 | 706 |
| Grenay Churchyard | 46 | E 12 | 707 |
| Grévillers British Cemetery | 51 | F 17 | 708 |
| Grévillers German Cemetery | 51 | E 17 | 709 |
| Gris-Pot British Cemetery, near Bois Grenier | 43 | F 9 | 710 |
| Grootebeek Cemetery, Reninghelst | 40 | E 7 | 711 |
| Grove Town British Cemetery, near Méaulte | 54 | D 19 | 712 |
| Guarbecque British Cemetery | 10 | G 3 | 713 |
| Guarbecque Churchyard | 10 | G 3 | 1904 |
| Guards' Burial Ground, Ginchy | 55 | F 18 | 714 |
| Guards' Cemetery, Combles | 55 | F 18 | 715 |
| Guards' Cemetery, Lesbœufs | 51 | F 18 | 1905 |
| Guards' Cemetery (Windy Corner) Cuinchy | 44 | E 11 | 716 |
| Guards' Grave, Villers-Cotterets Forest | 21 | H 8 | — |
| Guemappes British Cemetery | 49 | F 15 | 717 |
| Guildford Trench Cemetery, Tilloy-les-Mafflaines | 48 | E 14 | 718 |
| Guillemont British Cemetery | 55 | F 18 | — |
| Guillemont Road Military Cemetery | 55 | F 18 | 719 |
| Guizancourt Farm British Cemetery, Gouy | 11 | J 5 | 720 |
| Gun Farm Cemetery No. 2, Wytschaete | 41 | F 8 | 721 |
| Gunners' Farm Military Cemetery, Ploegsteert | 43 | F 8 | 723 |
| Gunners' Graveyard No. 1, Ypres | 41 | F 6 | 724 |

| Name of Cemetery. | Page. | Map Square. | No. on Map. |
|---|---|---|---|
| Gunners' Lodge, Zillebeke | 41 | F 7 | 726 |
| Guyencourt British Cemetery | 60 | — | 2173 |
| Gwalia British Cemetery, Poperinghe | 40 | E 6 | 727 |
| Habarcq Communal Cemetery Extension | 11 | G 4 | 728 |
| H.A.C. British Cemetery, Ecoust St. Mein | 51 | F 16 | 729 |
| Hagle Dump Cemetery, Elverdinghe | 40 | E 6 | 730 |
| Haillicourt Communal Cemetery | 11 | G 4 | 1906 |
| Hal Communal Cemetery | 5 | L 3 | 2029 |
| Halluin Communal Cemetery | 4 | H 3 | 731 |
| Hally Copse East Cemetery, St. Leger | 51 | F 16 | 732 |
| Hally Copse North Cemetery, St. Leger | 51 | F 16 | 733 |
| Hallines Churchyard | 3 | F 3 | 2030 |
| Ham British Cemetery, Muille, Villette | 21 | H 6 | 737 |
| Ham Communal Cemetery | 21 | H 6 | 1907 |
| Hamelet Australian Cemetery | 21 | G 6 | 735 |
| Hamelet Communal Cemetery Extension | 21 | G 6 | 736 |
| Hamelincourt Communal Cemetery Extension | 51 | E 16 | 739 |
| Hamel Military Cemetery | 50 | D 18 | 738 |
| Hancourt British Cemetery | 56 | H 20 | 740 |
| Hangard Communal Cemetery Extension | 21 | G 6 | 741 |
| Hangard Wood British Cemetery | 21 | G 6 | 742 |
| Hannescamp Churchyard | 50 | D 16 | 743 |
| Hannescamp New Military Cemetery | 50 | D 16 | 744 |
| Happy Valley British Cemetery, Monchy-le-Preux | 49 | F 14 | 745 |
| Hardecourt French Military Cemetery | 55 | F 19 | 747 |
| Hare Lane Cemetery, Fricourt | 54 | E 18 | 748 |
| Hargicourt British Cemetery | 57 | J 19 | 749 |
| Hargicourt Communal Cemetery Extension | 57 | J 19 | 750 |
| Hargicourt Sikh Cemetery | 57 | J 19 | 751 |
| Haringhe (Bandaghem) Military Cemetery, Rousbrugge-Haringhe | 3 | G 2 | 752 |
| Harlebeke Churchyard | 2 | J 2 | 2177 |
| Harley Street (No. 1), Cuinchy | 44 | E 11 | 754 |
| Harponville Communal Cemetery | 11 | G 5 | 755 |
| Harponville Communal Cemetery Extension | 11 | G 5 | 756 |
| Hasnon Communal Cemetery | 12 | J 4 | 759 |
| Haspres Communal Cemetery Extension | 12 | J 4 | 760 |
| Haspres Coppice Cemetery, Haspres | 12 | J 5 | 761 |
| Haubourdin Communal Cemetery (German) Extension | 43 | G 10 | 762 |
| Haubourdin German Cemetery | 43 | G 10 | — |
| Haucourt Communal Cemetery | 11 | J 5 | 763 |
| Haussy Communal Cemetery | 59 | L 15 | 764 |
| Haute-Avesnes British Cemetery | 48 | D 14 | 765 |
| Haute-Avesnes Communal Cemetery Extension | 48 | D 14 | 766 |
| Hautes Allaines German Cemetery, Bussu | 56 | G 19 | 1820 |
| Hautevesnes Communal Cemetery | 60 | — | 2031 |
| Hauteville Churchyard | 11 | G 5 | 1908 |
| Haverskerque British Cemetery | 11 | G 3 | 767 |
| Havrincourt Cottage Garden Cemetery | 52 | H 17 | 1830 |
| Havrincourt Wood Military Cemetery | 52 | H 17 | 1831 |
| Hawthorn Ridge No. 1, Beaumont-Hamel (V. Corps Cemetery No. 9) | 50 | D 17 | 769 |
| Hawthorn Ridge No. 2, Beaumont-Hamel (V. Corps Cemetery No. 12) | 50 | D 17 | 770 |
| Haynecourt British Cemetery | 11 | H 5 | 771 |
| Hazebrouck Communal Cemetery | 3 | G 3 | 772 |
| Heath Cemetery, Harbonnières | 21 | G 6 | 773 |
| Hebule Military Cemetery, Sailly-Saillisel | 55 | F 18 | 774 |
| Hébuterne Communal Cemetery | 50 | D 17 | 775 |
| Hébuterne Military Cemetery | 50 | D 17 | 776 |
| Hecq British Cemetery | 12 | J 5 | 777 |
| Hedauville Communal Cemetery Extension | 11 | G 5 | 778 |
| Hedge Row Trench Cemetery, Zillebeke | 41 | F 7 | 779 |
| Heilly Communal Cemetery | 11 | G 6 | 1909 |

| Name of Cemetery. | Page. | Map Square. | No. on Map. |
|---|---|---|---|
| Heilly Station Cemetery, Méricourt l'Abbé.. | 11 | G 6 | 781 |
| Helchin Communal Cemetery | 4 | J 3 | 2032 |
| Helena Trench Cemetery, Fampoux.. | 49 | F 14 | 782 |
| Hem Communal Cemetery | 55 | F 19 | — |
| Hem Farm Military Cemetery, Hem-Monacu | 55 | F 19 | 783 |
| Hengebaert Farm, Dickebusch | 41 | E 7 | 786 |
| Hénin British Cemetery | 49 | F 15 | 787 |
| Hénin Communal Cemetery Extension | 49 | F 15 | 788 |
| Hénin Crucifix British Cemetery | 49 | F 15 | 789 |
| Héninel Communal Cemetery Extension | 49 | F 15 | 793 |
| Hénin-Liétard Communal Cemetery | 11 | H 4 | 790 |
| Hénin North Cemetery | 49 | F 15 | 791 |
| Hénin-sur-Cojeul German Military Cemetery | 49 | F 15 | 792 |
| Henu Churchyard | 11 | G 5 | 796 |
| Herbecourt Communal Cemetery Extension | 55 | F 19 | 797 |
| Herchies Communal Cemetery | 12 | K 4 | 2033 |
| Hereford British Cemetery, Parcy Tigny | 60 | — | 798 |
| Herinnes Communal Cemetery | 4 | J 3 | 2034 |
| Hérissart Communal Cemetery | 10 | G 5 | 799 |
| Hermies Australian Cemetery | 52 | G 17 | 800 |
| Hermies British Cemetery | 52 | G 17 | 801 |
| Hermies Hill British Cemetery | 52 | G 17 | 802 |
| Hermonville Trench Military Cemetery, Berry-au-Bac | 60 | — | 2035 |
| Hersin Communal Cemetery Extension | 46 | D 12 | 803 |
| Hervin Farm British Cemetery,St. Laurent-Blangy.. | 49 | F 14 | 804 |
| Herzeele Churchyard | 3 | G 2 | 1910 |
| Hesbecourt Communal Cemetery Extension | 57 | H 19 | 805 |
| Hesdin Communal Cemetery, Marconne | 10 | F 4 | 2178 |
| Hestrud Churchyard | 12 | L 5 | 2036 |
| Heudecourt Communal Cemetery,German Extension | 56 | H 18 | 806 |
| Hexham Road Cemetery, Le Sars | 51 | E 17 | 807 |
| Hibers Trench British Cemetery, Wancourt | 49 | F 15 | 808 |
| High British Cemetery, Sailly-le-Sec | 54 | D 19 | 809 |
| Highland British Cemetery, Le Cateau | 59 | M 17 | 810 |
| Highland Cemetery, High Wood | 51 | E 18 | 811 |
| High Tree British Cemetery, Montbrehain | 12 | J 6 | 812 |
| Highway British Cemetery, Cappy | 55 | E 19 | 813 |
| Hill Side British Cemetery, Le Quesnel | 21 | G 6 | 814 |
| Hill Top Cemetery, Lesdain | 53 | J 17 | 815 |
| Hinges Military Cemetery | 44 | D 11 | 816 |
| Holnon British Cemetery | 21 | J 6 | 817 |
| Holnon Wood, Marteville | 21 | H 6 | 818 |
| Hon Hergies Communal Cemetery | 12 | K 4 | 2037 |
| Honnechy British Cemetery | 59 | L 17 | 819 |
| Honnechy Churchyard | 12 | J 5 | 1911 |
| Honnechy German Cemetery | 12 | J 5 | 1832 |
| Hooge Crater Cemetery, Zillebeke | 41 | F 7 | 820 |
| Hop Store, Vlamertinghe | 40 | E 6 | 821 |
| Hospice Cemetery, Locre | 40 | E 8 | 822 |
| Hospital Farm, Elverdinghe | 40 | E 6 | 823 |
| Hospital Military Cemetery, Dury | 20 | F 6 | 824 |
| Houchin British Cemetery | 46 | D 12 | 825 |
| Houchin Communal Cemetery | 46 | D 12 | 826 |
| Hordain Communal Cemetery, German Extension | 11 | J 5 | 1833 |
| Houdain Communal Cemetery | 12 | K 4 | 2038 |
| Houdain French Military Cemetery | 11 | G 4 | 827 |
| Houdain Lane British Cemetery,Tilloy-les-Mofflaines | 49 | F 14 | 828 |
| Houplines Communal Cemetery | 43 | F 9 | 829 |
| Houplines-Epinette Road Cemetery, Houplines | 43 | F 9 | 830 |
| Houplines New Military Cemetery | 43 | F 9 | 831 |
| Houplines Old Military Cemetery | 43 | F 9 | 832 |
| Hourges Military Cemetery | 21 | G 6 | — |
| Hourges Orchard Cemetery, Domart-sur-la-Luce | 21 | G 6 | 833 |
| Houtkerque Churchyard | 3 | G 2 | 1912 |
| Houlle Churchyard | 3 | F 3 | 2039 |

| Name of Cemetery. | Page. | Map Square. | No. on Map. |
|---|---|---|---|
| Houyet Churchyard | 13 | M 5 | 2040 |
| Huby St. Leu British Cemetery | 10 | F 4 | 2179 |
| Humbercamp Communal Cemetery | 11 | G 5 | 834 |
| Humbercamp Communal Cemetery Extension | 11 | G 5 | 835 |
| Hunters' Cemetery, Beaumont-Hamel | 50 | D 17 | 836 |
| Huts Military Cemetery, Dickebusch | 40 | E 7 | 837 |
| Huy Communal Cemetery | 14 | N 3 | 2041 |
| Hyde Park Corner (Royal Berks) Military Cemetery, Ploegsteert | 43 | F 8 | 838 |
| Imperial British Cemetery, Hendecourt-lez-Cagnicourt | 49 | G 15 | 839 |
| Inchy Communal Cemetery Extension | 59 | L 17 | 840 |
| Indian Village North Cemetery, Festubert | 44 | E 11 | 842 |
| Indian Village, Richebourg l'Avoue | 44 | E 11 | 841 |
| Inniskilling Cemetery, Dallon | 21 | J 6 | 843 |
| Irish Farm, St. Jean | 41 | F 6 | 844 |
| Irish House Cemetery, Kemmel | 41 | F 7 | 845 |
| Iwuy Communal Cemetery Extension | 11 | J 5 | 846 |
| Izel-les-Hameau Communal Cemetery | 11 | G 4 | 847 |
| Jeanbart British Cemetery, Sailly-au-Bois | 50 | D 17 | 1779 |
| Jeancourt Communal Cemetery Extension | 57 | H 19 | 849 |
| Jeancourt Indian Cemetery | 57 | H 19 | 850 |
| Jemelle Communal Cemetery | 14 | N 5 | 2042 |
| Jenlain Communal Cemetery | 58 | N 14 | 652 |
| John Copse British Cemetery No. 1, Hébuterne (V. Corps Cemetery No. 1) | 50 | D 17 | 851 |
| John Copse British Cemetery No. 2, Hébuterne (V. Corps Cemetery No. 2) | 50 | D 17 | 852 |
| Joinville le Pont Communal Cemetery | 29 | G 10 | 2180 |
| Jolimetz Communal Cemetery | 12 | J 5 | 1913 |
| Joncourt British Cemetery | 11 | J 6 | 853 |
| Joncourt Communal Cemetery | 11 | J 6 | 1834 |
| Joncourt Railway British Cemetery | 11 | J 6 | 854 |
| Kandahar Farm, Neuve Eglise | 43 | F 8 | 856 |
| Kangaroo British Cemetery, Sailly-le-Sec | 54 | C 19 | 855 |
| Kemmel Chateau Military Cemetery | 41 | E 7 | 857 |
| Kemmel Churchyard | 41 | E 8 | 858 |
| Ker Fautras Cemetery, Brest | — | — | — |
| Kezelberg Cemetery, Moorseele | 4 | H 3 | 859 |
| Kiboko Wood British Cemetery, Biaches | 55 | F 19 | 860 |
| King's Claire, Cuinchy | 44 | E 11 | 861 |
| King's Liverpool Graveyard, Cuinchy | 44 | E 11 | 863 |
| Kink Corner Cemetery, Zonnebeke | 41 | G 6 | 864 |
| Kite Crater, St. Laurent-Blangy | 48 | E 14 | 865 |
| Klein Vierstraat British Cemetery, Kemmel | 41 | E 7 | 866 |
| Knightsbridge Cemetery, Mesnil | 50 | D 17 | 867 |
| La Baraque British Cemetery, Bellenglise | 57 | J 19 | 869 |
| La Bassée Communal Cemetery, German Extension | 45 | E 11 | 1835 |
| L'Abbaye German Military Cemetery, Vermand (Aisne) | 57 | J 20 | 870 |
| La Belle Alliance Cemetery, Boesinghe | 41 | F 6 | 871 |
| Labourse Communal Cemetery | 46 | D 12 | 872 |
| La Boutillerie, Nantes | — | — | — |
| La Bouverie New Communal Cemetery | 12 | K 4 | 2043 |
| La Brique Military Cemetery No. 2 (West), St. Jean | 41 | F 6 | 874 |
| La Brique Military Cemetery, St. Jean | 41 | F 6 | 873 |
| La Broque (Verbrouk) German Cemetery | 14 | O 3 | 2044 |
| La Cauchie Communal Cemetery | 11 | G 5 | 1836 |
| La Chapelle Farm, Zillebeke | 41 | F 7 | 875 |
| La Chapellette British Cemetery, Péronne | 55 | F 20 | 876 |
| La Chapellette Indian Cemetery, Péronne | 55 | F 20 | 877 |
| La Clytte Military Cemetery, Reninghelst | 40 | E 7 | 878 |

( 127 )

| Name of Cemetery. | Page. | Map Square. | No. on Map. |
|---|---|---|---|
| La Cordonnerie Farm, near Fromelles | 43 | F 10 | 880 |
| La Cote Military Cemetery, Maricourt | 55 | E 19 | 879 |
| La Cour de Soupir Farm (52nd L.I. Cemetery), Soupir | 60 | — | 2181 |
| La Cour de Soupir Farm (Guards' Cemetery), Soupir | 60 | — | 2182 |
| La Cranière Military Cemetery, Le Forest | 55 | F 19 | 881 |
| Lagnicourt Australian Cemetery | 52 | G 16 | 882 |
| Lagnicourt Hedge Cemetery | 52 | G 16 | 883 |
| La Gorgue Communal Cemetery | 44 | D 10 | 884 |
| La Groise Communal Cemetery | 12 | K 5 | 1914 |
| La Haute Loge British Cemetery, Le Mesnil-en-Weppes | 43 | F 10 | 885 |
| Laherlière Communal Cemetery | 11 | G 5 | 1915 |
| Laherlière Military Cemetery | 11 | G 5 | 888 |
| La Hulpe Communal Cemetery | 5 | L 3 | 2045 |
| La Kreule British Cemetery, Hazebrouck | 3 | G 3 | 886 |
| La Laiterie Military Cemetery, Kemmel-Vierstraat Road | 41 | F 7 | 889 |
| La Longueville Communal Cemetery | 12 | K 4 | 2046 |
| La Louvière Communal Cemetery | 12 | L 4 | 2183 |
| Lamain Communal Cemetery | 11 | J 3 | 890 |
| Lambersart German Cemetery, Lambersart | 11 | H 3 | 892 |
| La Maisonette British Cemetery, Marfaux | 60 | — | — |
| La Motte Brebière Communal Cemetery | 20 | G 6 | 1916 |
| Lancashire Cemetery, Savy Wood | 21 | H 6 | 894 |
| Lancashire Cottage Military Cemetery, Ploegsteert | 43 | F 8 | 895 |
| Lancashire Support Farm, Warneton | 43 | F 8 | 897 |
| Lancer Lane British Cemetery, Fampoux | 49 | F 14 | 898 |
| Landrécies British Cemetery | 12 | K 5 | 899 |
| La Neuville aux Larris Military Cemetery | 60 | — | 1837 |
| La Neuville British Cemetery, Corbie | 11 | G 6 | 900 |
| La Neuville Communal Cemetery | 11 | G 6 | 901 |
| Langton Barracks Cemetery, Bouchavesnes | 55 | F 19 | 902 |
| Lankhof Chateau, Zillebeke | 41 | F 7 | 903 |
| La Plus Douve Farm, near Wulverghem | 43 | F 8 | 905 |
| La Première Borne, Ypres | 41 | F 7 | 906 |
| Lapugnoy Military Cemetery | 11 | G 4 | 907 |
| Larch Wood (Railway Cutting), Zillebeke | 41 | F 7 | 908 |
| Larriere British Cemetery, Bellicourt | 57 | J 19 | 909 |
| La Sentinelle Communal Cemetery | 58 | L 13 | 1917 |
| La Targette British Cemetery, Forenville | 11 | J 5 | 910 |
| Lauwe German Military Cemetery | 4 | G 3 | 1838 |
| La Vallée Mulâtre Communal Cemetery Extension, La Vallée | 12 | J 5 | 911 |
| Laventie Communal Cemetery | 42 | E 10 | 912 |
| Laventie Military Cemetery | 42 | E 10 | 913 |
| Laviéville Communal Cemetery | 11 | G 5 | 914 |
| L'Ebbe Farm, Poperinghe | 40 | D 6 | 915 |
| Le Bizet Convent, Ploegsteert | 43 | F 9 | 916 |
| Le Bucquière Communal Cemetery Extension | 52 | G 17 | 918 |
| Le Canet Cemetery, Marseilles | — | — | — |
| Le Cateau Communal Cemetery | 59 | M 17 | 919 |
| Le Cateau German Military Cemetery | 59 | M 17 | 920 |
| Le Catelet Communal Cemetery | 57 | J 18 | 1918 |
| Lecelles Communal Cemetery | 12 | J 4 | 1780 |
| Lécluse Crucifix Cemetery | 11 | H 4 | 921 |
| Lederzeele Churchyard | 3 | F 3 | 1919 |
| Le Fermont Military Cemetery, Rivière | 48 | D 15 | 924 |
| Le Forest Communal Cemetery | 11 | H 4 | 925 |
| Le Grand Beaumart British Cemetery, Steenwerck | 42 | E 9 | 926 |
| Le Grand Fayt Communal Cemetery | 12 | K 5 | 2047 |
| Le Grand Hasard Military Cemetery, Morbecque | 3 | G 3 | 927 |
| Leicester Camp Cemetery, Reninghelst | 40 | E 7 | 930 |
| Leipzig Farm Cemetery, Brielen | 41 | F 6 | 932 |
| Le Lièvre Cemetery, Boesinghe | 41 | F 6 | 931 |

| Name of Cemetery. | Page. | Map Square. | No. on Map. |
|---|---|---|---|
| Le Mans Grand Cemetery (Sarthe) | — | — | — |
| Lens Canadian Cemetery No. 1 | 47 | E 12 | 934 |
| Lens Canadian Cemetery No. 2 | 47 | E 12 | 935 |
| Lens Canadian Cemetery No. 3 | 47 | F 12 | 936 |
| Lens Communal Cemetery, Avion | 47 | F 12 | 937 |
| Le Petit Bavay British Cemetery, Pont-sur-Sambre | 12 | K 5 | 2185 |
| Le Peuplier Military Cemetery, Caestre | 3 | G 3 | 939 |
| Le Plantin Cemetery (Welsh Chapel), Festubert | 44 | E 11 | 940 |
| Le Plantin South Cemetery, Givenchy-lez-La Bassée | 44 | E 11 | 941 |
| Le Portel Communal Cemetery | 2 | E 3 | 2048 |
| Le Quennet Cemetery, Crèvecœur-sur-l'Escaut | 53 | J 17 | 942 |
| Le Quesnel Communal Cemetery Extension | 21 | G 6 | 943 |
| Le Quesnoy British Cemetery | 58 | N 15 | 944 |
| Le Quesnoy Communal Cemetery | 58 | N 15 | 945 |
| Le Rutoire British Cemetery, near Vermelles | 46 | E 12 | 948 |
| Le Rutoire German Cemetery, Vermelles | 47 | E 12 | 1839 |
| Le Sart Churchyard | 12 | K 5 | 2049 |
| Les Baraques Military Cemetery, Sangatte | 2 | E 2 | 2186 |
| Lesdain German Cemetery | 53 | K 17 | 949 |
| Les Haies Military Cemetery, Chaumuzy | 60 | — | 950 |
| Les Harisoirs British Cemetery, Mont Bernenchon | 44 | C 10 | 951 |
| Les Quatre Bras, Bachant, Communal Cemetery, Aymeries | 12 | K 5 | 2187 |
| Les Tuileries British Cemetery, Englefontaine | 59 | N 16 | 1840 |
| Le Touquet Railway Crossing, Ploegsteert | 43 | F 8 | 953 |
| Le Touret Military Cemetery, Richebourg l'Avoue | 44 | E 11 | 954 |
| Le Touquet-Paris Plage Communal Cemetery | 9 | E 4 | 2188 |
| Le Tréport Military Cemetery | 9 | D 5 | 2189 |
| Le Trou, near Fleurbaix | 45 | E 10 | 955 |
| Leuze Cemetery | 12 | J 3 | 2190 |
| Leval Communal Cemetery | 12 | K 5 | 2050 |
| Levallois Perret Communal Cemetery, Paris | 28 | F 9 | 2191 |
| Level Crossing British Cemetery, Fampoux | 49 | F 14 | 957 |
| Levergies Communal Cemetery | 11 | J 6 | 1841 |
| Le Verguier Communal Cemetery | 57 | J 19 | 958 |
| Le Vertannoy British Cemetery, Hinges | 44 | D 11 | 959 |
| Levi Cottage Cemetery, Zonnebeke | 41 | G 6 | 960 |
| L'Homme Mort Cemetery, Mory | 51 | F 16 | 928 |
| L'Homme Mort Cemetery, No. 2, Ecoust St. Mein | 51 | F 16 | 929 |
| Liéramont Communal Cemetery, German Extension | 56 | H 18 | 961 |
| Lieu St. Amand British Cemetery | 11 | J 4 | 962 |
| Lievin Station Cemetery | 47 | E 12 | 963 |
| Lignereuil Military Cemetery | 10 | G 4 | 964 |
| Ligny-en-Cambrèsis Communal Cemetery | 12 | J 5 | 1920 |
| Ligny-sur-Canche British Cemetery | 10 | F 4 | 2192 |
| Ligny St. Flochel British Cemetery | 10 | G 4 | 965 |
| Lijssenthoek Military Cemetery, Poperinghe | 40 | D 7 | 967 |
| Lijssenthoek Shrine, Poperinghe | 40 | D 7 | 968 |
| Lille Communal Cemetery | 11 | H 3 | 969 |
| Lillers Communal Cemetery and Extension | 10 | G 3 | 922 |
| Lille Southern Cemetery | 11 | H 3 | 970 |
| Lincolns' British Cemetery, St. Martin-sur-Cojeul | 49 | F 15 | 971 |
| Lindenhoek Chalet Military Cemetery | 41 | E 8 | 972 |
| Linen Factory, Bac St. Maur | 42 | E 9 | 973 |
| Linselles German Military Cemetery | 4 | H 3 | 974 |
| Little "Z" British Cemetery, Gommecourt | 50 | D 16 | 975 |
| Lives Churchyard | 13 | M 4 | 2051 |
| Lock 8 Cemetery, Voormezeele | 41 | F 7 | 976 |
| Locon Old Military Cemetery | 44 | D 10 | 979 |
| Locquignol Communal Cemetery Extension | 12 | K 5 | 2193 |
| Locre Churchyard | 40 | E 8 | 981 |
| Lomme Communal Cemetery | 43 | G 9 | 982 |
| London Cemetery, High Wood, Longueval | 51 | E 18 | 983 |
| London Cemetery, Neuville Vitasse | 48 | E 15 | 985 |

| Name of Cemetery. | Page. | Map Square. | No. on Map. |
|---|---|---|---|
| London Rifle Brigade Military Cemetery, Ploegsteert-Le Bizet Road | 43 | F 8 | 986 |
| London (6th) Cemetery, Loos | 47 | E 12 | 984 |
| Lone Cemetery, Roclincourt | 48 | E 14 | 991 |
| Lone Farm Cemetery, Givenchy | 44 | E 11 | — |
| Lone Farm Cemetery, Harbonnières | 54 | D 20 | 987 |
| Lonely British Cemetery No. 2, Colincamps | 50 | D 17 | 988 |
| Lonely British Cemetery, Sailly-au-Bois | 50 | D 17 | 989 |
| Lonely House British Cemetery, Gavrelle | 49 | F 14 | 990 |
| Lone Ridge British Cemetery, Longueval | 55 | E 18 | 992 |
| Lone Tree Cemetery, Spanbroekmolen, Wytschaete | 41 | F 8 | 993 |
| Longavesnes British Cemetery | 56 | H 19 | 994 |
| Longpré-les-Corps Saints British Cemetery No. 1 | 10 | F 5 | 2194 |
| Longpré-les-Corps-Saints British Cemetery No. 2 | 10 | F 5 | 2195 |
| Longtree Dump Military Cemetery, Sailly-Saillisel | 55 | F 18 | 995 |
| Longueau British Cemetery | 20 | G 6 | 996 |
| Longueau Communal Cemetery | 20 | G 6 | 1922 |
| Longueness Souvenir Cemetery | 3 | F 3 | 2196 |
| Longueval Road Cemetery | 55 | E 18 | 997 |
| Lonsdale Cemetery No. 1, Authuille Wood, Aveluy | 50 | D 18 | 998 |
| Lonsdale Cemetery No.2, Authuille Wood, Authuille | 50 | D 18 | 999 |
| Loos (Ennequin) Communal Cemetery | 11 | H 3 | 1000 |
| Lorette Ridge, Aix Noulette | 46 | E 13 | 1001 |
| Louez Military Cemetery, Duisans | 48 | E 14 | 1002 |
| Louvencourt Military Cemetery | 11 | G 5 | 1003 |
| Louverval Chateau Cemetery, Doignies | 52 | G 16 | 1004 |
| Louverval Military Cemetery, Doignies | 52 | G 16 | 1005 |
| Louvignies British Cemetery, Louvignies-lez-Quesnoy | 58 | N 15 | 1006 |
| Louvignies Churchyard | 59 | N 15 | 1923 |
| Lowrie British Cemetery, Havrincourt | 52 | H 17 | 1007 |
| Lucheux Military Cemetery | 10 | G 5 | 1008 |
| Luke Copse British Cemetery (V. Corps Cemetery No. 19) | 50 | D 17 | 1009 |
| Lumbres Communal Cemetery | 3 | F 3 | 2052 |
| Lumm Farm Cemetery, Wytschaete | 41 | F 8 | 1010 |
| Lynde Churchyard | 3 | G 3 | 1924 |
| McCormick's Post Cemetery, Flers | 51 | E 18 | 1011 |
| "Madame" Military Cemetery, Clery-sur-Somme | 55 | F 19 | 1012 |
| Madeleine Cemetery, Amiens | 10 | F 6 | 1014 |
| Magny-la-Fosse British Cemetery | 57 | K 19 | 1015 |
| Magny-la-Fosse Communal Cemetery | 57 | K 19 | 1016 |
| Maillen Communal Cemetery | 13 | M 4 | 2053 |
| Mailly-Maillet Communal Cemetery Extension | 50 | D 17 | 1017 |
| Mailly-Maillet Military Cemetery | 50 | D 17 | 1018 |
| Mailly Wood Cemetery | 50 | D 17 | 1019 |
| Maing Communal Cemetery Extension | 58 | L 14 | 1020 |
| Maisnil St. Pol Churchyard | 10 | G 4 | 1925 |
| Maison du Rasta, Langemarck | 41 | F 6 | 1099 |
| Malakoff Farm, Brielen | 41 | E 6 | 1022 |
| Malincourt German Cemetery | 11 | J 5 | 1023 |
| Malo-les-Bains Communal Cemetery | 3 | G 2 | 1024 |
| Malonne Communal Cemetery | 13 | M 4 | 2054 |
| Manancourt Churchyard | 56 | G 18 | 1025 |
| Manchester Cemetery, Riencourt-les-Bapaume | 51 | F 17 | 1026 |
| Manitoba British Cemetery (C.A.4), Beaufort | 21 | G 6 | 1027 |
| Manor Road Cemetery, Zillebeke | 41 | F 7 | 1028 |
| Mansard Farm Cemetery, Dadizeele | 43 | H 2 | 1029 |
| Maple Copse Military Cemetery, Zillebeke | 41 | F 7 | 1031 |
| Maple Leaf Cemetery, Romarin, Neuve Eglise | 43 | F 8 | 1030 |
| Malplaquet Communal Cemetery | 12 | K 4 | 2055 |
| Marbaix Communal Cemetery | 12 | K 5 | 2056 |
| Marchélepot New British Cemetery | 21 | H 6 | 1032 |
| Marchiennes New Communal Cemetery | 11 | J 4 | 1783 |
| Marche Communal Cemetery | 14 | N 4 | 2057 |

| Name of Cemetery. | Page. | Map Square. | No. on Map |
|---|---|---|---|
| Marcinelle Communal Cemetery | 13 | L 4 | 2058 |
| Marcoing Line British Cemetery, Sailly | 11 | H 5 | 1034 |
| Marcq Churchyard | 11 | J 4 | 1926. |
| Mardick Churchyard | 3 | F 2 | 1033 |
| Marengo Farm, Boesinghe | 41 | F 6 | 1035 |
| Maresches Communal Cemetery | 58 | M 14 | 1036 |
| Maretz British Cemetery | 12 | J 5 | 1037 |
| Maretz Communal Cemetery, German Extension | 12 | J 5 | 1038 |
| Marfaux British Cemetery | 60 | — | 1274 |
| Marfaux Churchyard Extension | 60 | — | 1039 |
| Maricourt Military Cemetery | 55 | E 19 | 1040 |
| Marles-les-Mines | 11 | G 4 | 1927 |
| Marloie Churchyard | 14 | N 5 | 2059 |
| Maroc British Cemetery, Grenay | 46 | E 12 | 1041 |
| Maroeuil British Cemetery | 48 | D 14 | 1042 |
| Maroilles Communal Cemetery | 12 | K 5 | 2060 |
| Marquaix German Cemetery | 56 | H 19 | 1043 |
| Marquion German Cemetery | 11 | H 5 | 1044 |
| Marteville Communal Cemetery | 21 | H 6 | 1045 |
| Martinpuich British Cemetery | 51 | E 18 | 1046 |
| Martinpuich Road Cemetery, Bazentin | 51 | E 18 | 1047 |
| Martinsart British Cemetery, near Mesnil | 54 | D 18 | 1048 |
| Masnières British Cemetery | 53 | J 17 | 1842 |
| Masnières-Crèvecœur Road Cemetery, Crèvecœur-sur-l'Escaut | 53 | J 17 | 1050 |
| Masnières German Cemetery | 53 | J 17 | 1051 |
| Matigny Communal Cemetery | 21 | H 6 | 1928 |
| Matringhem Churchyard | 10 | F 4 | 2061 |
| Maubeuge Communal Cemetery | 12 | K 4 | 2197 |
| Mazarques Cemetery, Marseilles | — | — | — |
| Mazingarbe Communal Cemetery | 46 | D 12 | 1053 |
| Mazingarbe Communal Cemetery Extension | 46 | D 12 | 1054 |
| Mazinghien Communal Cemetery | 12 | J 5 | 1055 |
| Meath British Cemetery, Villers Guislain | 57 | J 18 | 1056 |
| Méaulte Military Cemetery | 54 | D 19 | 1057 |
| Méaulte Triangle British Cemetery | 54 | D 19 | 1058 |
| Meaux Military Cemetery | 29 | H 9 | 2062 |
| Meerut Indian Cemetery, St. Martin-les-Boulogne | 2 | E 3 | 2063 |
| Meerut Military Cemetery, St. Martin-les-Boulogne | 2 | E 3 | 2198 |
| Melbourne British Cemetery, Montbrehain | 12 | J 6 | 1059 |
| Memorial British Cemetery, Vauvillers | 21 | G 6 | 1060 |
| Mendinghem British Cemetery, Proven | 40 | D 6 | 1061 |
| Mendon British Cemetery, Flaucourt | 55 | F 20 | 1062 |
| Menin Communal Cemetery | 4 | H 3 | 1065 |
| Menin Road South Military Cemetery, Ypres | 41 | F 7 | 1064 |
| Méricourt l'Abbé Communal Cemetery Extension | 11 | G 6 | 1066 |
| Merignolles British Cemetery, Proyart | 54 | E 20 | 1067 |
| Merville Communal Cemetery | 44 | D 9 | 1068 |
| Merville Communal Cemetery Extension | 44 | D 9 | 1069 |
| Mesnil Communal Cemetery | 50 | D 18 | 1070 |
| Mesnil Ridge Military Cemetery | 50 | D 17 | 1072 |
| Meteren Commnual Cemetery | 42 | D 8 | 1073 |
| Meteren Military Cemetery | 42 | D 8 | 1074 |
| Metz-en-Couture British Cemetery No. 2 | 52 | H 17 | 1075 |
| Metz-en-Couture German Extension | 52 | H 17 | 1076 |
| Meurchin Communal Cemetery | 47 | F 12 | 1077 |
| Mezières Communal Cemetery Extension | 21 | G 6 | 1078 |
| Middle Farm Cemetery, Wytschaete | 41 | F 8 | 1079 |
| Millain Churchyard | 3 | F 2 | 2064 |
| Mille Kapelleken Cemetery, Dickebusch | 40 | E 7 | 1081 |
| Millencourt Communal Cemetery | 54 | C 18 | 1086 |
| Millencourt Communal Cemetery Extension | 54 | C 18 | 1087 |
| Mill Road Cemetery No. 2, Thiepval | 50 | D 18 | 1083 |
| Mill Switch British Cemetery, Neuville St. Remy | 11 | H 5 | 1085 |
| Mindel Trench British Cemetery St. Laurent-Blangy | 48 | E 14 | 1088 |

| Name of Cemetery. | Page. | Map Square. | No. on Map. |
|---|---|---|---|
| Minty Farm Cemetery, St. Jean | 41 | F 6 | 1089 |
| Mirfield Cemetery, Boesinghe | 41 | F 6 | 1090 |
| Moggs Hall Cemetery, Neuve Chapelle | 45 | E 10 | 1091 |
| Moislains British Cemetery | 56 | G 19 | 1092 |
| Molenhoek Military Cemetery, Becelaere | 4 | H 2 | 1093 |
| Molinghem Communal Cemetery | 10 | G 3 | 1094 |
| Molliens-au-Bois Communal Cemetery | 10 | G 6 | 1095 |
| Moha Communal Cemetery | 14 | N 3 | 2065 |
| Monceau St. Waast Communal Cemetery | 12 | K 5 | 2066 |
| Monchaux-sur-Escaillon Communal Cemetery | 12 | J 4 | 1930 |
| Monchy-au-Bois British Cemetery | 50 | D 16 | 1096 |
| Monchy Breton Churchyard | 10 | G 4 | 1929 |
| Monchy British Cemetery, Monchy-le-Preux | 49 | F 15 | 1097 |
| Mondicourt Communal Cemetery | 10 | G 5 | 1098 |
| Mons British Cemetery | 12 | K 4 | 2199 |
| Mons Communal Cemetery Extension (New British Plot) | 12 | K 4 | 2200 |
| Montauban Road Cemetery, Carnoy | 55 | E 18 | 1101 |
| Montay-Amerval Road British Cemetery, Montay | 59 | M 16 | 1102 |
| Montay British Cemetery | 59 | M 17 | 1103 |
| Montay Communal Cemetery | 59 | M 17 | 1104 |
| Montay-Neuville Road British Cemetery | 59 | M 16 | 1105 |
| Mont Bernenchon British Cemetery, Gonnehem | 11 | G 3 | 1106 |
| Mont Bernenchon Churchyard | 11 | G 3 | 1107 |
| Montbliart Communal Cemetery | 12 | L 5 | 2067 |
| Montbrehain British Cemetery | 12 | J 6 | 1108 |
| Mont des Bruyères British Cemetery, St. Amand | 12 | J 4 | 1109 |
| Mont de Soissons Farm, near Serches | 60 | — | 1790 |
| Mont Gargon Communal Cemetery, Rouen | 19 | D 7 | 2201 |
| Mont Huon Cemetery, Le Tréport | 9 | D 6 | 2202 |
| Montigny British Cemetery | 11 | H 4 | 1112 |
| Montigny Communal Cemetery | 10 | G 6 | 1113 |
| Montigny Communal Cemetery Extension | 10 | G 6 | 1114 |
| Montignies-sur-Roc Churchyard | 12 | K 4 | 2068 |
| Mont Noir Military Cemetery, St. Jans Cappell | 40 | E 8 | 1115 |
| Montreal Cemetery, Givenchy-en-Gohelle | 46 | E 13 | 1116 |
| Montrembœuf Farm Cemetery, Vierzy | 60 | — | 1117 |
| Mont St. André Churchyard | 13 | M 3 | 2069 |
| Mont St. Eloy Military Cemetery | 46 | D 13 | 1118 |
| Mont St. Martin British Cemetery, Gouy | 57 | K 19 | 1119 |
| Mont Vidaigne, Westoutre | 40 | E 7 | 1120 |
| Moor British Cemetery, Edgehill, Dernancourt | 54 | D 19 | 1121 |
| Moorseele Convent Military Cemetery | 4 | G 2 | — |
| Morbecque British Cemetery, Morbecque | 11 | G 3 | 1122 |
| Morchies Australian Cemetery | 52 | G 17 | 1123 |
| Morchies British Cemetery | 52 | G 16 | 1124 |
| Morcourt Communal Cemetery Extension | 54 | D 20 | 1125 |
| Moreuil Communal Cemetery, Allied Extension | 21 | G 6 | 2070 |
| Morlancourt Military Cemetery | 54 | D 19 | 1127 |
| Morlancourt New British Cemetery | 54 | D 19 | 1126 |
| Morlanwelz Communal Cemetery | 12 | L 4 | 2203 |
| Morval British Cemetery | 55 | F 18 | 1128 |
| Morville Communal Cemetery | 13 | M 4 | 2082 |
| Mory Abbey British Cemetery | 51 | F 16 | 1129 |
| Mory Street British Cemetery, St. Leger | 51 | F 16 | 1130 |
| Motor Car Corner Military Cemetery, Ploegsteert | 43 | F 9 | 1131 |
| Moulin d' Ardre British Cemetery, Marfaux | 60 | — | 1013 |
| Moulle British Cemetery | 3 | F 3 | 2204 |
| Moussy Churchyard | 60 | — | 2205 |
| Mouvaux Communal Cemetery | 11 | H 3 | 1844 |
| Mouvaux Military Cemetery | 4 | H 3 | 1132 |
| Mud Corner Cemetery, Warneton | 43 | F 8 | 1133 |
| Mud Lane No. 2 Cemetery, Ploegsteert | 43 | F 8 | 1135 |
| Mud Lane, Ploegsteert | 43 | F 8 | 1134 |
| Munich Trench Cemetery (V Corps Cemetery No. 8), Beaumont-Hamel | 50 | D 17 | 1136 |

| Name of Cemetery. | Page. | Map Square. | No. on Map. |
|---|---|---|---|
| Namps-au-Val British Cemetery | 20 | F 6 | 2206 |
| Nanteuil Military Cemetery, Nanteuil-la-Fosse | 60 | — | 1138 |
| Nauroy Road British Cemetery, Bellicourt | 57 | J 19 | 1139 |
| Naval Trench British Cemetery, Gavrelle | 43 | F 14 | 1140 |
| Naves Communal Cemetery Extension | 11 | J 5 | 1141 |
| Needle Dump Cemetery, Lesbœufs | 51 | F 18 | 1142 |
| Needle Dump South Cemetery, Lesboeufs | 51 | F 18 | 1143 |
| Needle Wood Military Cemetery, Clery-sur-Somme | 55 | F 19 | 1144 |
| Néry Communal Cemetery | 21 | H 8 | 2207 |
| Nesle Communal Cemetery | 21 | H 6 | 1145 |
| Neuf Brisach Communal Cemetery Extension, Alsace | 37 | T 12 | 2071 |
| Neuilly-sur-Seine New Communal Cemetery, Paris | 28 | F 9 | 2209 |
| Neuve Chapelle Churchyard | 45 | E 10 | 1146 |
| Neuve Eglise Churchyard | 43 | E 8 | 1147 |
| Neuve Eglise North Cemetery | 43 | E 8 | 1148 |
| Neuville Bourjonval British Cemetery | 52 | G 17 | 1149 |
| Neufchâtel Churchyard | 9 | E 3 | 2208 |
| Neuville-sous-Montreuil Military Cemetery | 9 | E 4 | 2210 |
| Neuville-Vitasse Road Cemetery, St. Martin-sur-Cojeul | 49 | F 15 | 1151 |
| Neuvilly British Cemetery | 59 | M 17 | 1153 |
| Neuvilly British Cemetery No. 2 | 59 | M 16 | 1846 |
| Neuvilly Communal Cemetery Extension | 59 | M 16 | 1845 |
| Neuvilly Ravine British Cemetery No. 2 | 59 | M 16 | 1154 |
| New Cemetery, Ploegsteert Wood | 43 | F 8 | 1155 |
| New German Cemetery, Hautrage | 12 | K 4 | 2211 |
| New Irish Farm, St. Jean | 41 | F 6 | 1157 |
| New Munich Cemetery (V Corps Cemetery No. 25), Beaumont-Hamel | 50 | D 17 | 1158 |
| New Zealand Cemetery, Grevillers | 51 | E 17 | 1159 |
| New Zealand Cemetery No. 17, Favreuil | 51 | F 17 | 1160 |
| New Zealand Rifle Brigade Military Cemetery, Messines Hill | 43 | F 8 | 1161 |
| Niagara British Cemetery, Iwuy | 11 | J 5 | 1162 |
| Nielles Churchyard | 10 | F 3 | 2072 |
| Nieppe Bois (Rue du Bois) British Cemetery, Vieux Berquin | 11 | G 3 | 1163 |
| Nieppe Communal Cemetery | 43 | F 9 | 1164 |
| Nieuport Bains Military Cemetery | 3 | G 1 | 1847 |
| Nieuport Communal Cemetery | 3 | H 1 | 1165 |
| Nieuport Military Cemetery | 3 | G 1 | 1166 |
| Nil St. Vincent Communal Cemetery | 13 | M 3 | 2073 |
| Nine Elms British Cemetery, Poperinghe | 40 | D 7 | 1167 |
| Nine Elms British Cemetery, Thélus | 48 | E 14 | 1168 |
| Nivelles Communal Cemetery | 13 | L 3 | 2074 |
| Nœux-les-Mines Communal Cemetery | 46 | D 12 | 1170 |
| Nœux-les-Mines Communal Cemetery Extension | 46 | D 12 | 1171 |
| Noreuil Australian Cemetery | 52 | G 16 | 1172 |
| Noreuil British Cemetery No. 1 | 52 | G 16 | 1173 |
| Noreuil British Cemetery No. 2 | 52 | G 16 | 1174 |
| Norfolk Cemetery, Becordel-Becourt, near Fricourt | 54 | D 18 | 1175 |
| Nortbecourt Churchyard | 2 | F 3 | 2075 |
| North Bank Cemetery, Voormezeele | 41 | F 7 | 1176 |
| North British Cemetery, Raillencourt | 53 | J 16 | 1177 |
| North Cemetery, Festubert | 44 | E 11 | 1178 |
| North Cemetery, Givenchy-en-Gohelle | 47 | E 13 | 1179 |
| Northern Sap Cemetery, near Posen Street, Loos | 47 | E 12 | 1182 |
| North Maroc Churchyard | 46 | E 12 | 1180 |
| North Maroc Intercommunal Cemetery | 46 | E 12 | 1181 |
| Northumberland British Cemetery, Fampoux | 49 | F 14 | 1183 |
| Nortleulinghem Churchyard | 3 | F 3 | 2076 |
| Notre Dame Cemetery, Cambrai | 53 | J 16 | — |
| Nouvelles Communal Cemetery | 12 | K 4 | 2077 |
| Noyelles Communal Cemetery Extension, Noyelles-sur-l'Escaut | 53 | J 16 | 1184 |

( 133 )

| Name of Cemetery. | Page. | Map Square. | No. on Map. |
|---|---|---|---|
| Noyon British Cemetery | 21 | H 7 | 1185 |
| Nurlu Communal Cemetery, German Extension | 56 | G 18 | 1186 |
| Oak Dump Cemetery, Voormezeele | 41 | F 7 | 1187 |
| Obies Churchyard | 12 | K 4 | 2078 |
| Obies Communal Cemetery | 12 | K 4 | 2079 |
| Offoy Communal Cemetery | 21 | H 6 | 1931 |
| Oignies Communal Cemetery, German Extension | 11 | H 4 | 1189 |
| Oisy le Verger German Military Cemetery | 11 | H 5 | 1191 |
| Old British Front Line Cemetery, Faubourg St. Sauveur, Arras | 48 | E 14 | 1188 |
| Onnaing Communal Cemetery | 58 | M 13 | 1194 |
| Onraet Farm Cemetery, Wytschaete | 41 | F 7 | 1195 |
| Ontario British Cemetery, Sains-lez-Marquion | 52 | H 16 | 1196 |
| Oost Dunkerque Bains British Cemetery | 3 | G 1 | 1197 |
| Oost Hoek Military Cemetery, Adinkerke | 3 | G 2 | 1198 |
| Oostaverne German Cemetery | 41 | F 7 | 1850 |
| Oosttaverne Wood Cemetery No. 1, Wytschaete | 41 | F 7 | 1199 |
| Oosttaverne Wood Cemetery No. 2, Wytschaete | 41 | F 7 | 1200 |
| Orange Hill British Cemetery, Feuchy | 49 | F 14 | 1201 |
| Orange Trench British Cemetery, Feuchy | 49 | F 15 | 1202 |
| Orchard Dump Cemetery | 47 | F 13 | 1851 |
| Orchard of Smith's Villa, Fleurbaix | 43 | F 9 | 1203 |
| Orcq Communal Cemetery | 11 | J 3 | 1204 |
| Origny Military Cemetery | 22 | J 6 | 2080 |
| Orival Wood British Cemetery, Flesquières | 53 | H 17 | 1852 |
| Orleans Grand Cemetery | — | — | — |
| Orsinval Communal Cemetery | 58 | N 14 | 1932 |
| Ostend Military Cemetery | 3 | H 1 | 1192 |
| Ostreville Churchyard | 10 | G 4 | 1933 |
| Ouderdom Cemetery No. 2, Reninghelst | 40 | E 7 | 1205 |
| Oulchy-le-Chateau-Beugneux Road British Cemetery, Grand Rozoy | 60 | — | 1206 |
| Outlook, Philosophe, near Mazingarbe | 46 | E 12 | 1207 |
| Outtersteene Communal Cemetery, Bailleul | 42 | D 8 | 1208 |
| Outtersteene Communal Cemetery Extension, Bailleul | 42 | D 8 | 1209 |
| Ovillers British Cemetery | 54 | D 18 | 1210 |
| Ovillers Civil Cemetery Extension, Solesmes | 59 | M 16 | 1211 |
| Ovillers New Communal Cemetery, Solesmes | 59 | M 16 | 1853 |
| Oxford Road Cemetery No. 2, Ypres | 41 | F 6 | 1213 |
| Oxford Road Cemetery, Ypres | 41 | F 6 | 1212 |
| Packhorse Farm Cemetery, Wulverghem | 41 | E 8 | 1214 |
| Packhorse Farm Shrine, Wuverghem | 41 | E 8 | 1215 |
| Paillencourt British Cemetery | 11 | J 5 | 1216 |
| Paratonneres Farm Military Cemetery, Boesinghe | 41 | E 6 | 1784 |
| Pargny British Cemetery | 21 | H 6 | 1854 |
| Parvillers British Cemetery No. 1 | 21 | G 6 | 1220 |
| Parvillers British Cemetery No. 2 | 21 | G 6 | 1221 |
| Parvillers British Cemetery No. 3 | 21 | G 6 | 1222 |
| Pas Communal Cemetery | 10 | G 5 | 1223 |
| Peake Wood British Cemetery, Fricourt | 54 | E 18 | 1224 |
| Pelves Canadian Cemetery | 49 | F 14 | 1225 |
| Pepinster Communal Cemetery | 14 | O 3 | 2081 |
| Pernes British Cemetery, Pernes-en-Artois | 10 | F 4 | 1226 |
| Pernes Churchyard | 10 | G 4 | 1934 |
| Pernois British Cemetery, Halloy-les-Pernois | 10 | F 5 | 2213 |
| Péronne Communal Cemetery Extension | 56 | G 19 | 1228 |
| Péronne Road Cemetery, Bouchavesnes | 55 | F 19 | 1229 |
| Péronne Road Cemetery, Maricourt | 55 | E 19 | 1230 |
| Perth Cemetery, China Wall Extension | 41 | F 7 | 1855 |
| Perth Cemetery, China Wall, Zillebeke | 41 | F 7 | 1231 |
| Petit Cuincy | 11 | H 4 | 1935 |
| Phalempin Communal Cemetery | 11 | H 4 | 1233 |

| Name of Cemetery. | Page. | Map Square. | No. on Map. |
|---|---|---|---|
| Pheasant Trench, Langemarck | 41 | F 6 | — |
| Philosophe British Cemetery, Mazingarbe | 46 | E 12 | 1234 |
| Picantin Post Cemetery, Laventie | 45 | E 10 | 1235 |
| Picantin Post Graveyard, Laventie | 45 | E 10 | 1237 |
| Picquigny British Cemetery | 10 | F 6 | 2214 |
| Picquigny Communal Cemetery | 10 | F 2 | 2215 |
| Pierrefonds French Cemetery | 21 | H 8 | 2216 |
| Pietrebais Churchyard | 6 | M 3 | 2083 |
| Pigeon Ravine British Cemetery, Epéhy | 57 | J 18 | 1856 |
| Pilckem Road Cemetery, Boesinghe | 41 | F 6 | 1239 |
| Pinney Avenue Support Line, Fleurbaix | 43 | F 10 | 1241 |
| Ploegsteert Churchyard | 43 | F 8 | 1936 |
| Poeuilly British Cemetery | 57 | H 20 | 1242 |
| Point du Jour Military Cemetery No. 1, Athies | 49 | F 14 | 1248 |
| Point du Jour Military Cemetery No. 2, Athies | 49 | F 14 | 1249 |
| Point 75 British Cemetery, Gommecourt | 50 | D 16 | 1243 |
| Point 80 French Military Cemetery, Etinehem | 54 | D 19 | 1244 |
| Point 110 New Military Cemetery, Fricourt | 54 | E 19 | 1246 |
| Point 110 Old Military Cemetery, Fricourt | 54 | E 19 | 1247 |
| Poix du Nord Communal Cemetery Extension | 59 | N 16 | 1857 |
| Polygon Wood Cemetery, Zonnebeke | 41 | G 6 | 1250 |
| Pommereuil British Cemetery | 59 | M 17 | 1251 |
| Pommier Communal Cemetery | 50 | D 16 | 1252 |
| Ponche British Cemetery, Coyecque | 10 | F 3 | 2217 |
| Pond Farm Military Cemetery, Wulverghem | 41 | F 8 | 1253 |
| Pont Ballot Farm, Houplines | 43 | F 9 | 1254 |
| Pont d'Achelles, Nieppe | 43 | E 8 | 1255 |
| Pont de Briques Communal Cemetery, St. Etienne-au-Mont | 9 | E 3 | 2218 |
| Pont de la Lys Indian Cemetery, Estaires | 44 | D 10 | 1256 |
| Pont de Metz Communal Cemetery | 20 | F 6 | 2234 |
| Pont de Nieppe Communal Cemetery | 43 | F 9 | 1257 |
| Pont du Hem Military Cemetery, near La Gorgue | 44 | E 10 | 1258 |
| Pont Fixe Post Office Cemetery, Givenchy | 44 | E 11 | 1259 |
| Pont Logy (Shrine Farm), Richebourg l'Avoue | 44 | E 10 | 1260 |
| Pont Remy British Cemetery | 9 | F 5 | 2219 |
| Pont-sur-Sambre Communal Cemetery Extension | 12 | K 5 | 2220 |
| Poperinghe Communal Cemetery | 40 | E 6 | 1262 |
| Poperinghe East Line Cemetery | 40 | E 7 | 1263 |
| Poperinghe New Military Cemetery | 40 | E 7 | 1264 |
| Poperinghe Old Military Cemetery | 40 | E 6 | 1265 |
| Poplar British Cemetery | 50 | D 16 | 1266 |
| Porte de Paris Cemetery, Cambrai | 53 | J 16 | — |
| Posen Street Station Cemetery, Loos | 47 | E 12 | 1267 |
| Post Office Rifles Cemetery, Festubert | 44 | E 11 | 1268 |
| Potijze Burial Ground, Ypres | 41 | F 6 | 1269 |
| Potijze Chateau Grounds, Ypres | 41 | F 6 | 1271 |
| Potijze Chateau Lawn, Ypres | 41 | F 6 | 1272 |
| Potijze Chateau Wood Cemetery | 41 | F 6 | 1273 |
| Potijze Chateau, Ypres | 41 | F 6 | 1270 |
| Pourcy British Cemetery No. 2, Marfaux | 60 | — | 1275 |
| Pozières British Cemetery | 50 | E 18 | 1276 |
| Prayelle Farm Military Cemetery, Viesly | 12 | J 5 | 1277 |
| Premont British Cemetery | 12 | J 5 | 1278 |
| Prémont Cemetery, German Extension | 12 | J 5 | 1279 |
| Presbytery Garden, St. Jean | 41 | F 6 | 1280 |
| Préseau Communal Cemetery Extension | 58 | M 14 | 1281 |
| Preux-au-Bois British Cemetery | 12 | J 5 | 1282 |
| Priez Farm, Combles | 55 | F 18 | 1283 |
| Prisches Communal Cemetery | 12 | K 5 | 2084 |
| Prospect Hill British Cemetery, Gouy | 57 | K 18 | 1284 |
| Protestant Cemetery, The Hague, Holland | — | — | — |
| Prouvy Churchyard Cemetery | 12 | J 4 | 1937 |
| Proven Churchyard | 40 | D 6 | 1938 |
| Proville British Cemetery | 53 | J 16 | 1285 |
| Provincial Cemetery, Loos | 47 | E 12 | 1286 |

| Name of Cemetery. | Page. | Map Square. | No. on Map. |
|---|---|---|---|
| Prowse Point Lower Cemetery, Warneton | 43 | F 8 | 1287 |
| Prowse Point Military Cemetery, Warneton | 43 | F 8 | 1288 |
| Prowse Point New Military Cemetery, Warneton | 43 | F 8 | 1289 |
| Proyart Communal Cemetery Extension | 54 | E 20 | 1290 |
| Proyart Wood Military Cemetery | 54 | D 20 | 1291 |
| Puchevillers British Cemetery | 10 | G 5 | 1292 |
| Pys British Cemetery | 50 | E 17 | 1293 |
| Pys New British Cemetery | 50 | E 17 | 1294 |
| Quadrangle Cemetery, Bazentin | 54 | E 18 | 1295 |
| Quaregnon Communal Cemetery | 12 | K 4 | 2086 |
| Quarry British Cemetery, Fampoux | 49 | F 14 | 1296 |
| Quarry British Cemetery, Monchy-le-Preux | 49 | F 15 | 1298 |
| Quarry British Cemetery, Vermelles | 46 | E 11 | 1299 |
| Quarry Cemetery, Marquion | 11 | H 5 | 1297 |
| Quarry Cemetery, Montauban | 55 | E 18 | 1300 |
| Quarry Palace Cemetery, Thiepval | 50 | D 17 | 1301 |
| Quarry Post Cemetery, Authuille Wood, Ovillers-la Boisselle.. | 50 | D 18 | 1302 |
| Quarry Scottish Cemetery, Montauban | 55 | E 18 | 1859 |
| Quarry Wood British Cemetery, Sains-lez-Marquion | 52 | H 16 | 1303 |
| Quatre Vents Military Cemetery, Estrée-Cauchie | 46 | D 13 | 1304 |
| Quéant Communal Cemetery Extension | 52 | G 16 | 1305 |
| Quéant Road British Cemetery, Buissy | 52 | G 16 | 1306 |
| Quebec British Cemetery, Cherisy | 49 | F 15 | 1307 |
| Queen's Cemetery (V Corps Cemetery No. 4), Bucquoy | 50 | D 17 | 1308 |
| Queensland Cemetery, Warneton | 43 | F 8 | 1309 |
| Quérénaing Communal Cemetery | 58 | M 14 | 1310 |
| Querrieu British Cemetery | 10 | G 6 | 1311 |
| Quesnoy Communal Cemetery, Quesnoy-sur-Deûle | 4 | H 3 | 946 |
| Quesnoy Farm British Cemetery, Bucquoy | 50 | D 16 | 1312 |
| Quesques Churchyard | 2 | F 3 | 2087 |
| Quiéry La Motte British Cemetery | 11 | H 4 | 1313 |
| Quietiste British Cemetery, Le Cateau | 59 | M 17 | 1314 |
| Quievrain Communal Cemetery | 12 | K 4 | 1315 |
| Quiévrechaine Communal Cemetery.. | 12 | J 4 | 1939 |
| Quievy Communal Cemetery Extension | 12 | J 5 | 1316 |
| Rab's Road, St. Laurent-Blangy | 48 | E 14 | 1317 |
| Raillencourt British Cemetery | 53 | J 16 | 1318 |
| Railway Chateau Cemetery, Vlamertinghe | 41 | F 7 | 1319 |
| Railway Dugouts Burial Ground (Transport Farm), Zillebeke | 41 | F 7 | 1320 |
| Railway Hollow (V. Corps Cemetery No. 3), Hébuterne | 50 | D 17 | 1321 |
| Railway Siding, Neuve Eglise | 42 | E 8 | 1322 |
| Railway Triangle, North Point, St. Laurent-Blangy | 48 | E 14 | 1323 |
| Raismes Communal Cemetery | 12 | J 4 | 1324 |
| Ramegnies Churchyard Communal Cemetery, Ramegnies-Chin | 11 | J 3 | 1325 |
| Ramegnies Communal Cemetery | 11 | J 3 | 1326 |
| Ramicourt British Cemetery | 12 | J 6 | 1327 |
| Ramicourt Communal Cemetery Extension | 12 | J 6 | 1328 |
| Ramillies British Cemetery | 11 | J 5 | 1329 |
| Ramparts, Lille Gate, Ypres | 41 | F 7 | 1330 |
| Ramscappelle Road Military Cemetery, St. George's | 3 | H 1 | 1331 |
| Ram Wood Cemetery, Menin | 4 | H 3 | 1332 |
| Rancourt Military Cemetery | 55 | F 18 | 1333 |
| Ransart (M.D.S.) Cemetery | 48 | D 16 | 1334 |
| Raperie British Cemetery, Villemontoire | 60 | — | 1335 |
| Ration Dump Burial Ground, Zillebeke | 41 | F 7 | 1337 |
| Ration Farm (La Plus Douve) Annexe, Ploegsteert | 43 | F 8 | 1338 |
| Ration Farm New Military Cemetery, Bois Grenier | 43 | F 9 | 1339 |
| Ration Farm Old Military Cemetery Bois Grenier.. | 43 | F 9 | 1340 |
| Ravine British Cemetery, Neuvilly | 59 | M 16 | 1341 |
| Rebecq Rognon Communal Cemetery | 5 | L 3 | 2088 |

( 136 )

| Name of Cemetery. | Page. | Map Square. | No. on Map. |
|---|---|---|---|
| Recques Churchyard | 2 | F 3 | 2089 |
| Redan Ridge No. 1 (V Corps Cemetery No. 5), Beaumont-Hamel | 50 | D 17 | 1342 |
| Redan Ridge No. 2 (V Corps Cemetery No. 6), Beaumont-Hamel | 50 | D 17 | 1343 |
| Redan Ridge No. 3 (V Corps Cemetery No. 22), Beaumont-Hamel | 50 | D 17 | 1344 |
| Red Chateau, Courcelette | 50 | E 18 | 1345 |
| Red Cross Corner, Beugny | 51 | F 17 | 1346 |
| Red Cross Military Cemetery, Vlamertinghe | 40 | E 6 | 1347 |
| Red Dragon British Cemetery, Ovillers-la Boisselle | 54 | D 18 | 1348 |
| Red Farm British Cemetery, Vlamertinghe | 40 | E 7 | — |
| Red Farm Military Cemetery, Vlamertinghe | 40 | E 6 | 1349 |
| Regina Trench Cemetery, Courcelette | 50 | E 17 | 1350 |
| Rejet de Beaulieu Farm British Cemetery | 12 | J 5 | 1351 |
| Remilly Wirquin Churchyard | 10 | F 3 | 2090 |
| Remy British Cemetery | 49 | G 15 | 1352 |
| Reninghelst Churchyard | 40 | E 7 | 1353 |
| Reninghelst New Military Cemetery | 40 | E 7 | 1354 |
| Reservoir German Cemetery, Bapaume | 51 | F 17 | 1355 |
| Rest and be Thankful Farm, Kemmel | 41 | E 7 | 1356 |
| Riaumont Cemetery, Liévin | 47 | E 13 | 1357 |
| Ribécourt Railway British Cemetery | 53 | H 17 | 1358 |
| Ribécourt Road British Cemetery, Trescault | 52 | H 17 | 1359 |
| Ribemont Communal Cemetery, British Plot | 11 | G 6 | 1360 |
| Ribemont Communal Cemetery Extension | 11 | G 6 | 1860 |
| Ribemont Military Cemetery | 22 | J 6 | 2091 |
| Richebourg St. Vaast Churchyard | 44 | E 10 | 1361 |
| Ridgeway British Cemetery, Lihons | 21 | G 6 | 1362 |
| Ridgewood Military Cemetery, Voormezeele | 41 | F 7 | 1363 |
| Rieux British Cemetery | 11 | J 4 | 1364 |
| Rifle Brigade (13th) Cemetery, Achiet-le-Grand | 51 | E 16 | 1365 |
| Rifle House Military Cemetery, Ploegsteert, Warneton | 43 | F 8 | 1366 |
| Riquerval British Cemetery, Bohain | 12 | J 5 | 1367 |
| River British Cemetery, Neuvilly | 59 | M 16 | 1368 |
| River Douve Cemetery, Messines | 43 | F 8 | 1369 |
| Rivière British Cemetery, Bettencourt Rivière | 10 | F 5 | 2221 |
| Robecq Communal Cemetery | 11 | G 3 | 1940 |
| Robertsart | 59 | N 16 | 1941 |
| Roclincourt Communal Cemetery | 48 | E 14 | 1861 |
| Roclincourt Highland Cemetery | 48 | E 14 | 1374 |
| Roclincourt Military Cemetery | 48 | E 14 | 1373 |
| Rocquigny Road British Cemetery, Manancourt | 52 | G 18 | 1377 |
| Rœux British Cemetery | 49 | F 14 | 1378 |
| Roisel Communal Cemetery | 57 | H 19 | 1379 |
| Roisel Communal Cemetery Extension | 57 | H 19 | 1380 |
| Romeries Communal Cemetery Extension | 59 | M 15 | 1381 |
| Ronssoy Communal Cemetery Extension | 57 | J 19 | 1382 |
| Ronssoy Hill British Cemetery | 57 | H 19 | 1383 |
| Ronville British Cemetery, Arras | 48 | E 14 | 1384 |
| Ronville French Cemetery, Arras | 48 | E 14 | 1385 |
| Rookery British Cemetery, Héninel | 49 | F 15 | 1386 |
| Roosemberg Chateau Military Cemetery, Ploegsteert | 43 | F 8 | 1388 |
| Roosemberg Chateau Military Cemetery Extension, Ploegsteert | 43 | F 8 | 1389 |
| Rose Trench Cemetery, Lesbœufs | 51 | F 18 | 1387 |
| Rosières British Cemetery, Vauvillers | 21 | G 6 | 1390 |
| Rosières Communal Cemetery, Rosières-en-Santerre | 21 | G 6 | 1391 |
| Rosières Communal Cemetery Extension | 21 | G 6 | 1392 |
| Rossignol Cemetery, Hébuterne | 50 | D 17 | 1393 |
| Rossignol Estaminet, Kemmel | 41 | E 7 | 1394 |
| Rosult Communal Cemetery | 11 | J 4 | 1942 |
| Roulers German Cemetery | 4 | H 2 | 1395 |
| Roupy Communal Cemetery | 21 | H 6 | 1396 |
| Rousbrugge-Haringhe | 3 | G 2 | 1943 |
| Route de Loos (2e Cimitière Française) Extension, Grenay | 46 | E 12 | 1862 |

( 137 )

| Name of Cemetery. | Page. | Map Square. | No. on Map. |
|---|---|---|---|
| Rouvrel Communal Cemetery | 20 | G 6 | 2092 |
| Royal Berks Cemetery, Cuinchy | 44 | E 11 | 1397 |
| R.E. (Beaver) Farm, Kemmel | 40 | E 7 | 1398 |
| R.E. Cemetery, Epéhy | 57 | H 18 | 1785 |
| R.E. Farm Cemetery No. 1, Wytschaete | 41 | F 8 | 1399 |
| R.E. Farm Cemetery No. 2, Wytschaete | 41 | F 8 | 1400 |
| R.F.A. Cemetery, Ginchy | 55 | F 18 | 1401 |
| Royal Irish Cemetery, Armagh Wood, Zillebeke | 41 | F 7 | 1402 |
| Royal Irish Cemetery, near Ploegsteert | 43 | F 8 | 1404 |
| Royal Irish Rifles Graveyard, Laventie | 45 | E 10 | 1403 |
| Royal West Surrey's Cemetery | — | D 8 | 605 |
| Rozières Churchyard, Aisne | 60 | — | 1792 |
| Rubber House Cemetery, Nieuport | 3 | G 1 | 1408 |
| Rue Bapaume Military Cemetery, Arras | 48 | E 14 | 1409 |
| Rue Cailloux No. 1 Cemetery, Festubert | 44 | E 11 | 1410 |
| Rue Cailloux No. 2 Cemetery, Festubert | 44 | E 11 | 1411 |
| Rue Cailloux No. 3 Cemetery, Festubert | 44 | E 11 | 1412 |
| Rue David Military Cemetery, Fleurbaix | 43 | F 10 | 1413 |
| Rue de l'Epinette, Richbourg l'Avoue | 44 | E 11 | 1414 |
| Rue des Berceaux Military Cemetery, Richebourg l'Avoue | 44 | E 10 | 1415 |
| Rue des Boiteux Le Crombalot, Bois Grenier | 43 | F 9 | 1416 |
| Rue des Chavattes Indian Cemetery, Lacouture | 44 | E 11 | 1417 |
| Rue du Bacquerot No. 1 Military Cemetery, Laventie | 44 | E 10 | 1419 |
| Rue du Bacquerot (13th London) Graveyard, Laventie | 45 | E 10 | 1420 |
| Rue du Bacquerot (Wangerie Post) New Military Cemetery, Laventie | 45 | E 10 | 1421 |
| Rue du Bacquerot (Wangerie Post) Old Military Cemetery, Laventie | 45 | E 10 | 1422 |
| Rue du Bacquerot (Winchester Post) Military Cemetery, Laventie | 45 | E 10 | 1423 |
| Rue du Bacquerot (Winchester Post) New Military Cemetery, Laventie | 45 | E 10 | 1424 |
| Rue du Bois Military Cemetery, Fleurbaix | 45 | E 10 | 1425 |
| Rue du Bois No. 2 (King's Liverpool) Cemetery, Richebourg l'Avoue | 44 | E 10 | 1426 |
| Rue du Bois No. 3 Cemetery, Richebourg l'Avoue | 44 | E 10 | 1427 |
| Rue Masselot (2nd Lincolns) Cemetery, near Laventie | 45 | E 10 | 1428 |
| Rue Petillon Military Cemetery, Fleurbaix | 43 | F 10 | 1429 |
| Ruesnes Communal Cemetery | 58 | M 15 | 1430 |
| Rugby Corner Track, Boesinghe | 41 | F 6 | 1432 |
| Ruisseau Farm British Cemetery, Langemarck | 41 | F 6 | 1433 |
| Rumegies Communal Cemetery | 12 | J 4 | 1434 |
| Rumingham Chinese Cemetery | 3 | F 2 | 2222 |
| Sablonnières Communal Cemetery, 27 m. E. of Lyons | | | |
| Sailly-au-Bois Military Cemetery | 50 | C 17 | 1436 |
| Sailly-Labourse Communal Cemetery | 46 | D 11 | 1437 |
| Sailly-Labourse Communal Cemetery Extension | 46 | D 11 | 1438 |
| Sailly Laurette Military Cemetery | 54 | D 19 | 1439 |
| Sailly-le-Sec British Cemetery | 54 | C 19 | 1440 |
| Sailly-sur-la-Lys Churchyard | 42 | E 9 | 1441 |
| Sainghin-en-Melantois Churchyard | 11 | H 3 | 1944 |
| Sains-lez-Marquion British Cemetery | 52 | H 16 | 1442 |
| St. Acheul Town Cemetery, Amiens | 20 | F 6 | 1793 |
| St. Amand British Cemetery | 11 | G 5 | 1443 |
| St. Amand Communal Cemetery | 11 | G 5 | 1444 |
| St. Amand Communal Cemetery Extension | 11 | G 5 | 1446 |
| St. Amand-les-Eaux Communal Cemetery | 12 | J 4 | 1445 |
| St. André Communal Cemetery | 11 | H 3 | 1447 |
| St. Aubert British Cemetery | 12 | J 5 | 1448 |
| St. Aubin Churchyard | 12 | K 5 | 2093 |
| St. Augustine Cabaret Graveyard, Brielen | 41 | F 5 | 1449 |

| Name of Cemetery | Page. | Map Square. | No. on Map |
|---|---|---|---|
| St. Benin Communal Cemetery | 59 | M 17 | 1945 |
| St. Catherine British Cemetery | 48 | E 14 | 1450 |
| St. Cloud Communal Cemetery (Seine et Oise) | 28 | F 10 | 2223 |
| St. Cren British Cemetery, Mons-en-Chausée | 56 | G 20 | 1451 |
| St. Cren German Cemetery | 56 | G 20 | 1863 |
| St. Eloi Cemetery, Voormezeele | 41 | F 7 | 1452 |
| Ste. Emilie British Cemetery, Villers Faucon | 57 | H 19 | 1453 |
| Ste. Emilie Roadside German Cemetery, Villers Faucon | 57 | H 19 | 1864 |
| Ste. Emilie Valley British Cemetery, Villers Faucon | 57 | H 19 | 1454 |
| Ste Hélène British Cemetery, Pontruet | 57 | J 19 | 1456 |
| Ste. Marie Cemetery, Graville Ste. Honorine, Le Havre | 18 | B 7 | 2224 |
| St. Etienne-au-Mont Communal Cemetery | 9 | E 3 | 2225 |
| St. Etienne du Rouvray Communal Cemetery | 19 | D 8 | 2226 |
| St. Genois Communal Cemetery | 4 | J 3 | 2227 |
| St. Germain-au-Mont-d'Or Communal Cemetery and Extension, 8 m. N. of Lyons | — | — | — |
| St. Ghislain Communal Cemetery | 12 | K 4 | 2094 |
| St. Hilaire Communal Cemetery Extension, Frévent | 10 | F 5 | 1457 |
| St. Hilaire-lez-Cambrai British Cemetery | 12 | J 5 | 1458 |
| St. Hilaire-sur-Helpe Churchyard | 12 | K 5 | 2095 |
| St. Imoges Churchyard | 60 | — | 1459 |
| St. Julien Dressing Station Cemetery, Langemarck | 41 | F 6 | 1460 |
| St. Leger British Cemetery | 51 | F 16 | 1462 |
| St. Leger Wood Cemetery | 51 | F 16 | 1463 |
| St. Leonard Cemetery, Alençon | — | — | — |
| St. Marie-Cappel Churchyard | 3 | G 3 | 1946 |
| St. Martin-Calvaire British Cemetery | 49 | F 15 | 1464 |
| St. Mary's A.D.S., Hulluch | 47 | E 12 | 1465 |
| St. Nicholas British Cemetery, Arras | 48 | E 14 | 1466 |
| St. Olle British Cemetery, Raillencourt | 53 | J 16 | 1468 |
| St. Ouen Communal Cemetery Extension | 10 | F 5 | 2229 |
| St. Patrick Military Cemetery, Loos | 47 | E 12 | 1469 |
| St. Pierre Cemetery, Amiens | 10 | F 6 | 1472 |
| St. Pierre Divion Cemetery No. 1, Thiepval | 50 | D 17 | 1470 |
| St. Pierre Divion Cemetery No. 2, Thiepval | 50 | D 18 | 1471 |
| St. Pol British Cemetery, St. Pol | 10 | F 4 | 1473 |
| St. Pol Communal Cemetery Extension | 10 | F 4 | 1467 |
| St. Pol-sur-Mer Chinese Cemetery | 3 | F 2 | 1474 |
| St. Python Communal Cemetery Extension | 59 | L 16 | 1475 |
| St. Quentin Cabaret Military Cemetery, Wulverghem | 43 | F 8 | 1786 |
| St. Remy Chaussée Churchyard | 12 | K 5 | 2096 |
| St. Remy Chaussée Communal Cemetery | 12 | K 5 | 2230 |
| St. Remy-mal-bâti Communal Cemetery | 12 | K 5 | 2098 |
| St. Riquier British Cemetery | 10 | F 5 | 2231 |
| St. Sever Cemetery, Grand Quevilly, Rouen | 19 | D 8 | 2232 |
| St. Sever Cemetery, Petit Quevilly, Rouen | 19 | D 7 | 2233 |
| St. Souplet British Cemetery | 12 | J 5 | 1477 |
| St. Souplet Communal Cemetery | 12 | J 5 | 1947 |
| St. Vaast Communal Cemetery Extension | 12 | J 5 | 1479 |
| St. Vaast Post Indian Cemetery | 44 | E 10 | 1480 |
| St. Vaast Post Military Cemetery, Richebourg l'Avoué | 44 | E 10 | 1481 |
| St. Venant Communal Cemetery | 11 | G 3 | 1483 |
| St. Venant Communal Cemetery Extension | 11 | G 3 | 1482 |
| St. Venant-Robecq Road British Cemetery, Robecq | 11 | G 3 | 1484 |
| St. Waast-la-Vallée Communal Cemetery | 12 | K 4 | 2099 |
| Sameon Communal Cemetery | 11 | J 4 | 1485 |
| Samer Communal Cemetery | 9 | E 3 | 2100 |
| Sancourt British Cemetery | 11 | H 5 | 1486 |
| Sanctuary Wood Cemetery, Zillebeke | 41 | F 7 | 1487 |
| Sanders Keep Military Cemetery, Graincourt-les-Havrincourt | 52 | H 17 | 1488 |
| Sandpits British Cemetery, Labeuvrière | 11 | G 4 | 1489 |
| Sars Poteries | 12 | K 5 | 2101 |

| Name of Cemetery. | Page. | Map Square. | No. on Map. |
|---|---|---|---|
| Sassegnies Communal Cemetery | 12 | K 5 | 2102 |
| Sauchy-Cauchy Communal Cemetery Extension | 11 | H 5 | 1491 |
| Sauchy Lestrée German Military Cemetery | 11 | H 5 | 1492 |
| Saultain Communal Cemetery | 58 | M 14 | 1493 |
| Saulzoir Communal Cemetery Extension | 12 | J 5 | 1494 |
| Savy Communal Cemetery Extension | 21 | H 6 | 1495 |
| Savy Military Cemetery | 21 | H 6 | 1496 |
| Savy Wood North Cemetery | 21 | H 6 | 1497 |
| Sclayn Communal Cemetery | 13 | N 4 | 2103 |
| Scottish Rifles (2nd) Cemetery, Neuve Chapelle | 45 | E 10 | 1503 |
| Seaforth Cemetery, Buzancy | 60 | — | — |
| Seaforth Cemetery, Roeux | 49 | F 14 | 1498 |
| Sebourg British Cemetery | 58 | N 14 | 1500 |
| Sebourg Communal Cemetery | 58 | N 13 | 1501 |
| Sebourgquiaux British Cemetery | 58 | N 13 | 1502 |
| Selridge British Cemetery, Montay | 59 | M 17 | 1865 |
| Selvigny German Cemetery | 11 | J 5 | 1504 |
| Semousies Churchyard | 12 | K 5 | 2104 |
| Semousies Communal Cemetery | 12 | K 5 | 2235 |
| Senlecques Churchyard | 9 | F 3 | 2105 |
| Senlis Communal Cemetery | 11 | G 5 | 1506 |
| Senlis Communal Cemetery Extension | 11 | G 5 | 1507 |
| Seny Communal Cemetery | 14 | N 4 | 2106 |
| Sepmeries Communal Cemetery | 58 | M 14 | 1948 |
| Sequehart British Cemetery | 12 | J 6 | 1508 |
| Sequehart British Cemetery No. 2 | 11 | J 6 | 1866 |
| Serain Communal Cemetery Extension | 12 | J 5 | 1509 |
| Serques Churchyard | 3 | F 3 | 2107 |
| Serre Road Cemetery No. 1, Hébuterne | 50 | D 17 | 1510 |
| Serre Road Cemetery No. 2, Beaumont-Hamel | 50 | D 17 | 1511 |
| Serre Road Cemetery No. 3, Hébuterne | 50 | D 17 | 1512 |
| Seven Elms Dressing Station Cemetery, Martinpuich | 51 | E 18 | 1513 |
| Sezanne Communal Cemetery | 30 | K 10 | 2236 |
| Sivry Communal Cemetery | 12 | L 5 | 2108 |
| Shell Farm, Wytschaete | 41 | F 8 | 1515 |
| Shrine Cemetery, Bucquoy | 50 | D 16 | 1517 |
| Shrine Cemetery, Grévillers | 51 | E 17 | 1518 |
| Sign Post Lane, Laventie | 45 | E 10 | 1519 |
| Small Cemetery, Mazinghein | 12 | J 5 | 1521 |
| Snap Reserve Trench Cemetery, Villers Plouich | 52 | H 17 | 1523 |
| Soignies Communal Cemetery | 12 | K 3 | 2109 |
| Solesmes British Cemetery | 59 | L 16 | 1524 |
| Solesmes Communal Cemetery | 59 | M 16 | 1525 |
| Solferino Farm British Cemetery | 41 | F 6 | 1527 |
| Soire-le-Chateau Communal Cemetery and German Extension | 12 | K 5 | 2111 |
| Solre St. Gery Communal Cemetery | 12 | L 5 | 2110 |
| Somer Farm Cemetery, near Wytschaete | 41 | F 7 | 1528 |
| Somer Farm Cemetery No. 2, Wytschaete | 41 | F 7 | 1529 |
| Somerset L.I. Military Cemetery, Ploegsteert Wood, Warneton | 43 | F 8 | 1530 |
| Soumoy Communal Cemetery | 13 | L 5 | 2112 |
| Soupir Church Military Cemetery (Aisne) | 60 | — | 2237 |
| Soupir Communal Cemetery (Aisne) | 60 | — | 2238 |
| Sous-le-Bois Communal Cemetery | 12 | K 4 | 2239 |
| Southern Avenue Cemetery, Auchonvillers | 50 | D 17 | 1534 |
| Soyer Farm, Ploegsteert | 43 | F 8 | 1535 |
| Spa Communal Cemetery | 14 | O 4 | 2113 |
| Spanbroekmolen Cemetery, Wytschaete | 41 | F 8 | 1536 |
| Spiennes Communal Cemetery | 12 | K 4 | 2114 |
| Spoilbank Extension, Zillebeke | 41 | F 7 | 1538 |
| Spoilbank, Zillebeke | 41 | F 7 | 1537 |
| Spree Farm Cemetery, Langemarck | 41 | F 6 | 1539 |
| Spy Communal Cemetery | 13 | M 4 | 2115 |
| Staceghem Communal Cemetery | 4 | J 2 | 2240 |
| Station Road Cemetery, St. Aubert | 12 | J 5 | 1542 |

| Name of Cemetery. | Page. | Map Square. | No. on Map. |
|---|---|---|---|
| Steenkirk Belgian Military Cemetery | 3 | G 2 | 1543 |
| Steenvoorde French Military Cemetery | 3 | G 3 | 1921 |
| Steenwerck Communal Cemetery | 42 | E 9 | 1544 |
| Stirrup Lane Cemetery, Monchy-le-Preux | 49 | F 15 | 1545 |
| Strand Military Cemetery, Ploegsteert Wood | 43 | F 8 | 1546 |
| Strazeele Road Military Cemetery | 3 | G 3 | 1547 |
| Stump Road Cemetery, Grandcourt | 50 | E 17 | 1548 |
| Sucrerie British Cemetery, Epinoy | 11 | H 5 | 1549 |
| Sucrerie British Cemetery, Graincourt-les-Havrincourt | 52 | H 16 | 1550 |
| Sucrerie Cemetery, Ablain St. Nazaire | 46 | E 13 | 1551 |
| Sucrerie Military Cemetery, Colincamps | 50 | D 17 | 1552 |
| Suffolk Cemetery, near Vierstraat, Kemmel | 41 | F 7 | 1558 |
| Sumack Cemetery, Vimy | — | E 13 | 644 |
| Summit Trench British Cemetery, Croisilles | 49 | F 15 | 1553 |
| Sunken Road British Cemetery, Fampoux | 49 | F 14 | 1554 |
| Sunken Road Cemetery, Boisleux-St. Marc | 48 | E 15 | 1555 |
| Sunken Road Cemetery No. 2, Lesbœufs | 51 | F 18 | 1556 |
| Sunken Road Cemetery, near Pozières, Contalmaison | 54 | E 18 | 1557 |
| Sun Quarry British Cemetery, Cherisy | 49 | F 15 | 1559 |
| Sussex British Cemetery, Sailly Laurette | 54 | D 19 | 1560 |
| Sussex Cemetery, near Northern Sap, Loos Plain | 47 | E 12 | 1561 |
| Suzanne Communal Cemetery Extension | 55 | E 19 | 1562 |
| Suzanne French Military Cemetery No. 2 | 55 | E 19 | 1563 |
| Swan Trench (V Corps Cemetery No. 14), Puisieux-au-Mont | 50 | D 17 | 1564 |
| Sweveghem Churchyard | 4 | J 3 | 2241 |
| Tailles Wood British Cemetery, Etinehem | 54 | D 19 | 1567 |
| Taintignies Communal Cemetery | 11 | J 3 | 1568 |
| Talana Farm, Boesinghe | 41 | F 6 | 1569 |
| Talus Boisé German Cemetery Extension, Montauban | 55 | E 18 | 1571 |
| Tamines Communal Cemetery | 13 | M 4 | 2116 |
| Tancrez Farm Military Cemetery, Le Bizet-Le Touquet Road, Ploegsteert | 43 | F 9 | 1572 |
| Tank British Cemetery, Guémappe | 49 | F 15 | 1573 |
| Tannay British Cemetery, Thiennes | 10 | G 3 | 1574 |
| Targelle Ravine British Cemetery, Villers Guislain | 53 | H 18 | 1949 |
| Tea Farm, Wulverghem | 41 | F 8 | 1575 |
| Tees Trench British Cemetery No. 1, St. Laurent-Blangy | 48 | E 14 | 1576 |
| Tees Trench British Cemetery No. 2, St. Laurent-Blangy | 48 | E 14 | 1577 |
| Templeuve Communal Cemetery | 11 | J 3 | 1579 |
| Templeux-La Fosse German Cemetery | 56 | G 19 | 1580 |
| Templeux-La Fosse Military Cemetery | 56 | G 19 | 1581 |
| Templeux-Le Guerard British Cemetery | 57 | H 19 | 1582 |
| Templeux-Le Guerard Communal Cemetery and Extension | 57 | H 19 | 1583 |
| Tenth Avenue Cemetery, near Haisnes | 47 | E 12 | 1586 |
| Ten Tree Alley British Cemetery No. 2 (V Corps Cemetery No. 24), Beaucourt-sur-Ancre | 50 | D 17 | 1585 |
| Teofani Railway Crossing, Dadizeele | 4 | H 2 | 1587 |
| Terdeghem Churchyard | 3 | G 3 | 1950 |
| Terdeghem French Military Cemetery | 3 | G 3 | 1588 |
| Terlincthun British Cemetery, Wimille | 2 | E 3 | 2242 |
| Thélus Road British Cemetery, Roclincourt | 48 | E 14 | 1593 |
| Thennes Communal Cemetery | 21 | G 6 | 1951 |
| Theux Communal Cemetery | 14 | O 3 | 2117 |
| Thiant Communal Cemetery Extension | 12 | J 4 | 1594 |
| Thiennes British Cemetery, Morbecque | 10 | G 3 | 1595 |
| Thilloy Road British Cemetery, Beaulencourt | 51 | F 17 | 1597 |
| Thirteenth Corps Cemetery, St. Laurent-Blangy | 48 | E 14 | 1598 |
| Thistle Dump Cemetery, High Wood | 51 | E 18 | 1600 |
| Thun St. Martin British Cemetery | 11 | J 5 | 1601 |
| Tigris Lane Cemetery, Wancourt | 49 | F 15 | 1602 |

| Name of Cemetery. | Page. | Map Square. | No. on Map. |
|---|---|---|---|
| Tilloy British Cemetery, Tilloy-les-Mafflaines | 49 | E 15 | 1603 |
| Tilloy Quarry British Cemetery, Tilloy-les-Mafflaines | 49 | F 14 | 1605 |
| Tincourt British Cemetery, Tincourt-Boucly | 56 | G 19 | 1606 |
| Tincourt New British Cemetery, Tincourt-Boucly | 56 | G 19 | 1607 |
| Tinques Churchyard | 11 | G 4 | 1952 |
| Tombois Farm, Vendhuille | 57 | J 18 | — |
| Toronto Avenue Cemetery, Warneton | 43 | F 8 | 1608 |
| Toronto British Cemetery, Villers Bretonneux | 21 | G 6 | 1609 |
| Torreken Farm, Cemetery No. 1, Wytschaete | 41 | F 7 | 1610 |
| Tourcoing Communal Cemetery | 4 | H 3 | 1612 |
| Tourgeville Military Cemetery, Trouville | 18 | A 8 | 2243 |
| Tourlaville Cemetery, Cherbourg | — | — | — |
| Tournai Communal Cemetery | 12 | J 3 | 1614 |
| Tournai Communal Cemetery Extension | 12 | J 3 | 1613 |
| Toutencourt Communal Cemetery | 10 | G 5 | 1789 |
| Toutes Aides Cemetery, St. Nazaire | — | — | — |
| Track "X" British Cemetery, St. Jean | 41 | F 6 | 1616 |
| Tranchée de Mecknes Cemetery, Aix-Noulette | 46 | E 12 | 1618 |
| Trefcon British Cemetery, Caulaincourt | 21 | H 6 | 1619 |
| Trench Railway Cemetery, Verbrandenmolen, near Zillebeke | 41 | F 7 | 1620 |
| Triangle British Cemetery, Mœuvres | 52 | H 16 | 1621 |
| Triangle Cemetery, Petit Miraumont | 50 | E 17 | 1622 |
| Triez British Cemetery | 12 | J 4 | 1623 |
| Trois Arbres, Steenwerck | 42 | E 9 | 1624 |
| Troisvilles British Cemetery | 59 | L 17 | 1625 |
| Troisvilles Communal Cemetery Extension | 59 | L 17 | 1626 |
| Troyon Churchyard | 60 | — | 2244 |
| Tubize Communal Cemetery | 5 | L 3 | 2118 |
| Tuileries, The, Zillebeke | 41 | F 7 | 1629 |
| Two Tree Cemetery, Moyenneville | 51 | E 16 | 1628 |
| Tyne Cottage Cemetery, Passchendaele | 41 | G 6 | 1867 |
| Ugny l'Equipée Churchyard Cemetery | 21 | H 6 | 1953 |
| Underhill Farm Cemetery, Ploegsteert | 43 | F 8 | 1830 |
| Unicorn British Cemetery, Vendhuille | 57 | J 18 | 1787 |
| Uplands British Cemetery, Magny-la-Fosse | 57 | K 19 | 1631 |
| Upton Wood British Cemetery, Hendecourt-les-Cagnicourt | 49* | G 15 | 1632 |
| Urvillers German Military Cemetery | 21 | J 6 | 2119 |
| Vadencourt Chateau British Cemetery, Maissemy | 57 | J 20 | 1633 |
| Vadencourt New British Cemetery, Maissemy | 57 | J 20 | 1634 |
| Vaire Wood British Cemetery, Vaire-sous-Corbie | 21 | G 6 | 1635 |
| Valenciennes Communal Cemetery Extension | 58 | M 13 | 1636 |
| Valenciennes German Cemetery | 58 | M 13 | — |
| Valley British Cemetery, Villers Faucon | 57 | H 19 | 1637 |
| Valley Cemetery, Montauban | 55 | E 18 | 1638 |
| Valley Cemetery, Roclincourt | 48 | E 14 | 1639 |
| Valley Cemetery, Vis-en-Artois | 49 | F 15 | 1640 |
| Valley Cottages, near Zillebeke | 41 | F 7 | 1641 |
| Vanheule Farm, Langemarck | 41 | F 6 | 1656 |
| Vanheule Farm Cemetery | 41 | F 6 | 1642 |
| Varennes British Cemetery | 11 | G 5 | 1643 |
| Vaulx A.D.S. British Cemetery, Vaulx-Vraucourt | 51 | F 16 | 1645 |
| Vaulx Australian Cemetery, Vaulx-Vraucourt | 51 | F 16 | 1644 |
| Vaulx Churchyard British Extension, Vraucourt | 51 | F 16 | 1646 |
| Vaulx Hill British Cemetery, Vaulx-Vraucourt | 51 | F 16 | 1647 |
| Vauvillers Communal Cemetery | 21 | G 6 | 1868 |
| Vaux Andigny British Cemetery | 12 | J 5 | 1648 |
| Vaux Andigny Communal Cemetery Extension | 12 | J 5 | 1649 |
| Vaux-en-Amienois Communal Cemetery | 10 | F 6 | 2245 |
| Vauxhall Bridge Road Cemetery, Givenchy | 44 | E 11 | 1650 |
| Vaux Wood British Cemetery, Vaux | 55 | E 19 | 1652 |
| Vendegies-au-Bois British Cemetery | 59 | M 16 | — |

| Name of Cemetery. | Page. | Map Square. | No. on Map. |
|---|---|---|---|
| Vendegies Communal Cemetery | 59 | M 16 | 1653 |
| Vendegies Cross Roads, British Cemetery, Bermerain | 58 | M 15 | 1654 |
| Vendegies Cross-Roads German Cemetery | 58 | M 15 | 1869 |
| Vendellés Communal Cemetery Extension | 57 | H 20 | 1655 |
| Vendresse Communal Cemetery | 60 | — | 2246 |
| Verchain British Cemetery | 12 | J 4 | 1657 |
| Vermand Communal Cemetery | 57 | H 20 | 1658 |
| Vermelles British Cemetery | 46 | E 12 | 1659 |
| Vermelles Communal Cemetery | 46 | E 12 | 1660 |
| Verneuil Cemetery | 60 | — | 2247 |
| Verneuil Chateau Military Cemetery | 60 | — | 2248 |
| Vernon Street Cemetery (Squeak Forward Position) Carnoy | 55 | E 18 | 1661 |
| Verquin Communal Cemetery | 44 | D 11 | 1662 |
| Vertain Communal Cemetery Extension | 59 | M 15 | 1663 |
| Vertigneul Churchyard, Romeries | 59 | M 16 | 1664 |
| Vertus Communal Cemetery | 30 | K 9 | 2249 |
| Vicogne Communal Cemetery | 10 | F 5 | 1956 |
| Vicq Communal Cemetery | 12 | J 4 | 1957 |
| Vieil Arcy British Cemetery | 60 | — | 2250 |
| Vieille Chapelle Churchyard | 44 | D 10 | 1665 |
| Vieille Chapelle New Military Cemetery | 44 | D 10 | 1666 |
| Vieille Chapelle Old Military Cemetery | 44 | D 10 | 1667 |
| Viesly Communal Cemetery, German Extension | 59 | L 16 | 1668 |
| Vignacourt British Cemetery | 10 | F 5 | 2251 |
| Vijverhoek Brasserie Cemetery | 41 | F 7 | 1788 |
| Villa Wood Cemetery, Contalmaison | 54 | E 18 | 1670 |
| Villeneuve St. George's Communal Cemetery | 28 | G 10 | 2252 |
| Villereau Churchyard | 12 | J 4 | 1958 |
| Villers-au-Bois French Military Cemetery | 46 | D 13 | 1671 |
| Villers-Bocage Communal Cemetery | 10 | F 5 | 1672 |
| Villers-Bocage Communal Cemetery Extension | 10 | F 5 | 1673 |
| Villers-Bretonneux Communal Cemetery | 21 | G 6 | 1674 |
| Villers-Bretonneux Communal Cemetery Extension | 21 | G 6 | 1675 |
| Villers-Bretonneux Military Cemetery | 21 | G 6 | 361 |
| Villers-en-Cauchies Communal Cemetery | 12 | J 5 | 1676 |
| Villers Faucon Communal Cemetery | 57 | H 19 | 1677 |
| Villers Faucon Communal Cemetery Extension | 57 | H 19 | 1678 |
| Villers-Guislain Communal Cemetery | 53 | H 18 | 1679 |
| Villers-Guislain German Cemetery | 53 | H 18 | 1680 |
| Villers Hill Cemetery, Villers-Guislain | 57 | J 18 | 1681 |
| Villers-Plouich Communal Cemetery | 53 | H 17 | 1682 |
| Villers Pol Communal Cemetery Extension | 58 | N 14 | 1683 |
| Villers Station Military Cemetery | 46 | D 13 | 1684 |
| Ville-sur-Ancre Communal Cemetery | 54 | D 19 | 1685 |
| Ville-sur-Ancre New British Cemetery | 54 | D 19 | 1686 |
| Vimy Canadian Cemetery No. 1 | 47 | E 13 | 1687 |
| Vimy Canadian Cemetery No. 2 | 47 | E 13 | 1688 |
| Vimy Communal Cemetery, Farbus | 47 | E 13 | 1689 |
| Vis-en-Artois British Cemetery, Haucourt | 49 | G 15 | 1691 |
| Vlamertinghe Military Cemetery | 40 | E 6 | 1692 |
| Vlamertinghe New Military Cemetery | 40 | E 7 | 1693 |
| Vogenée Communal Cemetery | 13 | L 4 | 2120 |
| Voormezeele Enclosure No. 1 | 41 | F 7 | 1694 |
| Voormezeele Enclosure No. 2 | 41 | F 7 | 1695 |
| Voormezeele Enclosure No. 3 | 41 | F 7 | 1696 |
| Voormezeele Enclosure No. 4 | 41 | F 7 | 1697 |
| Voyennes Churchyard Cemetery | 21 | H 6 | 1960 |
| Voyennes Communal Cemetery | 21 | H 6 | 1959 |
| Vraignes Communal Cemetery | 56 | H 20 | 1698 |
| Vraucourt Copse British Cemetery, Vaulx-Vraucourt | 51 | F 16 | 1699 |
| Vrély Communal Cemetery Extension | 21 | G 6 | 1700 |
| Waggon Road (V. Corps Cemetery No. 10), Beaumont-Hamel | 50 | D 17 | 1701 |
| Wailly Military Cemetery | 48 | E 15 | 1702 |

| Name of Cemetery. | Page. | Map Square. | No. on Map. |
|---|---|---|---|
| Wailly Orchard Cemetery | 48 | E 15 | 1703 |
| Wallon-Cappel Churchyard | 3 | G 3 | 1961 |
| Wambaix Communal Cemetery | 11 | J 5 | 1962 |
| Wancourt British Cemetery | 49 | F 15 | 1704 |
| Wancourt Road British Cemetery, Neuville Vitasse | 49 | F 15 | 1705 |
| Wanquetin Communal Cemetery | 11 | G 4 | 1707 |
| Wanquetin Communal Cemetery Extension | 11 | G 4 | 1708 |
| Warcoing Communal Cemetery | 4 | J 3 | 2121 |
| Wargnies-le-Grand Churchyard | 12 | J 4 | 1709 |
| Wargnies-le-Petit Chateau | 12 | J 4 | 1711 |
| Wargnies-le-Petit Communal Cemetery | 12 | J 4 | 1710 |
| Warlincourt Halte British Cemetery, Saulty | 11 | G 5 | 1712 |
| Warloy-Baillon Communal Cemetery | 11 | G 5 | 1713 |
| Warloy-Baillon Communal Cemetery Extension | 11 | G 5 | 1714 |
| Warquignies Communal Cemetery | 12 | K 4 | 2122 |
| Warry Copse Cemetery, Courcelles-le-Comte | 51 | E 16 | 1715 |
| Warvillers Churchyard Extension | 21 | G 6 | 1716 |
| Wassigny Communal Cemetery | 12 | J 5 | 1963 |
| Waterloo Farm Cemetery, Paaschendaele | 41 | G 6 | 1718 |
| Watou Churchyard | 3 | G 2 | 1964 |
| Watten Churchyard | 3 | F 3 | 2123 |
| Wattrelos Communal Cemetery | 4 | H 3 | 1717 |
| Wavans British Cemetery | 10 | F 5 | 2253 |
| Wavrans Churchyard | 10 | F 3 | 2125 |
| Wavre Communal Cemetery | 5 | M 3 | 2124 |
| Wavrin Communal Cemetery | 45 | G 10 | 1719 |
| Wellington Cemetery, Ploegsteert | 43 | F 8 | 1720 |
| Wellington Cemetery, Rieux | 11 | J 5 | 1721 |
| Welsh Cemetery, Cæsar's Nose, Boesinghe | 41 | F 6 | 1722 |
| Welsh Cemetery, Longueval | 51 | E 18 | 1723 |
| West Cemetery, Richebourg St. Vaast | 44 | E 10 | 1725 |
| Westhof Farm, Neuve Eglise | 42 | E 8 | 1726 |
| Westoutre British Cemetery | 40 | E 7 | 1728 |
| Westoutre Churchyard | 40 | E 7 | 1727 |
| Westoutre Churchyard Extension | 40 | E 7 | 1729 |
| West Yorkshires' Cemetery, Equancourt | 52 | G 18 | 1730 |
| White Chateau British Cemetery, Cachy | 21 | G 6 | — |
| White City, Bois Grenier | 43 | F 9 | 1732 |
| White House, Menin Road, Ypres | 41 | F 7 | 1734 |
| White House, St. Jean | 41 | F 6 | 1735 |
| Wieltje Farm Cemetery, St. Jean | 41 | F 6 | 1736 |
| Wieltje Road Cemetery, Langemarck | 41 | F 6 | 1737 |
| Wilde Wood Cemetery, Zonnebeke | 41 | F 6 | 1738 |
| Willems Communal Cemetery | 11 | J 3 | 1739 |
| Willow British Cemetery, Boiry St. Rictrude | 50 | E 16 | 1740 |
| Wiltshire Farm, Ridgewood, near Dickebusch | 41 | F 7 | 1741 |
| Wimereux Communal Cemetery | 2 | E 3 | 2254 |
| Winchester Road Cemetery, Laventie | 45 | E 10 | 1742 |
| Windmill British Cemetery, Monchy-le-Preux | 49 | F 15 | 1743 |
| Winnezeele Churchyard | 3 | G 3 | 1965 |
| Wizernes Churchyard | 3 | F 3 | 2126 |
| Woburn Abbey, Cuinchy | 44 | E 11 | 1744 |
| Wood British Cemetery, Wiencourt-Equipée | 21 | G 6 | 1746 |
| Woods Military Cemetery, Zillebeke | 41 | F 7 | 1747 |
| Wormhoudt Communal Cemetery | 3 | G 2 | 1966 |
| Wulverghem Churchyard | 43 | F 8 | 1748 |
| Wulverghem-Lindenhoek Road, Military Cemetery | 43 | F 8 | 1749 |
| Wytschaete Cemetery | 41 | F 7 | 1750 |
| "X" Farm, Chapelle d'Armentières | 43 | F 9 | 1751 |
| "Y" Farm Military Cemetery, Touquet-des-Mages-Femmes, near Bois Grenier | 43 | F 10 | 1752 |
| "Y" Ravine British Cemetery No. 1 (V Corps Cemetery No. 17), Beaumont-Hamel | 50 | D 17 | 1753 |

| Name of Cemetery. | Page. | Map Square. | No. on Map. |
|---|---|---|---|
| "Y" Ravine German Cemetery, No. 2, Beaumont-Hamel | 50 | D 17 | 1755 |
| York British Cemetery, Haspres | 12 | J 5 | 1756 |
| Yorkshire Cemetery (Zouave Villa), St. Jean | 41 | F 6 | 1757 |
| Ypres Reservoir Middle Cemetery | 41 | F 6 | 1759 |
| Ypres Reservoir North Cemetery | 41 | F 7 | 1760 |
| Ypres Reservoir South Cemetery | 41 | F 7 | 1761 |
| Ytres Churchyard Cemetery | 52 | G 17 | 1764 |
| Ytres German Cemetery | 52 | G 17 | 1765 |
| Zelobes Indian Cemetery, Lacouture | 44 | D 10 | 1766 |
| Zouave Valley British Cemetery, Souchez | 46 | E 13 | 1767 |
| Zouave Villa Strong Post, Boesinghe | 41 | F 6 | 1768 |
| Zudausques Churchyard | 3 | F 3 | 2127 |
| Zuydcoote Military Cemetery | 3 | G 2 | 1769 |

THE WHITE CROSS INSURANCE ASSOCIATION LTD.

## LIST OF
# "WHITE CROSS"
## SPECIAL POLICIES FOR PRIVATE CARS

THE "WHITE CROSS" DOCTOR'S POLICY.
    For the Medical Profession.
    Compensation provided for Loss of Use of Car during Repair.

THE ROYAL AUTOMOBILE CLUB POLICY.
    For Associate-Members and Members of the Royal Automobile Club.
    The "White Cross" are specially authorised by the Club to issue this Policy.

THE AMERICA-EUROPE TOURISTS POLICY.
    For Tourists in Great Britain and Ireland, any Country in Europe, and in Algeria, Tunis, Malta, or Egypt.
    Sea Transit risk between U.S.A. or Canada and United Kingdom or France.

SPECIAL POLICIES FOR DIFFERENT MAKES OF CAR.

| | |
|---|---|
| A.B.C. POLICY | HUMBER POLICY |
| ANGUS SANDERSON POLICY | MINERVA POLICY |
| ARROL-JOHNSTON POLICY | NAPIER POLICY |
| AUSTIN POLICY | OVERLAND CAR POLICY |
| BERLIET POLICY | RENAULT CAR POLICY |
| CROSSLEY POLICY | ROLLS ROYCE CAR POLICY |
| DAIMLER POLICY | ROVER POLICY |
| DARRACQ POLICY | STELLITE CAR POLICY |
| DE DION POLICY | STRAKER SQUIRE POLICY |
| DELAUNAY BELLEVILLE POLICY | STUDEBAKER POLICY |
| FIAT POLICY | SUNBEAM POLICY |
| FORD CAR POLICY | WOLSELEY POLICY |

**Prospectus on Application.**

# INDEX

TO

## PHOTOGRAPHS OF TOWNS VILLAGES ETC., IN FRANCE AND BELGIUM.

| | |
|---|---|
| ALBERT—Cathedral, showing falling Statue .. | .. 154 |
| AMIENS—Ruins of Railway Station | .. 155 |
| ARRAS—Interior of Cathedral before Destruction | .. 148 |
| ARRAS—Interior of Cathedral after Destruction | .. 149 |
| BAPAUME—General View | .. 153 |
| LA BASSEE—Ruins from the Square .. | .. 151 |
| LILLE—Street Scene showing Ruins and Church | .. 150 |
| MONS—Canadians entering | 152 |
| MONTDIDIER—General View of Ruined Road to Roye | .. 156 |
| SOISSONS—Destroyed Bridge | .. 157 |
| ST. MIHIEL—General View | .. 159 |
| VERDUN—General View showing Canal and Cathedral | .. 158 |
| VERSAILLES—View of Palace from he Air .. | .. 160 |

ARRAS - Interior of Cathedral before the War.

ARRAS - Interior of Cathedral after the War.

LILLE - Street Scene, showing Ruins and Church.

LA BASSEE. Ruins from the Square.

MONS : Canadians Entering.

BAPAUME - General View.

ALBERT CATHEDRAL - Showing falling Statue

AMIENS - Ruins of Railway Station.

MONTDIDIER - General View of ruined road to Roye

SOISSONS - Destroyed Bridge.

VERDUN - General View showing Canal and Cathedral.

ST. MIHIEL - General View.

PALACE OF VERSAILLES - General view from the Air.

THE WHITE CROSS INSURANCE ASSOCIATION LTD.

# COMMERCIAL MOTOR VEHICLES

FOR EVERY DESCRIPTION OF

## Mechanically-Propelled Vehicle

Including

LIGHT AND HEAVY GOODS VEHICLES
TRACTORS, TRACTION ENGINES
THREE-WHEEL CARRIERS
FIRE BRIGADE VEHICLES, AMBULANCES
HEARSES, PRISON VANS, DUST CARTS
DISINFECTANT CARTS, WATER CARTS
ROAD SWEEPERS, TOWER WAGONS
AGRICULTURAL MACHINES
PLOUGHING ENGINES, ROAD ROLLERS

PASSENGER VEHICLES, viz.,
    Cars (of Private Type) for Private Hire, Public Hire
    Char-a-bancs and Wagonettes
    Vehicles used by Hotels, Hydros and Golf Clubs
    Omnibuses and Taxi Cabs

For Purposes of Premium each Vehicle is considered individually, according to its particular features, such as Horse Power and Value, District, Trade and the Purposes for which the Vehicle is used.

**Prospectus on Application.**

THE WHITE CROSS INSURANCE ASSOCIATION LTD.

THE

# WHITE CROSS
## MOTOR TRADERS POLICY

for

MOTOR DEALERS AND AGENTS
MOTOR GARAGE PROPRIETORS

etc.

Policies are issued under Alternative Schemes adapted to the particular requirements of each Individual Trader.

All types of Mechanically Propelled Vehicles (Cars, Vans, Lorries, Motor Cycles, etc.) are insured under one Policy, whilst used for the purposes of the Assured's business, including:

DEMONSTRATION　　　TRIALS　　　TESTING
DRIVING OF CUSTOMERS' CARS　　DELIVERY OF GOODS
TOWING　　TUITION
PRIVATE HIRE
(for Vehicles seating not more than six passengers).

---

THE

# WHITE CROSS
## MOTOR CYCLE POLICY

for

Motor Cycles (with or without Sidecars)
used for

PLEASURE and riding to and from business.
PLEASURE AND BUSINESS by Individual Owners.
BUSINESS by Firms or Commercial Travellers, including carrying of goods.

Prospectus on Application.